Coping with Crisis: Europe's Challenges and Strategies

How has the economic and financial crisis that started in 2007 affected European integration? Observers have been speculating about whether the crisis will ultimately lead to a strengthening or weakening of the European Union. This book studies the effects of the crisis on EU policy-making and institutional arrangements on one hand, and citizens' EU attitudes and political parties' electoral strategies on the other. It concludes that, at least in the short run, the crisis has overall created an opportunity for European integration rather than an obstacle. First, it has triggered events of proposed and actual far-reaching policy and institutional change. Second, negative effects on public opinion have not (yet) systematically translated into tendencies of stagnation or disintegration. The book brings together established scholars of European integration whose diverse research expertise contributes to an improved theoretical and empirical understanding of how the economic and financial crisis has affected EU policies, institutions and citizens.

This book was previously published as a special issue of the *Journal of European Integration*.

Jale Tosun holds a PhD in Social Science from the University of Konstanz. She is currently an Assistant Professor of International and Comparative Political Economy at the University of Heidelberg.

Anne Wetzel received her PhD at ETH Zurich and is currently a Postdoctoral Fellow at the Mannheim Centre for European Social Research (MZES).

Galina Zapryanova holds a PhD in Political Science from the University of Pittsburgh and is currently a Postdoctoral Fellow at the MZES.

Journal of European Integration Special Issues

Series editors:
Thomas Christiansen, Maastricht University, Netherlands
Simon Duke, European Institute of Public Administration, Netherlands

The *Journal of European Integration* book series is designed to make our Special Issues accessible to a wider audience. All of the themes covered by our Special Issues and the series are carefully selected with regard to the topicality of the questions addressed in the individual volumes, as well as to the quality of the contributions. The result is a series of books that are sufficiently short to appeal to the curious reader, but that also offer ample depth of analysis to appeal to the more specialist reader, with contributions from leading academics.

Coping with Crisis: Europe's Challenges and Strategies
Edited by Jale Tosun, Anne Wetzel and Galina Zapryanova

Globalization and EU Competition Policy
Edited by Umut Aydin and Kenneth Thomas

Redefining European Economic Governance
Edited by Michele Chang, Georg Menz and Mitchell P. Smith

PREVIOUSLY PUBLISHED BOOKS FROM THE JOURNAL

The Maastricht Treaty: Second Thoughts after 20 Years
Edited by Thomas Christiansen and Simon Duke

Europe after Enlargement
Edited by Yannis Stivachtis and Mark Webber

Euroscepticism within the EU Institutions
Diverging Views of Europe
Edited by Nathalie Brack and Olivier Costa

The Performance of the EU in International Institutions
Edited by Sebastian Oberthür, Knud Erik Jørgensen and Jamal Shahin

Functional and Territorial Interest Representation in the EU
Edited by Michèle Knodt, Christine Quittkat and Justin Greenwood

European Neighbourhood through Civil Society Networks?
Policies, Practices and Perceptions
Edited by James Wesley Scott and Ilkka Likanen

European Parliament Elections after Eastern Enlargement
Edited by Hermann Schmitt

The Common Agricultural Policy
Policy Dynamics in a Changing Context
*Edited by Grace Skogstad and
Amy Verdun*

The External Dimension of Justice and Home Affairs
A Different Security Agenda for the European Union?
Edited by Sarah Wolff, Nicole Wichmann and Gregory Mounier

Policy Coherence and EU Development Policy
Edited by Maurizio Carbone

The Future of European Foreign Policy
*Edited by Erik Jones and
Saskia van Genugten*

The EU as a Global Player
The Politics of Interregionalism
*Edited by Fredrick Söderbaum and
Luk Van Langenhove*

Coping with Crisis: Europe's Challenges and Strategies

Edited by
Jale Tosun, Anne Wetzel and
Galina Zapryanova

LONDON AND NEW YORK

First published 2015
by Routledge

2 Park Square, Milton Park, Abingdon, Oxfordshire OX14 4RN
711 Third Avenue, New York, NY 10017

Routledge is an imprint of the Taylor & Francis Group, an informa business

First issued in paperback 2018

Copyright © 2015 Taylor & Francis

All rights reserved. No part of this book may be reprinted or reproduced or utilised in any form or by any electronic, mechanical, or other means, now known or hereafter invented, including photocopying and recording, or in any information storage or retrieval system, without permission in writing from the publishers.

Notice:
Product or corporate names may be trademarks or registered trademarks, and are used only for identification and explanation without intent to infringe.

British Library Cataloguing in Publication Data
A catalogue record for this book is available from the British Library

ISBN 13: 978-1-138-81564-3 (hbk)
ISBN 13: 978-1-138-38386-9 (pbk)

Typeset in Sabon
by RefineCatch Limited, Bungay, Suffolk

Publisher's Note
The publisher accepts responsibility for any inconsistencies that may have arisen during the conversion of this book from journal articles to book chapters, namely the possible inclusion of journal terminology.

Disclaimer
Every effort has been made to contact copyright holders for their permission to reprint material in this book. The publishers would be grateful to hear from any copyright holder who is not here acknowledged and will undertake to rectify any errors or omissions in future editions of this book.

Contents

Citation Information   ix

1. Introduction: The EU in Crisis: Advancing the Debate   1
   Jale Tosun, Anne Wetzel & Galina Zapryanova

2. The Unexpected Winner of the Crisis: The European Commission's Strengthened Role in Economic Governance   19
   Michael W. Bauer & Stefan Becker

3. The Impact of the Euro Crisis on Citizens' Support for the European Union   37
   Daniela Braun & Markus Tausendpfund

4. 'We No Longer Love You, But We Don't Want To Leave You': The Eurozone Crisis and Popular Euroscepticism in Greece   53
   Ben Clements, Kyriaki Nanou & Susannah Verney

5. Politicizing Europe in Hard Times: Conflicts over Europe in France in a Long-term Perspective, 1974–2012   73
   Swen Hutter & Alena Kerscher

6. 'Beggars can't be Choosers': The European Crisis and Chinese Direct Investment in the European Union   89
   Sophie Meunier

7. Crisis and Citizens' Trust in the European Central Bank — Panel Data Evidence for the Euro Area, 1999–2012   109
   Felix Roth, Daniel Gros & Felicitas Nowak-Lehmann D.

8. European Integration in the Euro Crisis: The Limits of Postfunctionalism   127
   Frank Schimmelfennig

Index   145

Citation Information

The chapters in this book were originally published in the *Journal of European Integration*, volume 36, issue 3 (April 2014). When citing this material, please use the original page numbering for each article, as follows:

Chapter 1
Introduction: The EU in Crisis: Advancing the Debate
Jale Tosun, Anne Wetzel & Galina Zapryanova
Journal of European Integration, volume 36, issue 3 (April 2014). pp. 195–211

Chapter 2
The Unexpected Winner of the Crisis: The European Commission's Strengthened Role in Economic Governance
Michael W. Bauer & Stefan Becker
Journal of European Integration, volume 36, issue 3 (April 2014). pp. 213–229

Chapter 3
The Impact of the Euro Crisis on Citizens' Support for the European Union
Daniela Braun & Markus Tausendpfund
Journal of European Integration, volume 36, issue 3 (April 2014). pp. 231–245

Chapter 4
'We No Longer Love You, But We Don't Want To Leave You': The Eurozone Crisis and Popular Euroscepticism in Greece
Ben Clements, Kyriaki Nanou & Susannah Verney
Journal of European Integration, volume 36, issue 3 (April 2014). pp. 247–265

Chapter 5
Politicizing Europe in Hard Times: Conflicts over Europe in France in a Long-term Perspective, 1974–2012
Swen Hutter & Alena Kerscher
Journal of European Integration, volume 36, issue 3 (April 2014). pp. 267–282

Chapter 6
'Beggars can't be Choosers': The European Crisis and Chinese Direct Investment in the European Union
Sophie Meunier
Journal of European Integration, volume 36, issue 3 (April 2014). pp. 283–302

CITATION INFORMATION

Chapter 7
Crisis and Citizens' Trust in the European Central Bank — Panel Data Evidence for the Euro Area, 1999–2012
Felix Roth, Daniel Gros & Felicitas Nowak-Lehmann D.
Journal of European Integration, volume 36, issue 3 (April 2014). pp. 303–320

Chapter 8
European Integration in the Euro Crisis: The Limits of Postfunctionalism
Frank Schimmelfennig
Journal of European Integration, volume 36, issue 3 (April 2014). pp. 321–337

Please direct any queries you may have about the citations to
clsuk.permissions@cengage.com

INTRODUCTION

The EU in Crisis: Advancing the Debate

JALE TOSUN*, ANNE WETZEL** & GALINA ZAPRYANOVA**

*Institute for Political Science, University of Heidelberg, Heidelberg, Germany;
**MZES, University of Mannheim, Mannheim, Germany

ABSTRACT The European Union (EU) has experienced an unprecedented economic and financial crisis since 2007, the effects of which form the object of analysis in this Special Issue. In particular, it addresses the questions of whether and how the crisis has served as an obstacle or an opportunity for further integration. It concentrates on two broad types of implications for the EU that are central elements of theories on integration and policy and public opinion change. First, the crisis has triggered events of proposed and actual change of policies and institutions. Second, the crisis and the EU's response to it have had an impact on how citizens perceive the EU and its democratic legitimacy. Based on the contributions by scholars of European integration, this Special Issue concludes that, at least in the short run, the crisis has (overall) created an opportunity structure for European integration rather than an obstacle. At the same time, the contributions show the need for further research on the nexus of public opinion and politicization on the one side and institutional and policy change on the other.

Introduction

The global financial crisis of 2007 and 2008 led to a significant downturn in economic activity and caused a recession that has adversely affected the European Union (EU) on the whole. The politically most meaningful consequence of the global financial crisis is the Eurozone crisis — a combination of a government debt and banking crisis in the European Monetary Union (EMU) countries — that began to unfold in late 2009. This led to a politically critical situation in which some Eurozone countries experienced difficulties to service existing debt and to finance further budget deficits, while other Eurozone countries — together with the European Central Bank (ECB) and the International Monetary Fund (IMF) — had to provide bailout loans. The activation of the various bailout packages was made conditional on the receiving countries' agreement to implement a series of painful austerity measures that most basically aimed to cut government spending and to generate additional revenue (for an overview, see Walter 2013).

In the receiving countries, the austerity measures caused social unrest and undermined the functioning of democratic politics since electorally accountable national policy-makers had effectively lost their ability to choose among alternative policy options (Armingeon and Baccaro 2012). In the countries financially shouldering the bailout programmes, a clear majority of the population opposes the financial transfers (Bechtel, Hainmueller, and Margalit Forthcoming), which induces re-election seeking policy-makers in these countries to further insist on the receiving countries implementing harsh austerity measures.

The unprecedented volume of financial transfers and the controversial public debates surrounding them in both the receiving and the giving Eurozone countries induced the President of the European Council, van Rompuy (2012), to speak about a 'first test of solidarity' for the EU and to remind forcefully that such joint efforts were indispensable since 'the European project itself is at stake.'

What are the consequences of this extraordinary event for European integration? This is the overarching research question that guides the contributions to this Special Issue. In addressing this research question, all articles take the causes and faces of the economic and financial crisis as given and shed light on the implications of the crisis for EU institutions, citizens, and policy-making. The findings — provided by this collection of articles — serve as a basis for assessing, to what extent the economic and financial crisis has been both an obstacle and an opportunity for further integration.

This article is structured as follows. We first provide more detailed background on the economic and financial crisis in preparation for the subsequent discussion of its implications for European integration. We then proceed with an overview of theoretical approaches that allow for making predictions about exogenous shocks as opportunity for or obstacle to further integration. In the next step, we review the existing literature on the consequences of the economic and financial crisis and place the individual contributions to this Special Issue within this field. Finally, we discuss the implications of the authors' findings for the ways in which the economic and financial crisis poses an obstacle and an opportunity for further integration.

Economic and Financial Crisis: Main Characteristics and Conceptual Clarifications

When studying the effects of the crisis in this Special Issue, we subsume a whole range of events and aspects under this term. Chronologically, the starting point is marked by the collapse of the subprime mortgage market in the United States in 2007, the connected bankruptcy of the New Century Financial Corporation, and the subsequent freezing of interbank markets (Baldwin and Wyplosz 2012, 528). The effects of these events did not remain restricted to the United States. Europe saw a bank run in the United Kingdom and the ECB's first emergency liquidity measure in the same year (Hodson and Quaglia 2009, 940–1), which induced some authors to date the onset of the economic and financial crisis in Europe on 9 August 2007 (Hodson and Puetter 2013, 369). The subsequent collapse of the US investment bank Lehman Brothers 'triggered the worst financial crisis since 1929' (Baldwin and Wyplosz 2012, 528) and required government interventions to bailout the banks affected in both EU and non-EU states such as Iceland. Pursuant to these events, Hungary became the first EU member state to seek financial assistance and although a non-Eurozone member, the ECB provided emergency support (Hodson and Quaglia 2009, 941–2). The ECB put additional measures in place in 2008/2009 as a response to the global financial crisis (Hodson and Quaglia 2009, 943). The series of bailout of European banks, however, did not curtail the crisis. To the contrary, budget deficits grew dramatically. In the Eurozone, almost all countries exceeded the 3% of Gross Domestic Product deficit reference value fixed in the Stability and Growth Pact in 2009 — with particularly high values in Ireland, Greece, Spain, and Portugal (Hodson 2010, 229–30). In combination with the consequences of negative economic growth, this led to a fast increase in public debts,[1] which is widely regarded as 'the immediate cause of the next crisis, the Eurozone debt crisis' (Baldwin and Wyplosz 2012, 530).

Debt crises became particularly problematic in the Mediterranean. The most prominent and dramatic example is Greece, which 'served as the catalyst for the crisis of the euro' (Tsoukalis 2011, 26). As early as its entrance in the Eurozone in 2001, the country was so indebted that the size of the debt actually exceeded the size of the nation's entire economy. When, however, in 2008, the newly elected government of Giorgos Papandreou revised the expected budget deficit for the coming year from 3.7 to 12.7% and the debt had increased further, concerns about Greece's creditworthiness started to grow (Baldwin and Wyplosz 2012, 532; Hodson 2010, 234). Becoming skeptical of the debt situation in Greece, financial market actors demanded higher yields on the country's bonds, which raised the cost of the country's debt burden. It gradually became clear that the Greek government would not be able to cope with this situation alone. Furthermore, the other Eurozone members started to fear domino effects for the other highly indebted countries and currency fluctuations in the case of a Greek exit from the EMU. Eventually, 'Eurozone governments were ready to ignore the "no-bail-out clause" and other constraints of the Maastricht Treaty in order to save the euro at any cost' (Scharpf 2012, 22). In May 2010, the European Council agreed on a rescue operation for Greece that involved the EU — represented by the European Commission — the ECB, and the IMF (known as the 'Troika'). Many observers saw this decision as 'not so much the beginning of the end for the eurozone's sovereign debt crisis as the end of the beginning' (Hodson 2011, 231). It was followed by a series of bailouts in response to concerns of the financial markets regarding the public finances of other Eurozone members, namely Cyprus, Ireland, Portugal, and Spain (see Apostolides 2013; Eichler 2012; Enderlein and Verdun 2010). In 2012, Mario Draghi, President of the ECB, announced that 'the ECB is ready to do whatever it takes to preserve the euro'.[2]

Not only is the chronology of crisis-related events complex (and could only very briefly be outlined here) but also multidimensional. It involves a banking crisis, a sovereign debt crisis and macroeconomic crisis, which are closely interlinked (Hodson and Puetter 2013, 368; Shambaugh 2012; Walter 2013). When speaking of 'the crisis' in this Special Issue, we refer to the developments in the realm of banking, public debts, and macroeconomics in the EU — not only in the Eurozone — that were triggered by the collapse of the subprime mortgage market in the United States in 2007. Building on this multifaceted understanding of the crisis, we do not promote a particular understanding of 'effects' of the crisis nor do we restrict our view to a certain level at which effects may occur. With a crisis of such magnitude, it is not surprising that a variety of effects can be discerned. For instance, social unrest across the EU became a rather frequent feature of the sociopolitical landscape and governments' ability to effectively govern was challenged by both the rise of more extreme oppositional parties and plummeting public trust in national political institutions. The EU did not escape the spotlight either (particularly due to the controversial bailouts) and the new fiscal treaty which Euro-sceptic actors condemned as another step towards deeper integration and loss of national sovereignty. The common currency came under strong criticism and, for the first time since its creation, the question of EMU dissolution was debated in the press as a legitimate option (Crum 2013). Euroscepticism rose in the political realm manifested, for example, by the formation of the first-ever explicitly Euro-sceptic party in Germany where most forms of Euroscepticism had remained taboo for decades. Thus, the effects of the crisis are not restricted to the economic realm but have greater political and social implications for governments and governance at both the national and EU level.

All of these visible effects of the crisis unfolded gradually, in some states faster than others, thus increasing the complexity of comparisons. Examining these effects presents several conceptual and empirical issues. It is a particular challenge to separate the effects of the crisis from those of all other political developments happening at the same time (see Meunier 2014). These challenges should not, however, prevent us from examining important large-scale events and can be minimized by adopting approaches suitable to the particular study in question. For example, public opinion studies can use equivalent data pre and post the cut-off years, or survey questions worded a specific way, or experimental designs to demonstrate a crisis-linked pattern (see, e.g. Bechtel, Hainmueller, and Margalit Forthcoming; Wälti 2012). Studies interested in institutional and policy change may use longitudinal data for a rigorous quantitative assessment, and those analyzing new policies and institutions or seeking to illuminate the governments' strategies for implementing macroeconomic adjustments usually adopt a process-tracing approach for a refined qualitative assessment (see, e.g. Walter 2013). The contributions to this Special Issue make use of a range of methodological approaches to uncover how the economic and financial crisis has affected policies, institutions, and citizens in Europe.

Exogenous Shocks as Opportunities for or Obstacles to Integration: Theoretical Expectations

Theoretical work has extensively dealt with the consequences of exogenous shocks for policies, institutions, and citizens. In this section, we give a brief overview of the main lines of argumentation advanced in different theoretical perspectives and we seek to formulate some general expectations. We begin with integration theories and then turn to theories of policy and institutional change before presenting theories of public opinion change.

Integration Theories

The natural starting point for theorizing about the consequences of the economic and financial crisis in the EU is provided by theories of European integration (Schimmelfennig 2014; for an overview, see Schimmelfennig and Rittberger 2006). Somewhat remarkably, however, integration theories have not put too much emphasis on the implications of crises and exogenous shocks. An important exception is Schmitter's (1970, 840) further development of the neofunctionalist theory of integration, which includes considerations about 'exogenous tensions or process-generated contradictions.' According to Schmitter (1970, 841), these 'tensions' have two types of consequences. First, they affect the scope of the issue to be resolved jointly. And second, the level of authority for the supranational institutions for addressing them. Based on this reasoning, crises can either strengthen or weaken the scope or level of the supranational institutions' authority vis-à-vis national institutions. While the ultimate outcome depends on the strategies adopted by the national and supranational institutions, two extremes can be identified. One extreme is disintegration in the case that 'a given regional process fails to generate or respond to crises' and the second one is self-maintenance 'if it responds by reasserting previous strategies' (Schmitter 1970, 842). From this perspective, the crisis could both represent an opportunity for and obstacle to further integration.

Liberal intergovernmentalism — the second classic grand theory of EU integration — gives way to more moderate expectations about the occurrence and the scope of changes in particular. Liberal intergovernmentalism focuses on bargaining, national interests, and two-level games (Moravcsik 1993, 1998), which would predict difficulty in compromising between EU member states with divergent or sometimes contradictory (e.g. 'donors' vs. 'recipients') national interests. European economies do not always have the same degree or type of crisis-related problems and could hence require different economic 'cures' or political reforms. Thus, the crisis would be expected to be an obstacle rather than an opportunity for further integration.

Finally, postfunctionalism is the newest theoretical approach to European integration. It advocates an increased empirical and theoretical focus on public attitudes and party politics in the individual member states because these factors can effectively constrain the ability of governments to shape European integration (Hooghe and Marks 2005, 2009). With increases in Euroscepticism and more discernible anti-EU rhetoric by mainstream political parties, one would therefore expect far-reaching negative consequences for European integration.

Theories of Policy and Institutional Change

The four main theories of policy change regard exogenous shocks or — as more prominently used in this literature — 'focusing events', which are events that induce citizens and policy-makers to pay attention to a public problem (Birkland 1997), as central drivers of policy dynamics. Thus, all of the presented theories would expect the crisis to serve as an opportunity for policy change. The advocacy coalition framework views policies as the result of the competition between coalitions of actors who advocate beliefs about certain policy options (Sabatier and Jenkins-Smith 1999; Weible, Sabatier, and McQueen 2009). Against this background, policy change may principally result from two sources. Firstly, policy change can occur due to learning processes. Secondly, focusing events may lead to changes in the power distribution among advocacy coalitions. The policy subsystem adjustment model put forward by Howlett and Ramesh (2002) emphasizes that policy change is most likely if there are focusing events that draw new attention to a policy sector. Similarly, the multiple streams framework by Kingdon (2002) and the punctuated equilibrium framework by Baumgartner and Jones (1993) and True, Jones, and Baumgartner (2007) point to the importance of focusing events for major policy change.

The overarching expectation that exogenous shocks lead to changes is shared by neoinstitutionalist theories (for an overview, see Hall and Taylor 1996). While usually emphasizing institutional stability, even scholars of historical institutionalism posit that extraordinary events may lead to institutional change. Most essentially, historical institutionalism stresses the 'enduring impact of choices made during critical junctures in history,' which 'close off alternative options and lead to the establishment of institutions that generate self-reinforcing path-dependent processes' (Capoccia and Kelemen 2007, 341). In this regard, Gocaj and Meunier (2013) argue that the 'euro crisis of 2010–2012 provides an instance of historical institutionalism [...] in action, whereby the institutional creation decided at the critical juncture of the initial reaction to the crisis transformed the path of options available at subsequent attempts to tackle the crisis [...]' (240).

Theories of Public Opinion Change

Citizens form an opinion about political matters by becoming knowledgeable about topics. There are two main ways for people to gain political knowledge. One way is through direct experiences with a given issue and the other way is indirectly through exposure to information provided by other people and news media (Visser, Holbrook, and Krosnick 2008, 129). In the case of European integration, Hooghe and Marks (2005) distinguish between the economic model, the social identity model, and the cue model of public opinion.

The economic model of public opinion posits that citizens evaluate the economic consequences of European integration for themselves and for the socioeconomic groups to which they belong. Following this perspective, changes in public opinion towards European integration can occur if the direct experiences or the exposure to information in the news media suggest that the economic and financial crisis alters the cost-benefit calculus. Since the crisis has had strong negative socioeconomic effects in a range of EU member states and has produced scepticism about financial transfers, this perspectives lead to a hesitant view regarding the prospects of further integration. The social identity model, in contrast, emphasizes the importance of attachment to symbolic categories such as one's nation or the EU (Hooghe and Marks 2005, 422). Since identities are often stable and formed as a result of a long-term process of socialization, one would expect rather moderate changes to public opinion even given exogenous shocks. Finally, the gist of the cue model is that citizens' values and interests need to be primed to make them become politically salient, which in European polities is mostly done by political parties (Hooghe and Marks 2005, 425). Consequently, changes in public opinion on European integration pursuant to the crisis should depend on whether and how political parties address this issue. With the increase in Euro-sceptic actors, the cue model would predict rising Euroscepticism among the publics as well — thus presenting an obstacle for further integration.

Overview of the State of Research

Understanding current patterns of change or continuity in European institutions and societies is vital to having a roadmap for the future of European integration. While this has always been at the center of EU studies, recent events have received enhanced scholarly attention, culminating in the development of a rich literature within a remarkably short period of time. An inspection of the still growing body of research shows that the vast majority of studies of the political and social consequences of the economic and financial crisis focus on three broad themes — policies, governance, and democracy, which are examined either separately or in conjunction with one another.

Implications for Policies

While long-term effects of the crisis cannot be ascertained yet, studies of policy change have produced some surprising initial results. Despite the predictions of the main theories of policy change, the financial and economic crisis has not brought about rapid or radical changes in all policy areas concerned. Instead, the literature points to wide variation in the pace and scope of policy changes. De Ville and Orbie (2011), for instance, find that despite expectations of paradigmatic change, EU trade policy has not become more protectionist — in fact the opposite is happening. The European Commission's framing of the crisis has led to a strengthening of the trade liberalization paradigm dominant among EU institutional actors. Likewise, Tosun (Forthcoming) points to moderate changes regarding the absorption rules for regional funds triggered by the crisis, mainly consisting of extended application deadlines and a lowering of the co-financing requirements. Kudrna (2012) found only modest initial changes to the EU banking policies. Since then, further steps have been taken at the EU level, which shows that some changes may take more time than others.

The picture looks markedly different for hedge fund regulations, which did not exist at the European level prior to the crisis. In 2009, the European Commission organized a High-Level Conference on Private Equity and Hedge Funds, which brought together representatives of the hedge fund and private equity industries, investors, members of the regulatory community, and other experts in an initiative to review the adequacy of supervisory and regulatory arrangements for all financial market actors in the context of the crisis.[3] As Quaglia (2012) argues, the European Commission did not take this step due to changed interests but because the crisis challenged the 'market-making' and 'competition friendly' paradigm and instead favored the 'market-shaping' approach of the pro-regulation countries.

Whitman and Juncos (2012) address the dimension of the EU's enlargement and foreign policy and conclude that the official commitment to enlargement and the European Neighborhood Policy remains unaffected. But there are now practical problems that are caused by the crisis that limited the time and attention spent on these policies as well as the range of tools available.

In sum, the case studies indicate that there is a variation with regard to the scope and timing of change in different policy areas. While EU banking and trade policies have (initially) experienced moderate changes only, the EU-wide regulation of hedge funds represents a policy change of considerable scope. With respect to EU's enlargement and foreign policies, the effects of the crisis would take longer to discern. While official policy agendas remain the same or similar, their implementation is encountering greater obstacles.

Implications for Institutions and Governance

Changes in governance concern both changes at the level of the EU institutions and governance at sectoral level. As to the first, several studies conclude that under the pressure of the crisis, it was in particular the European Council who became 'the central leader and agenda setter in the EU' (Schwarzer 2012, 31). As Dinan (2011) summarizes, 'the crisis put the European Council front and centre of the EU' and 'revealed clearly where the real centre of power in the EU lay' (119). These developments are particularly beneficial for the big member states and generally promote intergovernmental tendencies (Schwarzer 2012). At the same time, the crisis accelerated the loss of decision-making leverage of other EU institutions. Regarding the architecture of the Council of the EU, Schwarzer (2012, 31) finds that the sectoral councils and their rotating presidency lost influence concerning agenda setting. Also, the European Commission's role as an agenda setter is found to have weakened, especially when it comes to long-term policy orientations and strategic directions (Schwarzer 2012, 31–2). On the other hand, the Commission's 'operational role' has been strengthened by the 'Six Pack' legislative package and the introduction of the 'European semester' (Schwarzer 2012, 32). All in all, Schwarzer (2012) concludes that 'the change of the role of the European Commission in the governance structures of the euro area that is underway can best be described as redirection' (32). The findings of analyses of the role of the European Parliament are equally mixed. Despite gaining new competences due to the Lisbon Treaty, the European Parliament has been excluded from crisis management and the development of long-term strategies (Schwarzer 2012, 32–3).

The institution that certainly saw the biggest change of its role in the EU's governance structure is the ECB. It has significantly gained importance in the institutional arrangements of the EMU, including the leverage of political influence in the Euro area (Schwarzer 2012, 34). Authors applying an institutionalist lens conclude that the ECB underwent two profound changes. Firstly, 'a limited process of *redirection* of its instruments and its advisory role' in the sense that it now uses 'a larger spectrum of policy tools aimed at an unchanged ultimate objective,' and has become involved in the new advisory activities of country-specific missions. Secondly, the creation of the European Systemic Risk Board marks a process of *layering*, which is the addition of a new institutional structure (Salines, Glöckler, and Truchlewski 2012, 668–70).

Turning to the sectoral level, the vast majority of scholars concur that the economic and financial crisis exposed the weaknesses of the EMU which operated on an 'incomplete, imbalanced set of rules' (Featherstone 2011). Fiscal meltdowns such as the Greek sovereign debt crisis 'acted as an authentic stress-test of EMU and generated an impressive list of policy responses' (Buti and Carnot 2012). From a neofunctionalist perspective, the financial and economic constraints generated by the crisis led to a functional pressure that acted as a catalyst for further integration. While functional dissonances between supranationalised monetary policy and integrated financial markets on the one hand and intergovernmental fiscal policy and national supervisory authorities on the other have persisted before the outbreak of the crisis, the latter bundled functional spillovers and changed the motives of policy-makers towards deeper integration (Fehlker, Demosthenes, and Niemann 2013).

As EU governments agreed to greater centralized monitoring of national budgets, stricter punishments for non-compliance and domestic structural reforms (mostly by means of the European Semester), integration scholars suggest that these steps towards a much closer fiscal union may have far-reaching consequences for several policy areas. The nature of these consequences remains contested however. Some see the fiscal changes brought forth by the financial crisis as a 'decisive stage on the road to "ever closer union"' (Buti and Carnot 2012) and expect that the reforms eventually 'require a major step of political integration' (Schwarzer 2012, 40). Others warn that without greater economic convergence of EMU-related policies and reform of the private sector, the 'long-term economic fundamentals are stacked against success' (Moravcsik 2012, 65) or express concerns about how the fiscal philosophy promoted by Germany will harm the European social model and EU's global performance (Laulom *et al.* 2012). Another sceptic view maintains that the dynamics of incremental decision-making prevent a solution to the crisis and only address its symptoms. The joint decision trap that is characteristic of the EU hinders effective crisis management through either further integration or disintegration (Genschel and Jachtenfuchs 2013). While differing on their predictions and prescriptions, studies mostly agree on the importance of the new fiscal framework and its potential extensions as a key moment in European integration that also has consequences for the future of political integration. However, Salines *et al.* (2012), for instance, argue that '[t]he reform of economic governance is dominated by the *redirection* of existing instruments and the *layering* of two additional instruments' (672) and thus representing an incremental change in line with the concept of path dependency in historical institutionalism.

Implications for Democracy

The third broad theme of interest to scholars and practitioners alike is the effects of the crisis on democracy in Europe — the difficulties in reconciling institutional authority in the multilevel EU governance structure with public pressures and democratic notions of legitimacy and accountability. Governance and democracy are of course two sides of the same coin — any policy initiatives or changes in governance structures brought forth by the crisis need to withstand much higher public scrutiny than day-to-day EU economic activity prior to 2007. While the increasing politicization of European integration has long been noted (see, e.g. Hooghe and Marks 2005, 2009; Hutter and Kerscher 2014), studies suggest that the ongoing economic crisis exacerbates this trend and brings European integration onto the political agenda (De Wilde and Zürn 2012). Euro-sceptic rhetoric, once relegated to the political fringe, is becoming incorporated in mainstream politics as parties engage the EU dimension for electoral or ideological purposes (Taggart and Szczerbiak 2013). With increased contestation of EU policies, this strand of literature thus broadly focuses on the implication of the crisis for EU democracy and legitimacy. The empirical focus tends to be political parties, citizens, or the relationship between the two.

Findings so far suggest some interesting patterns. Hobolt (2012) demonstrates that individuals evaluate EU democracy primarily through their confidence (or lack thereof) in European institutions rather than their views of national institutions. Surprisingly, the study also finds that economic factors related to perceived EU performance were far less important in determining individual-level satisfaction with EU democracy than trust in institutions. This pattern is corroborated by additional research which finds that despite increased Euroscepticism during the economic and financial crisis, contestation of EU matters is not primarily guided by economic considerations (see, e.g. Fligstein, Polyakova, and Sandholtz 2012; Serricchio, Tsakatika, and Quaglia 2013). In this context, Bechtel, Hainmueller, and Margalit (Forthcoming), for instance, show that the best predictors for German voters' support for crisis responses are their social dispositions, of which altruism and cosmopolitanism particularly matter.

All these findings imply that increased politicization may mean the EU cannot count on output legitimacy alone as the prescription for improving its standing with European publics. This may prove a particular challenge in the aftermath of the crisis because evidence shows trust in EU institutions declined immediately following the crisis with the ECB in particular receiving record low ratings among European publics (Gros and Roth 2010; Roth 2009; Roth, Gros, and Nowak-Lehmann D 2014; Wälti 2012).

While much remains to be empirically explored regarding changing electoral and attitudinal patterns in the context of the crisis, the consequences of the crisis for EU democracy from a normative point of view are also subject to a scholarly debate. Diverging views on the matter mirror the classic debate about whether and to what extent European integration suffers from a 'deficit of democracy.' In the aftermath of the crisis' outbreak, scholars have given conflicting assessments of the state of EU democracy. Scharpf (2012) paints the most pessimistic picture where the economic and financial crisis and the subsequent EU-driven reforms destroyed member states' ability to control their own economic fate and hence eroded the democratic legitimacy the EU had prior to the crisis. Armingeon and Baccaro (2012, 267) reach a similar conclusion by arguing that in Eurozone members that benefitted from bailouts different political parties could not propose distinctive policy alternatives and citizens could not affect the policies despite taking part in elections. Likewise, Bellamy and Kroeger (2013) contend that the EU suffers from a 'representation surplus' where the overrepresentation of various groups dilutes accountability and hinders governance, which results in a democratic deficit. Longo and Murray (2011) further argue that the EU's legitimacy problem pre-crisis 'has seriously impinged on the capacity of EU institutions to deal with current existential problems such as the debt crisis' (688). Hence, the democracy-crisis linkage may go both ways — tenuous democratic legitimacy hinders EU's ability for collective action in a crisis, while any perceived failures to confront the crisis decrease its legitimacy among the public even further.

A more positive assessment of the state of European democracy is provided by Nicolaïdis (2012, 2013) who calls for conceiving of the EU as a 'demoicracy' — a democracy, albeit an imperfect one, created by different nation states who govern together. Even further, Moravcsik (2012) discounts the 'democratic deficit' issue as non-existent and argues that if the Eurozone was to collapse, it would be because of rather too much than too little democracy — due to the necessity of broad consensus among member states before any major reforms are undertaken. In sum, while the democracy theme runs through much of the scholarly research on the effects of the financial crisis, vast normative disagreements remain about the meaning and quality of EU democracy.

Characterization of the Contributions in Light of the State of Research

How has the economic and financial crisis influenced EU policies and institutions? How has the economic and financial crisis affected citizens' EU attitudes? By addressing both research questions, the contributions assess to what extent the economic and financial crisis presents an *opportunity for* or *obstacle to* European integration.

The first three articles concentrate on the manifestations of policy and institutional change induced by the economic and financial crisis. The analysis by Frank Schimmelfennig challenges postfunctionalist integration theory by providing an institutionalist explanation for EU-level policy-making in the aftermath of the Eurozone crisis. The author argues that despite the 'postfunctionalist moment' of the Eurozone crisis, there have been major integration steps, which can largely be explained by a neofunctionalist account. Michael Bauer and Stefan Becker then take the level of analysis from overaching reforms of the EU political and institutional design to the changing role of a key institution — the European Commission. More precisely, the authors illustrate the European Commission's role in managing the crisis by concentrating on financial stability support, economic policy surveillance, coordination of national polices, and financial supervision. Coordination and decision-making within supranational economic governance systems is a key challenge to European integration and has been the subject of debate. While the authors show that the European Commission's agenda-setting powers have diminished due to the crisis, it now has increased its implementation competences. Sophie Meunier's study complements this first group of papers by demonstrating how the economic and financial crisis has helped to lower political resistance to Chinese inward investment. The resulting policy change, however, took place in the individual member states and was obstructed by the Council at the EU level, which provides support to the reasoning of liberal intergovernmentalism. The paper speaks to the previous article by Bauer and Becker by showing how the European Commission's political power has become transformed but not necessarily increased during the economic and financial crisis.

The second set of articles shifts the focus from policies and institutions to citizens and political parties as the units of analysis. Daniela Braun and Markus Tausendpfund use both individual-level and country-level variables to explain how the economic and financial crisis has affected citizens' attitudes towards European integration. The authors' most crucial finding is that in times of crisis, economic indicators and perceptions play the key role in explaining support for the EU which qualifies postfunctionalist reasoning. This finding also relates to Meunier's argument that the economic and financial crisis has facilitated policies intending to stimulate economic growth. Put differently, Braun and Tausendpfund provide the microfoundation for the macrolevel phenomenon illustrated by Meunier.

The next two contributions then bring more details to specific cases of interest. Felix Roth, Daniel Gros, and Felicitas Nowak-Lehmann shift the focus on the effect of the crisis to trust in the ECB. In line with the existing research (e.g. Wälti 2012), the authors show that the ECB has experienced loss in public trust across all Eurozone countries. This, however, does not represent an obstacle to integration given that the ECB is the institution whose public salience increased the most during the Euro crisis and whose leverage in EU decision-making has increased. Moreover, the authors are optimistic about further European integration since the majority of citizens do support the Euro despite the crisis, which should help to trigger policy change in the future. The contribution by Ben Clements, Kyriaki Nanou, and Susannah Verney is directly related to the previous two papers but is at the same time more specific as it sheds light on public opinion in Greece. Similar to Roth, Gros, and Nowak-Lehmann D, and Clements, Nanou, and Verney find that Greek citizens' attitudes towards the Euro run counter to the general negative trend. Support for the single currency has increased between 2007 and 2011 and is now higher in Greece than the EU as a whole — indicating that the Greeks do not entirely reject European integration. Furthermore, Clements, Nanou, and Verney support the findings of Braun and Tausendpfund that economic variables matter the most in explaining public support for European integration.

Finally, the study by Swen Hutter and Alena Kerscher helps to connect the three articles on public opinion with those on policy and institutional change by addressing the issue of politicization. The analysis of how the crisis has affected the long-term trends of politicization in France helps to illustrate how citizens' changing preferences along with changing patterns of party contestation amidst the crisis may affect the future of European integration. Examining politicization of the EU through a focus on French elections is of particular value as a country case study due to France's central role as a driver and agenda setter of European integration along with Germany (for the latter, see Bechtel, Hainmueller, and Margalit Forthcoming). Developments in French elections have thus higher probability of affecting the course of European integration than those in smaller EU member states. This is why it is remarkable that the authors find evidence for increased politicization as a result of the Eurozone crisis. At the same time, they are reluctant to conclude that this automatically leads to tighter constraints to integration. They show that the concrete impact of polarization on integration may depend on the particular constellation of the three dimensions that make up politicization.

In review, the contributions to this Special Issue develop further the state of research. First, the contributions provide considerations about how policy-makers at the EU level or in individual member states respond to public opinion. In this context, the article by Schimmelfennig deserves credit for shedding light on the strategies of elected politicians to facilitate EU-level reform despite public contestation. These strategies include euro-compatible government formation, avoidance of referendums, and delegation to technocratic supranational organizations (see also Walter 2013). Equally insightful in this regard is the study by Hutter and Kerscher as they provide a much needed exploration into the scope and types of EU politicization in the aftermath of the crisis. Second, the systematic analysis of the changes to the institutions' political power and the forms of governance pursuant to the crisis as provided by Bauer and Becker go beyond the analyses in the literature by characterizing the 'redirection' of European Commission's role (see Schwarzer 2012, 32). Third, Meunier's contribution brings in a completely new perspective on the study of the economic and financial crisis, namely how interactions with external economic partners can be an important catalyst affecting long-term economic conditions in the EU. Fourth, the studies on public opinion by Braun and Tausendpfund, Roth, Gros, and Nowak-Lehmann D and Clements, Nanou, and Verney advance the state of research by linking general public opinion models to European integration theory and providing insights into the state of democratic legitimacy in the EU. In this way, these studies serve as the microlevel foundations for the macrolevel explanations that address instances of policy and institutional change.

Concluding Remarks

The majority of findings in the Special Issue suggest that the economic and financial crisis has produced continuous but incremental changes in EU institutions and policies. While the European Commission has experienced a 'redirection' of its role, the ECB has broadened its mandate. Fiscal and financial policy reforms have resulted in strengthened integration. With a view to the integration theories presented above, these developments correspond most closely with the expectations based on neofunctionalism. Yet, as the case of foreign inward investment policy shows, intergovernmentalism is relevant, too.

With regard to EU support and trust in European institutions, the articles show that while it is negatively affected, the overall support for key achievements of European integration — most notably the Euro — remains unchallenged. Moreover, in spite of the decline, they are still higher than approval of national institutions. So far, negative effects on public opinion have not systematically translated into tendencies of stagnation or even disintegration at the level of policies and institutions. Still, policy-makers should continue to develop strategies to overcome the economic and final crisis. As several authors conclude, the dynamics may change and even reverse in the longer run. Also, if the crisis has indeed exacerbated the 'democratic deficit' in the EU — as evidenced for example by the all-time low of public trust in the ECB — then more extensive policy changes than the current institutional readjustments may be necessary. All in all, the findings of this Special Issue allow for the conclusion that at least in the short run the economic and financial crisis has created an opportunity structure for European integration rather than an obstacle.

With regard to public opinion theory, the contributions show the need for nuanced further research. The contributions highlight both some of the strengths and limitations of postfunctionalist approaches to European integration. On one hand, the results provide support for postfunctionalist tenets, which means that integration is indeed becoming progressively more politicized and loses public support. These developments hold the potential to reshape the direction, or at least the pace, of European integration. On the other hand, the link between increased politicization of integration and policy/institutional change at the EU level is not straightforward to establish. We therefore invite further research to better analyze how public opinion affects policy and institutional change in the EU and assess the explanatory power of integration theories.

Acknowledgments

This Special Issue is the outcome of a workshop that took place on 3 and 4 June 2013 at the Mannheim Centre for European Social Research (MZES). We gratefully acknowledge funding for this event by the MZES and the Lorenz von Stein Foundation. We would also like to express our gratitude to all workshop participants. Stefanie Walter deserves credit for commenting on the draft versions of the papers. We thank Marina Arz and Constanze Nickel for their support in organizing the workshop, Cornelius Eich for helping us in formatting the manuscript, and James Ferrell for language editing. The usual disclaimer applies.

Notes

1. See also: http://epp.eurostat.ec.europa.eu/portal/page/portal/euroindicators/peeis for selected principal economic indicators and http://epp.eurostat.ec.europa.eu/tgm/table.do?tab=table&plugin=1&language=en&pcode=tsdde410 for public debts.
2. http://www.ecb.int/press/key/date/2012/html/sp120726.en.html.
3. http://ec.europa.eu/internal_market/investment/alternative_investments/index_en.htm.

References

Apostolides, A. 2013. Beware of German gifts near elections: how Cyprus got here and why it is currently more out than in the Eurozone. *Capital Markets Law Journal* 8, no. 3: 300–18.
Armingeon, K., and L. Baccaro. 2012. Political economy of the sovereign debt crisis: the limits of internal devaluation. *Industrial Law Journal* 41, no. 3: 254–75.
Baldwin, R., and C. Wyplosz. 2012. *The economics of European integration*. London: McGraw-Hill.
Baumgartner, F.R., and B.D. Jones. 1993. *Agendas and instability in American politics*. Chicago, IL: University of Chicago Press.
Bechtel, M., J. Hainmueller, and Y. Margalit. forthcoming. Preferences for international redistribution: the divide over the Eurozone bailouts. *American Journal of Political Science*.
Bellamy, R., and S. Kroeger. 2013. Representation deficits and surpluses in EU Policy-making. *Journal of European Integration* 35, no. 5: 477–97.
Birkland, T.A. 1997. *After disaster: agenda setting, public policy, and focusing events*. Washington, DC: Georgetown University Press.
Buti, M., and N. Carnot. 2012. The EMU debt crisis: early lessons and reforms. *Journal of Common Market Studies* 50, no. 6: 899–911.
Capoccia, G., and R.D. Kelemen. 2007. The study of critical junctures: theory, narrative, and counterfactuals in historical institutionalism. *World Politics* 59, no. 03: 341–69.
Crum, B. 2013. Saving the Euro at the cost of democracy? *Journal of Common Market Studies* 51, no. 4: 614–30.
De Ville, F., and J. Orbie. 2011. The European Union's trade policy response to the crisis: paradigm lost or reinforced? *European Integration online Papers* 15: 1–22.
De Wilde, P., and M. Zürn. 2012. Can the politicization of European integration be reversed? *Journal of Common Market Studies* 50, no. 1: 137–53.

Dinan, D. 2011. Governance and institutions: implementing the Lisbon treaty in the shadow of the Euro crisis. *Journal of Common Market Studies* 49, no. S1: 103–21.

Eichler, S. 2012. Financial crisis risk, ECB "Non-standard" measures, and the external value of the Euro. *The Quarterly Review of Economics and Finance* 52, no. 3: 257–65.

Enderlein, H., and A. Verdun (eds.). 2010. *EMU and political science: what have we learned?* London: Routledge.

Featherstone, K. 2011. The JCMS Annual Lecture: The Greek Sovereign Debt Crisis and EMU: A Failing State in a Skewed Regime. *Journal of Common Market Studies* 49, no. 2: 193–217.

Fehlker, C., I. Demosthenes, and A. Niemann. 2013. Die Errichtung einer europäischen Finanzmarktunion: Ein Fall von funktionalem spillover [Building a European financial market union: a case of neofunctionalist spillover]. *Zeitschrift für Internationale Beziehungen* 20, no. 1: 105–24.

Fligstein, N., A. Polyakova, and W. Sandholtz. 2012. European integration, nationalism and European identity. *Journal of Common Market Studies* 50, no. S1: 106–22.

Genschel, P., and M. Jachtenfuchs. 2013. Alles ganz normal! Eine institutionelle Analyse der Euro-Krise [Politics as usual! An institutional analysis of the Euro crisis]. *Zeitschrift für Internationale Beziehungen* 20, no. 1: 75–88.

Gocaj, L., and S. Meunier. 2013. Time will tell: the EFSF, the ESM, and the Euro crisis. *Journal of European Integration* 35, no. 3: 239–53.

Gros, D., and F. Roth. 2010. The financial crisis and citizen trust in the European central bank. *CEPS Working Document* No. 334.

Hall, P.A., and R.C. Taylor. 1996. Political Science and the three new institutionalisms. *Political Studies* 44, no. 5: 936–57.

Hobolt, S.B. 2012. Citizen satisfaction with democracy in the European Union. *Journal of Common Market Studies* 50, no. 1: 88–105.

Hodson, D. 2010. The EU economy: the Euro area in 2009. *Journal of Common Market Studies* 48, no. S1: 225–42.

Hodson, D. 2011. The EU economy: the Eurozone in 2010. *Journal of Common Market Studies* 49, no. S1: 231–49.

Hodson, D., and U. Puetter. 2013. The European Union and economic crisis. In *European Union politics*, eds. M. Cini and N. Pérez-Solórzano Borragán, 367–79. Oxford: Oxford University Press.

Hodson, D., and L. Quaglia. 2009. European perspectives on the global financial crisis: introduction. *Journal of Common Market Studies* 47, no. 5: 939–53.

Hooghe, L., and G. Marks. 2005. Calculation, community and cues: public opinion on european integration. *European Union Politics* 6, no. 4: 419–43.

Hooghe, L., and G. Marks. 2009. A postfunctionalist theory of European integration: from permissive consensus to constraining dissensus. *British Journal of Political Science* 39, no. 1: 1–23.

Howlett, M., and M. Ramesh. 2002. The policy effects of internationalization: a subsystem adjustment analysis of policy change. *Journal of Comparative Policy Analysis* 4, no. 1: 31–50.

Hutter, S., and A. Kerscher. 2014. Politicizing Europe in Hard Times: conflicts over Europe in France in a long-term perspective, 1974–2012. *Journal of European Integration* 36, no. 3. doi: 10.1080/07036337.2014.885752.

Kingdon, J.W. 2002. *Agendas, alternatives, and public policies*. New York: Longman.

Kudrna, Z. 2012. Cross-border resolution of failed banks in the European Union after the crisis: business as usual. *Journal of Common Market Studies* 50, no. 2: 283–99.

Laulom, S., E. Mazuyer, Ch. Teissier, C.E. Triomphe, and P. Vielle. 2012. *How has the crisis affected social legislation in Europe?* Policy Brief No. 2/2012. Brussels: ETUI.

Longo, M., and P. Murray. 2011. No ode to joy? Reflections on the European Union's legitimacy. *International Politics* 48, no. 6: 667–90.

Meunier, S. 2014. "Beggars can't be choosers": the European crisis and Chinese direct investment in the European Union. *Journal of European Integration* 36, no. 3. doi: 10.1080/07036337.2014.885754.

Moravcsik, A. 1993. Preferences and power in the European community: a liberal intergovernmentalist approach. *Journal of Common Market Studies* 31, no. 4: 473–524.

Moravcsik, A. 1998. *The choice for Europe*. Ithaca, NY: Cornell University Press.

Moravcsik, A. 2012. Europe after the crisis, how to sustain a common currency. *Foreign Affairs* 91, no. 3: 54–68.

Nicolaïdis, K.A. 2012. The idea of European Demoicracy. In *Philosophical Foundations of European Union Law*, eds. J. Dickson and P. Eleftheriadis, 247–74. Oxford: Oxford University Press.

Nicolaïdis, K. 2013. European Demoicracy and its crisis. *Journal of Common Market Studies* 51, no. 2: 351–69.

Quaglia, L. 2012. The 'Old' and 'New' political economy of hedge fund regulation in the European Union. *West European Politics* 34, no. 4: 665–82.

van Rompuy, H. 2012. Speech at the Ambrosetti forum. Cernobbio, 8 September (PRESSE 370).

Roth, F. 2009. The effect of the financial crisis on systemic trust. *Intereconomics* 44, no. 4: 203–8.

Roth, F., D. Gros, and F. Nowak-Lehmann D. 2014. Crisis and citizens' trust in the European Central Bank - panel data evidence for the Euro area, 1999 to 2012. *Journal of European Integration* 36, no. 3. doi: 10.1080/07036337.2014.886400.

Sabatier, P.A., and H.C. Jenkins-Smith. 1999. The advocacy coalition framework: an assessment. In *Theories of the policy process*, ed. P.A. Sabatier, 117–66. Boulder: Westview Press.

Salines, M., G. Glöckler, and Z. Truchlewski. 2012. Existential crisis, incremental response: the Eurozone's dual institutional evolution 2007–2011. *Journal of European Public Policy* 19, no. 5: 665–81.

Scharpf, F.W. 2012. *Legitimacy intermediation in the multilevel european polity and its collapse in the Euro crisis* (No. 12/6). MPIfG Discussion Paper.

Schimmelfennig, F., and B. Rittberger. 2006. Theories of European integration. Assumptions and hypotheses. In *European Union. Power and policy-making*, ed. J. Richardson, 73–95. London: Routledge.

Schmitter, P.C. 1970. A revised theory of regional integration. *International Organization* 24, no. 4: 836–68.

Schwarzer, D. 2012. The Euro area crises, shifting power relations and institutional change in the European Union. *Global Policy* 3, no. S1: 28–41.

Serricchio, F., M. Tsakatika, and L. Quaglia. 2013. Euroscepticism and the global financial crisis. *Journal of Common Market Studies* 51, no. 1: 51–64.

Shambaugh, J.C. 2012. The Euro's three crises. *Brookings Papers on Economic Activity* 44, no. 1: 157–231.

Taggart, P., and A. Szczerbiak. 2013. Coming in from the cold? Euroscepticism, government participation and party positions on Europe. *Journal of Common Market Studies* 51, no. 1: 17–37.

Tosun, J. forthcoming. Absorption of regional funds: a comparative analysis. *Journal of Common Market Studies*, doi: 10.1111/jcms.12088.

True, J.L., B.D. Jones, and F.R. Baumgartner. 2007. Punctuated equilibrium theory: explaining stability and change in American policymaking. In *Theories of the policy process*, ed. P.A. Sabatier, 155–88. Boulder: Westview Press.

Tsoukalis, L. 2011. The JCMS annual review lecture. The shattering of illusions – and what next? *Journal of Common Market Studies* 49, no. S1: 19–44.

Visser, P.S., A.L. Holbrook, and J.A. Krosnick. 2008. Knowledge and attitudes. In *Handbook of public opinion research*, eds. W. Donsbach and M.W. Traugott, 127–40. Thousand Oaks, CA: Sage.

Walter, S. 2013. *Financial crises and the politics of macroeconomic adjustments*. Cambridge: Cambridge University Press.

Wälti, S. 2012. Trust no more? The impact of the crisis on citizens' trust in Central banks *Journal of International Money and Finance* 31, no. 3: 593–605.

Weible, C.M., P.A. Sabatier, and K. McQueen. 2009. Themes and variations: taking stock of the advocacy coalition framework. *Policy Studies Journal* 37, no. 1: 121–40.

Whitman, R.G., and A.E. Juncos. 2012. The Arab spring, the eurozone crisis and the neighbourhood: a region in flux. *Journal of Common Market Studies* 50, no. S1: 147–61.

The Unexpected Winner of the Crisis: The European Commission's Strengthened Role in Economic Governance

MICHAEL W. BAUER & STEFAN BECKER

German University of Administrative Sciences, Speyer, Germany

ABSTRACT Since the latest financial and economic crisis took hold of the European Union (EU), its economic governance architecture has been undergoing crucial changes. Research into the institutional consequences of these reforms is still fragmented — especially with regard to the function of the European Commission. This article seeks to fill this void by analysing the supranational executive's role in the four areas that have witnessed the most important changes: financial stability support, economic policy surveillance, coordination of national polices and supervision of the financial sector. The empirical evidence suggests that the Commission continues to be a powerful player in EU economic governance, but its primary role is changing. While its agenda-setting power is decreasing, most decisions in economic governance depend on the Commission to make them work. With more and stronger implementation competences, it may be less visible. But it is not less important. This finding qualifies the degree of intergovernmentalism in economic governance.

1. Introduction

Faced with the most severe financial and economic crisis in decades, the European Union (EU) has taken great pains to reform its economic governance architecture in order to provide immediate relief and prevent further emergencies. After what can be described as a 'step change' (Schimmelfennig 2014), it now features financial stability support with strong conditionality for troubled member states, a tighter grip on domestic economic policies, a clearer focus on competitiveness in the coordination of other national policies and an emerging regime for the regulation of the financial sector. While the *policy* substance of these reforms is widely debated, their *polity* consequences are only beginning to be understood (see Salines, Glöckler, and Truchlewski 2012; Schwarzer 2012 for first assessments).

The role of the European Commission is particularly unclear — more so as these reforms come at a time It has almost become conventional wisdom that this institution, once considered to be the ultimate engine for an ever closer union, is gradually losing political clout (Peterson 2012). Against the background of an empowered European Parliament, progressive political leadership by the European Council and the proliferation of new regulatory institutions, the EU executive's influence has been repeatedly called into question (see further references to this debate in Kassim and Menon 2004; Kassim *et al.* 2013). At first glance, the EU's response to the current financial and economic crisis seems to aggravate this alleged decline. Early accounts argue that agenda-setting has been dominated by intergovernmental institutions (Hodson 2013), while the Commission has been described as being 'not very visible in early crisis management' (Puetter 2012, 172) and as remaining rather 'indecisive and uninspiring' thereafter (Menz and Smith 2013, 202). As a consequence, many observers see it successively turning into a mere secretariat for the member states (Ondarza 2011), and 'intergovernmentalism' is the key term for describing the EU's crisis management (e.g. Fabbrini 2013).

While the empirical observations are valid, some conclusions are disputable. The concepts of intergovernmentalism and supranationalism are the theoretical standard of evaluating European integration. However, intergovernmentalism and supranationalism are difficult to apply to an economic governance architecture that is growing more complex. Differences are to be expected across policy areas and policy phases. The role of the Commission seems to be a strong case in point: it can convincingly be argued that the Commission has remained rather cautious during the early phases of crisis response (see also Copeland and James 2014), but such a narrow analytical focus runs the risk of underestimating this institution's overall importance and thereby neglecting crucial dynamics in EU politics. After all, policy-making involves more than just agenda-setting; policies have to be formulated, implemented and (ideally) evaluated.

The Commission role in these dimensions of the reformed economic governance architecture is hardly elaborated. The term 'secretariat' is actually prone to obfuscate the significance of 'one of the most mature and powerful international bureaucracies worldwide' (Trondal 2010, 17). Especially when it comes to implementing the numerous reforms brought about by the crisis, it is intuitive that the Commission will bear lots of responsibility. So even if institutional changes are results of intergovernmental bargaining, they can involve or empower supranational institutions in deliberate or unforeseen ways. It is thus worthwhile to study the Commission's role in established and emerging policy areas of economic governance in order to provide a more complete picture.

For this purpose, this article briefly reminds us of the manifold functions the Commission already fulfils in European politics and develops a modest analytical framework for capturing its role in economic governance in and after the crisis. The empirical section then considers the Commission's tasks in four areas: financial stability support, economic policy surveillance, coordination of national policies and supervision of the financial sector. It is argued that the Commission is — at least in the policy areas under discussion — indeed undergoing a profound change. But rather than being in decline, it is entrusted with ever wider and deeper implementation tasks that are of high political importance. During the crisis, the Commission may have kept a rather low profile, but its role in the reformed economic governance architecture appears not to be diminished but strengthened. The supranational element of crisis reform is thus not to be underestimated — even if some of the measures take intergovernmental form.

2. Analysing the Multifunctional Commission

Many analyses of the Commission focus on its ability to provide political leadership and set the agenda of EU politics — rightly so, given the treaty stipulation that it 'shall promote the general interest of the Union and take appropriate initiatives to that end' (Article 17 TEU). But its functions go far beyond this mandate. As per the treaties, it is also responsible for ensuring the application of primary and secondary EU law, executing the budget and managing programmes as well as coordinating, executive and management functions. In practical terms, this has caused a proliferation of Commission tasks. As regards economic governance before the crisis, Brussels bureaucrats were already involved in activities as different as applying state aid control, monitoring budget deficits and benchmarking national social policies — just to name a few. With the EU now strengthening its role in established policy fields and expanding its involvement into new areas, the list of Commission activities can be expected to grow even more complex. It therefore seems appropriate to take stock of the recent changes in the Commission's task portfolio.

Two theoretical approaches are to guide our analysis. Firstly, the policy cycle approach serves as a heuristic background, according to which the ideal typical policy process can be divided into more or less four major stages (Anderson 1975; Jones 1970): (1) problems are identified and set on the political agenda, (2) policy options are drawn up and eventually decided on, (3) the selected policies are specified and implemented and (4) they go through evaluation, after which they are maintained, reformed or dismantled (see also Knill and Tosun 2011). Empirically, these phases are neither distinct nor do they necessarily follow this sequence. But they allow for a more structured analysis of all reforms related to the financial and economic crisis. The implementation phase — or third major stage in the policy cycle approach – is crucial for the impact of reforms but, as of yet, under-researched in the field of economic governance. And it will thus make up the core of this article.

So secondly, the assessment of the Commission's role in this implementation phase is based on an adaptation of Börzel's (2005) differentiation between the breadth and depth of integration.[1] The former relates to the range of its involvement, taking into account the policy areas in which the EU — and with it the Commission — has a say. Expansions in breadth can be obvious when a policy field is becoming a matter of EU competence for the first time, or it can be subtle when further elements of this particular policy are added or made more prominent. The depth of Commission's involvement depends on its relevance. Its authority varies depending on the decision-making procedures governing the respective policy field. It is, for instance, quite independent in enforcing the single market, whereas it only plays an auxiliary role in the coordination procedures that are to guide national reforms. There are, by now, quite many governance practices besides and in between the Community Method and intergovernmental procedures. The following empirical account will carefully assess the breadth and depth of Commission involvement in different dimensions of EU economic governance. In so doing, it will also assess the degree to which these policy areas feature supranational elements.

3. Empirical Evidence from the Policy Areas

3.1. Financial Stability Support

Since the crisis first took hold in Europe, the policy area of financial stability support for EU member states has witnessed rapid and remarkable institutionalization. The Commission has been and continues to be involved in multiple ways. This represents an enormous expansion of Commission activity having not been extensively dealing with this policy area before the crisis. As the first Greek bail-out package was provided by bilateral loans and financing by the International Monetary Fund (IMF), the Commission was only entrusted with coordinating and administrating the pooled bilateral loans, including their disbursement (European Commission 2013a). However, when the European stability architecture emerged, its competences grew more complex. This architecture currently features four facilities for granting financial assistance to troubled member states, which are basically based on two governance arrangements.

3.1.1. Balance of Payments assistance and European Financial Stabilization Mechanism. The Balance of Payments (BoP) assistance is a relatively modest facility that is only open to non-euro countries, but the decisions for granting financial support to Hungary (2008), Latvia (2008) and Romania (2009) have arguably been the first responses to the unfolding financial crisis in the EU. Ultimately based on Article 143 TFEU, BoP assistance was already established in 1988 (Council Regulation (EEC)

No. 1969/88). It was then modified in 2002 with 14.5 billion having been granted until fall 2013 (Council Regulation (EC) No. 332/2002).

As concerns the governance of BoP assistance, the Commission is usually part of all relevant phases. It first conducts negotiations with other potential international donors in order to elicit multilateral assistance options. After securing such an arrangement, the Commission is responsible for drafting a decision proposal on a member state's actual request for BoP assistance that the Council has to vote on. If this is agreed in principle, it negotiates a memorandum of understanding with the applicant state and monitors compliance if an agreement has been reached. What is most remarkable about the BoP assistance is the Commission's mandate to manage the financial assistance by borrowing on the capital markets — the EU budget being an implicit guarantee and safeguarding the best rating possible — and lending to the member states in question.

Apart from these direct competences, its old mandate of guarding the treaties is also playing a role when granting BoP assistance. In the case of Hungary, which applied for a second precautionary programme in 2011, the Commission's role in monitoring compliance with EU law was of considerable importance. After starting an infringement procedure regarding, among other issues, the independence of the Hungarian Central Bank in early 2012 (European Commission 2012a), it was not before the Hungarian Prime Minister promised several reforms that the negotiations about a second assistance programme would begin. The implicit understanding was that these reforms would have to be implemented before the negotiations can be concluded (European Commission 2012b). This incident shows that BoP assistance not only involves the Commission in crucial phases, but also empowers its old mandate of guarding the treaties by adding another incentive for member states to comply with EU law.

When the financial crisis escalated in 2010, two new funding instruments were quickly established to offer financial assistance to troubled euro member states that failed to raise money at competitive rates on the capital market. One of them was the European Financial Stabilization Mechanism (EFSM), which is modelled on the BoP assistance and has the same institutional underpinning. This framework has been proposed by the Commission and endorsed by the Council (Regulation (EU) No. 407/2010). For its short-lived existence, the EFSM raised funds up to 48.5 billion for Portugal and Ireland — and it is, once again, the Commission who is in charge of borrowing and lending.

The Commission's financial responsibilities in both the EFSM and the BoP assistance should, however, not be overestimated because the Council always has to approve the terms. This was, for example, the case in 2011, when the Commission suggested reduced interest rate margins and extended maturities for loans granted to Ireland and Portugal (European Commission 2011a), a proposal the Council eventually adopted (Council of the European Union 2011). The Commission has thus no discretion in financial matters. This has to be kept in mind when analysing the following funding instruments, where member states decided to delegate the management of resources to other bodies.

3.1.2. European Financial Stability Facility and European Stability Mechanism. In case of the European Financial Stability Facility (EFSF), borrowing and lending to euro member states, up to 440 billion in total, was delegated to a new organization in the form of a public-limited company in Luxemburg. The same is true for the newer European Stability Mechanism, which is now replacing the EFSF (and the EFSM). Both arrangements also have a distinct intergovernmental treaty basis.

Still, Commission expertise is employed at various stages in the process of granting assistance through the ESM, mostly along with the European Central Bank (ECB) and the IMF (so-called *troika*). First, when a member state requests support, the Commission (along with the ECB) is entrusted with assessing the situation concerning the risk to the overall financial stability, the sustainability of the applicant's public debt and the actual or potential financing needs (Article 13 (1) ESM Treaty). Second, following a general decision by the Board of Directors to grant support, it is the Commission's task (as part of the *troika*) to negotiate a memorandum of understanding with the applicant state (Article 13 (2) ESM Treaty) — and sign it if the memorandum is accepted by the creditor states. Third, the Commission and its *troika* partner institutions are responsible for monitoring compliance with the memorandum of understanding (Article 13 (7) ESM Treaty).

It certainly stands to question how much autonomy the *troika* enjoys vis-à-vis the lender states and also how power and expertise are actually distributed within this group. The European Parliament's hearing (2013) on the working methods of the troika supports early anecdotal evidence from missions to Greece, Ireland and Portugal that sees the Commission having a prominent role alongside the IMF, when assessing the countries' financing needs and actually taking the lead when designing reform plans (Merler, Pisani-Ferry, and Wolff 2012, 7). This impression of the division of labour in the *troika* is also substantiated by the IMF's dissatisfaction with the group's performance in Greece. Its respective report (IMF 2013) condemned the Commission's successful insistence on austerity (see also Lütz and Kranke 2011). This shows that its mandate is far from being an administrative matter; its decisions can have significant political and social repercussions.

As in the BoP assistance scheme, granting financial support through the ESM is also linked to the Commission's mandate of guarding the treaties. The programme for Spain calls for a close monitoring of state aid rules, which is naturally up to the EU's executive. The respective clauses concern the restructuring of Spanish banks and the disbursement of funds for safeguarding their stability. Once again, the Commission plays a crucial role for the decision of granting assistance. In this case, it eventually accepted Spain's plans and the restructuring got under way (European Commission 2012c).

Taken together, the governance architecture of financial stability support involves the Commission in various capacities. It proposes decisions on granting assistance, negotiates conditionality agreements and monitors compliance. The EU executive thus fulfils crucial tasks in all phases of this particular policy cycle. Against the background of the ESM replacing both EFSF and EFSM, it can be argued that the Commission has been kept at arm's length when the crisis called for firewalls with more financial leverage (Hodson 2013), but it stands to question if the technical task of handling loans is all that important. Moreover, the policy programmes attached to financial stability support involve the Commission in its old mandate as guardian of the treaties.

The depth of Commission involvement in the area of financial stability support has thus hardly been reduced, while the breadth of its involvement (in light of the financial resources now being re-allocated) has been greatly expanded during the financial crisis. The newer lending facilities may have intergovernmental bases, but as indicated by the competences of the Commission — and those of the ECB — their daily operation features strong supranational elements because most tasks that are to be accomplished before and after the decisions are delegated to such institutions. As any act of delegation, this provides agents with some leeway. It comes as no surprise that the *troika*'s performance — with it the policy prescription heavily designed by the Commission — is coming under closer scrutiny.

3.2. Economic Policy Surveillance

Apart from introducing these emergency measures, the EU has also passed important reforms aimed at preventing debt crises. In the last two years, there have been crucial changes to all procedures that steer national economic and fiscal policies. Most of these are now streamlined under the 'European Semester' that has already been put in place in 2010. This framework is important in itself in that it improves the stringency of EU economic policy-making, providing clear timelines and combining 'hard' and 'soft' measures (Hallerberg, Marzinotto, and Wolff 2012). It thereby provides political and institutional linkages that could strengthen the Commission's position overall. This section considers the reforms made in regard to 'hard' surveillance with possible sanctions while coordination by 'soft' law is dealt with in the next section.

3.2.1. Six-Pack. Agenda-setting and policy formulation in the field of economic and fiscal surveillance has been hard fought between the Commission and the van Rompuy Task Force which was commissioned by the European Council (2010). The former's right of initiative in this field notwithstanding, the Commission was particularly eager to underline its policy entrepreneurial role. It therefore issued its legislative proposals one month before the Task Force published its report (Schwarzer 2012, 19). The so-called Six-Pack has then been quickly passed through the ordinary legislative channels in 2011. It is made up of five regulations and one directive[2] aimed at reinforcing the Stability and Growth Pact (SGP) that has proven to be ineffective in the run-up to the crisis.

As regards to the governance architecture of the SGP, the most important reform is certainly the introduction of the 'reverse qualified majority voting' for sanctions when member states do not comply with recommendations. From now on, a qualified majority of member states have to vote *against* sanctions, whereas before they had to vote *for* them. In combination with fines and sanctions being now possible much earlier in the process, this adds significant political weight to the recommendations of the Commission, which continues to be in charge of monitoring national progress and proposing actions against deviant member states.

The Six-Pack further reinforces the economic policy surveillance regime in two important ways. First, the Excessive Deficit Procedure is strengthened by the operationalization of the debt criterion[3] and the introduction of the development of national expenditures into the monitoring regime. These reforms leave the Commission's assessments and recommendations with more power, as it is now, for instance, able to issue early warnings to member states if their expenditures grow faster than their GDP. Second, the newly introduced Macroeconomic Imbalance Procedure features the Commission in its preventive and corrective arm — with the former being of particular interest. The Commission now follows macroeconomic trends in an early warning system, made operational by a scoreboard that currently consists of 11 indicators.[4] In cases where member states are above certain statistical thresholds, there are in-depth reviews to be conducted by the Commission (and the ECB where appropriate). This qualitative approach goes beyond 'doing the numbers'; it even includes the possibility of on-site missions by Brussels bureaucrats. These arrangements leave the Commission with strong interpretative authority for the assessment of imbalances. If member states are eventually found to have excessive imbalances, the Commission is yet again responsible for drafting a recommendation for corrective measures.

The first significant results of these reforms were a long time coming. At one point in 2013, there were 20 countries under closer observation in the Excessive Deficit Procedure, but these procedures predated the Six-Pack reforms. In all cases, the Commission so far refrained from employing stronger measures. On the contrary, it proposed the extension of six deadlines for fiscal adjustments (European Commission 2013b). This can be read as either being hesitant to move toward sanctions or deliberately using its discretion to emphasize its 'softer' reform recommendations (see the case of France below). Under the Macroeconomic Imbalance Procedure, the Commission attended to its duties and conducted in-depth reviews of 12 member states in 2012 and 13 member states in 2013. Spring 2014 saw in-depth reviews for 16 countries, involving not only Spain and Slovenia as the most imperilled economies but also Germany, which caused some irritation within the latter state. As far the preconditions for these reviews go, the Commission had to launch this review. It remains to be seen whether and when any excessive imbalance procedures are actually opened — but the Commission is certainly on the lookout.

3.2.2. *Two-Pack.* The so-called Two-Pack, which has also been passed by the ordinary legislative procedure and is made of two regulations,[5] takes effect in 2014. It basically amplifies the measures brought by the Six-Pack and the Fiscal Compact (see below) in regard to the *ex ante* coordination of fiscal policies and the monitoring of financially troubled countries. Starting in fall each year, the surveillance procedure focuses on the budgetary plans of euro area member states for the forthcoming year. It is the Commission's responsibility to assess the 'fit' of the draft budgets with the SGP in general and last year's country-specific recommendations in particular. While the Commission cannot infringe on national sovereignty on budget issues, this procedure does add to its 'toolbox for making recommendations' (European Commission 2013c) in that these early opinions can later be used when deciding on placing member states in the Excessive Deficit Procedure.

In short, this procedure empowers the Commission to offer budgetary guidance much earlier than before. Its general budgetary outlook for the upcoming year is to stimulate further debate among governments and parliaments. In addition, the Two-Pack introduces tougher monitoring procedures for member states that are receiving financial assistance or have just finished structural adjustment programmes. These tasks are, once again, delegated to the Commission and (where appropriate) the ECB. The same is true for the provision of technical assistance when member states have insufficient capacities.

3.2.3. Fiscal Compact. Other than the foregoing reforms, which have been realized by ordinary legislative acts, the Treaty on Stability, Coordination and Governance (TSCG) — also referred to as the Fiscal Compact — is of intergovernmental nature. But this agreement — aimed at further strengthening fiscal discipline and intensifying policy surveillance within the euro area — involves supranational institutions as well.[6]

On the one hand, the treaty stipulates that the correction mechanisms, which are to be triggered automatically if the deficit criteria are breached, are to be based on common principles put forward by the Commission (Article 3 (2) TSCG).[7] On the other hand, the Commission is once again responsible for monitoring compliance. According to Article 8 TSCG, the 'Commission is invited to present in due time to the Contracting Parties a report on the provisions adopted by each of them [...]. If [it] concludes in its report that such Contracting Party has failed to comply [...], the matter will be brought to the Court of Justice of the EU by one or more Contracting Parties'. While a negative opinion by the Commission is not required for bringing a matter to the Court of Justice, the guardian of the EU treaties plays a corresponding role in this intergovernmental agreement by providing crucial information for the member states to decide on. The nature of the treaty, brought about by the resistance of the United Kingdom and the Czech Republic, should not obliterate its supranational characteristics. It stands to question if a legal basis in the EU treaties would have taken a wholly different form as regards the governance architecture.

The Fiscal Compact also intensifies the Excessive Deficit Procedure. Article 7 TGSC states that 'the Contracting Parties whose currency is the euro commit to supporting the proposals or recommendations submitted by the European Commission', unless a qualified majority votes against it. This means that the Fiscal Compact extends 'reversed qualified majority voting' to all stages of the Excessive Deficit Procedure, even if not mentioned in the

Six-Pack reforms, effectively adding further weight to the Commission's assessments.

The reforms aimed at preventing future fiscal crises are thus expanding both the depth and breadth of Commission involvement in economic policy surveillance. It is now responsible for additionally monitoring overall public debt, the development of national expenditures and macroeconomic imbalances. Due to its complex nature, the latter undertaking involves a more qualitative approach, a new instrument for the Commission. Its assessments and recommendations are now also carrying additional weight. The introduction of 'reversed qualified majority' voting when it comes to fines and sanctions can be considered a notable increase in the depth of Commission competences and an important step away from intergovernmental dominance in the SGP (Schimmelfennig 2012, 406). Economic policy surveillance in the context of the treaties has thus seen a clear strengthening on the supranational level. Even the Fiscal Compact, seen by some observers as the prime example of the new intergovernmentalism, employs the Commission and the European Court of Justice in crucial ways and thus has much supranational substance.

3.3. Coordination of National Policies

Apart from economic policy surveillance with possible sanctions, there are also coordination procedures that are to steer national policies by soft law. These are aimed at fostering reforms in policy areas of common interest but utmost national sovereignty, such as social security and employment. Obviously, these policy areas have received greater attention during the financial crisis.

There are two broader initiatives in this regard. The first one is Europe 2020, the successor of the Lisbon Strategy that ran until 2010. As its predecessor, Europe 2020 is a broad growth strategy that touches upon several policy fields. The second initiative was the Euro Plus Pact, adopted in 2011 by the euro zone members and six other states. Its aims are to improve competitiveness, create employment and contribute to sustainable public debt by reinforcing and refining member states' commitments made in the context of the Europe 2020 strategy. Both of these initiatives make use of procedures that broadly resemble the Open Method of Coordination.

This mode of governance is based on soft law, such as guidelines and recommendations, which are to guide the member states' reform initiatives. There are no hard sanctions. Rather, this procedure aims at benchmarking, persuasion through naming and shaming as well as policy learning through best practices. The Commission is a crucial provider of information in both initiatives. At the beginning of the year, it produces an annual growth survey that outlines the progress made and the challenges to overcome in general terms. Ideally, these priorities are considered when member states draw up their national stability (under the SGP) and reform (under the Europe 2020 strategy) programmes. After evaluating the national documents, the Commission proposes country-specific recommendations that the Council has to endorse. It also assesses the progress made in terms of the Euro

Plus Pact commitments, once again providing information for the European Council that is ultimately in charge of the political monitoring. In cooperation with Eurostat, it also operates a scoreboard of the progress on Europe 2020's eight headline indicators.

The Commission's role in these coordination procedures should, however, not be overstated because the European Council provides policy guidance. This does not only concern the overall orientation of the Europe 2020 strategy that was mainly outlined by the European Council, which outrivalled the Commission by narrowly focusing on jobs and growth and dismissing claims for a broader approach (Ondarza 2011, 20). Member state institutions are also strong in the implementation phase. In fact, during the first cycle of the European Semester, member states were eager to diminish some of the Commission's recommendations (Hallerberg, Marzinotto, and Wolff 2012), and there have been strong doubts about policy coordination without sanctions in general (e.g. de la Porte and Pochet 2012).

However, in light of the current crisis, soft law might become stronger than before. The recommendations for France in 2013 are a case in point. The suggestions for reforming — *inter alia* — the French labour market and pension system were given special meaning by the simultaneous proposal to extend the country's deadline for fiscal adjustment under the SGP (European Commission 2013b). This gave the impression that the reforms were a precondition for the extension, displayed by the French President's harsh reaction to the recommendations. While critical observers are eager to emphasize the Commission's legal inability to enforce these reforms, this was certainly one of the most discussed cases of soft law yet. Given the new 'comply or explain' rule that commits the Council to publish its reasons when changing the recommendations (Council of the European Union 2013), this trend is likely to continue.

If the Euro Plus Pact as well the Europe 2020 strategy are taken more seriously by their respective member states, they widen the depth and breadth of Commission involvement through closer monitoring, clearer benchmarking and more specific recommendations. Persuasion as well as naming and shaming will always be less forceful than the threat of monetary sanctions, but in times of contagious crises national governments are coming under more pressure to argue their cases. This puts the Commission in a more prominent position, and so far it seems as if it is trying to use its authority. And it can be argued that the symbolic linking with the SGP monitoring regime represents a small self-empowerment by the Commission.

3.4. *Supervision of the Financial Sector*

As regards to the supervision of the financial sector, the pace of reforms has been slower than in other areas. Two initiatives are, however, worth noting: the European System of Financial Supervision (ESFS) and the banking union that has finally begun to take shape with the introduction of the Single Supervisory Mechanism (SSM).

Other than delivering the proposals for the ESFS in 2009, the Commission is not much involved in this area of financial supervision. Tasks are delegated to four new institutions that took up their work in 2011: three European supervisory authorities[8] for micro-prudential oversight and a European Systemic Risk Board for macro-prudential oversight. The former are mainly responsible for coordinating and monitoring national authorities (but without the right to interfere in their work); the latter can ultimately result in non-binding recommendations to member states and specific national or EU authorities. The Commission is merely represented on the respective boards, but it does play an evaluative role in this domain. The different regulations contain clauses that entitle it to review the structure and performance of the overall oversight system.

The SSM can be considered a more important step towards European banking union. Governments of the euro area called upon the Commission to propose respective legislation in June 2012. Only about 75 days later, the proposal (COM (2012) 511 final) was published. Based on this document, an agreement was reached in the Council at the end of 2012, with the parliament — after some bargaining with the Council under mediation of the Commission — generally agreeing in the Spring of 2013. Details are still to be clarified before the regulations for this undertaking are finally passed, but the overall structure is already observable at this point. The SSM will be located in the ECB, which will be entrusted with direct supervision of the most significant banks (as well as those receiving direct financial assistance from EU facilities) and monitoring of national supervision of less significant banks. The Commission will only be granted observer status on its supervisory board. It will, however, once again be responsible for evaluating this new mechanism. As it is stated in the proposed regulation, the Commission shall publish a report on its application after three years and shall make accompanying proposals.

The Commission further fulfilled its duty of formulating policy and proposed legislation for a Single Resolution Mechanism (SRM). The Commission describes its own role in this arrangement as deciding 'on the basis of the Single Resolution Board's recommendation, or on its own initiative, [...] whether and when to place a bank into resolution' and setting 'out a framework for the use of resolution tools' (European Commission 2013d). Interestingly, it is — as of yet — not clear who will make the final decisions. This competence could be transferred to the Commission, which sees itself as the only EU institution with adequate legal authority.

So far, the Commission is mainly fulfilling its old mandates of policy developing and evaluation when it comes to the supervision of the financial sector. Its competences in this field have thus widened a bit, but they have not grown deeper in regulatory terms. If the SRM eventually took the shape the Commission proposes (for this, it has the backing of the European Parliament), its depth of involvement would increase considerably. Still, as the supervision of the financial sector is slowly moving from soft law to hard rules (Hennessy 2014), its supranational element is obvious. And this has strengthened another actor on this level: the ECB.

Table 1. Overview of changes in Commission's role in economic governance

Financial stability support (EFSM, EFSF, ESM)	Economic policy surveillance (Six-Pack, Two-Pack, Fiscal Compact)	Coordination of national policies (Europe 2020, Euro Plus Pact)	Supervision of financial sector (SSM, SRM)
Breadth: +++ Wider involvement due to increased financial support in more countries through new lending facilities	*Breadth:* ++ Wider monitoring regime through inclusion of national expenditures, macroeconomic trends, overall debt and budgetary plans	*Breadth:* + Slightly wider coordinating functions through introduction of further procedures focused on competitiveness	*Breadth:* + Slight widening of evaluative role; further expansion, if SRM features Commission as prominently as currently envisioned
Depth: ++ Stronger position in terms of negotiating and monitoring due to prominent role in *troika*; contraction in administrative role because of new lending facilities	*Depth:* +++ Stronger opinions and recommendations by virtue of RQMV, introduction of macroeconomic scoreboard and in-depth reviews	*Depth:* ++ Slightly stronger recommendations by symbolic coupling with 'harder' surveillance and 'comply or explain' rule, operation of scoreboard	*Depth:* 0 No change; possibly strong monitoring role, if SRM features Commission as envisioned

Notes: +++ = strong expansion, ++ = medium expansion, + = little expansion, 0 = no change, – = decrease

This overview of crisis-related reforms and their implications for the Commission has revealed that this institution has been entrusted with ever more implementation tasks in the economic governance architecture, which effectively expands the breadth (in terms of policy areas) and depth (in terms of competence) of its involvement. Its role does, however, vary between policy areas, as is summarized in Table 1. Financial stability support and economic policy surveillance rely heavily on the EU's executive, the coordination of national policies only to certain extent and the supervision of the financial sector — so far — hardly at all.

4. Conclusion

This close reading of institutional change during the crisis has revealed that the Commission is far from being absent in EU economic governance. As the rules for member states are growing ever stricter, the EU's executive plays a pivotal role in enforcing them. While its agenda-setting power has been curbed during the crisis, it continues to formulate policy, and more importantly its role in implementation has grown substantially. It now covers a much broader scope of policies and is, in some cases, equipped with stronger competences. What does this tell us about EU economic governance in general and the Commission in particular?

First of all, regarding the central theme of this special issue, i.e. long-term consequences of the crisis and their theoretical implications for EU studies (Tosun, Wetzel, and Zapryanova 2014), it is safe to say that EU economic governance is changing incrementally. What at first appears to be an institutional big-bang is rather following the established architecture (see also Salines, Glöckler, and Truchlewski 2012). As EU economic governance currently features quite different modes of governance in all relevant policy areas, there is no clear intergovernmental or supranational model. However, the foregoing analysis on the Commission shows that supranational actors play an ever more important role, although its involvement varies depending on the policy area and the institutional paths taken before the crises. It has become evident that even intergovernmental frameworks — such as the Fiscal Compact and the ESM — do not bar intense Commission involvement; on the contrary, they heavily rely on the EU's central executive.

For the Commission, this means that it is successively shifting from policy entrepreneurship to policy management (Bauer 2006). This trend has been envisioned by Laffan as early as 1997, and the two main reasons cited then still sound familiar today: the level of integration achieved and a less benign environment. While it is true that economic governance was and continues to be less supranational than other policy areas, there was already much to be managed by the Commission under the policy surveillance and coordination regimes — leaving little room for policy entrepreneurship in the advent of the crisis. Add to that the 'constraining dissensus' across the EU (Hooghe and Marks 2008), which entails historically low trust in supranational institutions, as well as little experience in the field of financial stability support and supervision, and it comes as no surprise that the Commission refrained from putting forward bold integration plans in both areas.

Still, the member states' strategy of 'delegation to non-majoritarian, technocratic supranational organizations' (Schimmelfennig 2014) left the Commission on a stronger footing than before, because the delegated tasks are not purely administrative matters. It is a highly political activity to deliver opinions and recommendations — be it in terms of financial stability support or policy surveillance — for the member states to decide on. Negotiating memoranda of understanding is also quite political, as evidenced by the controversies surrounding the conditionality for creditor states. Even monitoring compliance with requirements laid down in the memoranda of understanding or the reformed SGP leaves the Commission with strong discretion, as does its role as an information hub between the member states in the coordination of national policies. Finally, putting forward legislative proposals, even if 'commissioned' by the member states, remains a highly influential activity.

For the Commission, its new role will entail further challenges. Its early record in the *troika* shows that negotiating as well as monitoring strict conditionality under precarious circumstances is a delicate task, for which the Commission will have to build up further expertise. Its interpretative authority in the European Semester will demand careful recommendations as to not excessively agitate member states. To a certain extent, it is up to the Commission to safeguard the loose coupling of 'harder' surveillance and 'softer' coordination. Generally, the EU's executive is, so far, only equipped with potential leverage; whether and how it is used remains to be seen.

This is, at the same time, the main implication for future research. Rather than putting too much weight on agenda-setting and grand EU policy initiatives, the Commission's role in implementation has to be taken more seriously, in economic governance and beyond. Otherwise, EU studies run the risk of underestimating the many little 'pockets of power' Brussels bureaucrats are equipped with. This will not be an easy exercise; disentangling the influences inside the *troika* would require intensive research. However, it might not only be in economic governance but also in the implementation of other policies that Commission activity might be more salient and might show more political weight than what has been studied under the heading of policy entrepreneurship so far.

In sum, the Commission's importance in the European economic integration process has not been diminished, but its role has shifted. The current crisis might well prove to be a catalyst accelerating changes which so far have gone by and large unobserved. Given that the EU system is constantly maturing, entrepreneurship as neo-functionalists conceive it will most likely become ever rarer. Analysts might thus be well advised not to assess the changing Commission role on decreasing entrepreneurial spirit but to embrace the challenge to analyse its political room of manoeuvre in supervising and steering policy implementation. The emerging economic governance regime offers new opportunities for supranational influence, and the Commission might well use its new implementation powers politically in similar terms as it has used policy entrepreneurship in the past.

Notes

1. Börzel draws on the works of Lindberg and Scheingold (1970), Schmitter (1970) and Scharpf (2001).
2. Regulation (EU) No. 1173/2011, Regulation (EU) No. 1174/2011, Regulation (EU) No. 1175/2011, Regulation (EU) No. 1176/2011, Council Regulation (EU) No 1177/2011 and Council Directive 2011/85/EU.
3. From now on, member states can be put in the deficit procedure, when the 60% reference for the debt-to-GDP ratio is not respected, even if the deficit is below 3%. However, the assessment will take into account 'all relevant factors and the impact of the economic cycle' and the gap between a member state's debt level and the 60% reference must *not* be reduced by 1/20th annually (on average over three years) in order to trigger the deficit procedure (European Commission 2011b).
4. The legal basis for this monitoring system is Regulation (EU) No. 1176/2011.
5. Regulation (EU) No. 473/2013 and Regulation (EU) No 472/2013.
6. Much of its substance mirrors the Six-Pack reforms and will therefore not be discussed.
7. These principles were published in June 2012 (COM (2012) 342 final).
8. These are the European Banking Authority, the European Securities and Markets Authority and the European Insurance and Occupational Pensions Authority.

References

Anderson, J.E. 1975. *Public policy-making*. New York: Holt-Preager.
Bauer, M.W. 2006. Co-managing programme implementation: conceptualizing the European Commission's role in policy execution. *Journal of European Public Policy* 13, no. 5: 717–35.

Börzel, T.A. 2005. Mind the gap! European integration between level and scope. *Journal of European Public Policy* 12, no. 2: 217–36.

Copeland, P., and S. James. 2014. Policy windows, ambiguity and commission entrepreneurship: explaining the relaunch of the European Union's economic reform agenda. *Journal of European Public Policy* 21, no. 1: 1–19.

Council of the European Union. 2011. *Press release*. 3119th Council Meeting, General Affairs. Luxemburg, 11 October 2011, 15336/11.

Council of the European Union. 2013. *Explanatory note, accompanying document to council recommendations to member states under the European semester 2013*. 11336/13.

European Commission. 2011a. *Press release*, Brussels, 14 September 2011. MEMO/11/602.

European Commission. 2011b. *Press release*, Brussels, 12 December 2011. MEMO/11/898.

European Commission. 2012a. *Press release*, Brussels, 17 January 2012. IP/12/24.

European Commission. 2012b. *Press release*, Brussels, 25 April 2012. IP/12/407.

European Commission. 2012c. *Press release*, Brussels, 18 November 2012. IP/12/1277.

European Commission. 2013a. *Financial assistance to Greece*, http://ec.europa.eu/economy_finance/assistance_eu_ms/greek_loan_facility/index_en.htm (accessed 31 August 2013).

European Commission. 2013b. *Press release*, Brussels, 29 May 2013. MEMO/13/463.

European Commission. 2013c. *Press release*, Brussels, 12 March 2013. MEMO/13/196.

European Commission. 2013d. *Press release*, Brussels, 10 July 2013d. IP/13/674.

European Council. 2010. *Conclusions of the European Council*. 25/26 March 2010. EUCO 7/10.

Fabbrini, S. 2013. Intergovernmentalism and its limits: assessing the European Union's answer to the Euro crisis. *Comparative Political Studies* 46, no. 9: 1003–29.

Hallerberg, M., B. Marzinotto, and G.B Wolff. 2012. *On the effectiveness and legitimacy of EU economic policies*, Bruegel Policy Briefs, Issue 4/2012.

Hennessy, A. 2014. Redesigning financial supervision in the European Union (2009–2013). *Journal of European Public Policy* 21, no. 2: 151–68.

Hodson, D. 2013. The little engine that wouldn't: supranational entrepreneurship and the Barroso Commission. *Journal of European Integration* 35, no. 3: 301–14.

Hooghe, L., and G. Marks. 2008. A Postfunctionalist theory of European integration: from permissive consensus to constraining dissensus. *British Journal of Political Science* 39: 1–23.

International Monetary Fund. 2013. *Greece: ex post evaluation of exceptional access under the 2010 stand-by arrangement*, IMF Country Report No. 13/156.

Jones, C.O. 1970. *An introduction to the study of public policy*. Belmont, CA: Wadsworth.

Kassim, H., and A. Menon. 2004. EU member states and the Prodi Commission. In *The changing European Commission*, ed. D.G. Dimitrakopoulos, 89–104. Manchester: Manchester University Press.

Kassim, H., J. Peterson, M.W. Bauer, S. Connolly, R. Dehousse, L. Hooghe, and A. Thompson. 2013. *The European Commission of the twenty-first century*. Oxford: Oxford University Press.

Knill, C., and J. Tosun. 2011. Policy-making. In *Comparative politics*, ed. D. Caramani, 373–88. Oxford: Oxford University Press.

Laffan, B. 1997. From policy entrepreneur to policy manager: the challenge facing the European Commission. *Journal of European Public Policy* 4, no. 3: 422–38.

Lindberg, L.N., and S.A. Scheingold. 1970. *Europe's would-be polity*. Englewood Cliffs, NJ: Prentice-Hall.

Lütz, S., and M. Kranke. 2011. *The paradox of weakness in crisis lending: how the European Commission prevails over the IMF*, Mimeo, 11 April 2011.

Menz, G., and M.P. Smith. 2013. Kicking the can down the road to more Europe? Salvaging the Euro and the Future of European Economic Governance, *Journal of European Integration* 35, no. 3: 195–206.

Merler, S., J. Pisani-Ferry, and G.B. Wolff. 2012. *The role of the ECB in financial assistance: some early observations*, European Parliament-IP/A/ECON/NT/2012-04.

Ondarza, N. v. 2011. *Koordinatoren an der Spitze: Politische Führung in den reformierten Strukturen der Europäischen Union* [Coordinators at the top: political leadership in the reformed strucutres of the European Union], SWP-Studie.

Peterson, J. 2012. The college of commissioners. In *The institutions of the European Union*, 3rd ed. eds. J. Peterson and M. Shackleton, 96–123. Oxford: Oxford University Press.

de la Porte, C., and P. Pochet. 2012. Why and how (still) Study the open method of co-ordination (OMC)? *Journal of European Social Policy* 22, no. 3: 336–49.

Puetter, U. 2012. Europe's deliberative intergovernmentalism: the role of the Council and European Council in EU economic governance. *Journal of European Public Policy* 19, no. 2: 161–78.

Salines, M., G. Glöckler, and Z. Truchlewski. 2012. Existential crisis, incremental response: the eurozone's dual institutional evolution 2007–2011. *Journal of European Public Policy* 19, no. 5: 665–81.

Scharpf, F.W. 2001. Notes toward a theory of multilevel governing in Europe. *Scandinavian Political Studies* 24, no. 1: 1–26.

Schimmelfennig, F. 2012. Zwischen Neo-und Postfunktionalismus: Die Integrationstheorien und die Eurokrise [Between neo- and postfunctionalism: integration theories and the euro crisis]. *Politische Vierteljahresschrift* 53, no. 3: 394–413.

Schimmelfennig, F. 2014. European integration in the euro crisis: the limits of postfunctionalism. *Journal of European Integration*.

Schmitter, P.C. 1970. A revised theory of regional integration. *International Organization* 24, no. 4: 836–68.

Schwarzer, D. 2012. The euro area crises, shifting power relations and institutional change in the European Union. *Global Policy* 3, no. 1: 28–41.

Tosun, J., A. Wetzel, and G. Zapryanova. 2014. Coping with crisis: Europe's challenges and strategies. *Journal of European Integration*.

Trondal, J. 2010. *An emergent European executive order*. Oxford: Oxford University Press.

The Impact of the Euro Crisis on Citizens' Support for the European Union

DANIELA BRAUN* & MARKUS TAUSENDPFUND**

*Geschwister-Scholl Institute for Political Science, University of Munich, München, Germany;
**Department of Political Science, University of Hagen, Hagen, Germany

ABSTRACT Our paper investigates the impact of the global and the Euro crisis on citizens' attitudes towards the European Union (EU). We measure the impact of the Euro crisis on two different levels: First, the crisis itself at the contextual level and second, and more importantly, at the individual level, referring to citizens' perceptions of the crisis. Our main assumption is that during the crisis, economic explanations find their way back into the study of EU support. We test our hypotheses with 27 EU member states using different Eurobarometer surveys and apply descriptive statistics as well as multi-level regression analyses. Three conclusions emerge from the analysis: First, the impact of the Euro crisis is stronger than in the case of the global financial crisis. Second, support for the EU depends on both the contextual and the individual level although effects of the latter are more prevalent. Third, the effect of the individual perception of the crisis on EU support is stronger in Euro countries as well as in economically powerful countries. Altogether and contrary to major assumptions following post-functional arguments, our findings show that in times of the crisis economic factors again play a major role in the explanation of support for the EU. This leads to a rather critical evaluation for the future of the European integration process.

Introduction

The current economic crisis is one the most far-reaching events in the last decades. One can easily assume that these events severely challenged both national political systems and the supranational entity of the European

Union (EU) (Scharpf 2011). The latter is of particular importance for the future of the European integration process. In the preceding chapters, this has been investigated with a particular eye on institutional changes through the crisis, e.g. changes in general governance structures or with respect to the role of the European Commission (Bauer and Becker 2014). Nevertheless, the crisis is supposed to affect not only polities and policies, but also the dimension of politics. Most scholars agree that citizens' support plays an important role within the integration process (Hix and Høyland 2011, 105; Hooghe and Marks 2009) — in particular after the end of the so-called 'permissive consensus' (Down and Wilson 2008; Hooghe and Marks 2009; Schäfer 2006). Hence, it is at least as relevant to study how the crisis affects this dimension.

Against this background, we aim to study whether the crisis erodes citizens support for the EU and thus might represent a threat to the further integration process (Tosun, Wetzel and Zapryanova 2014). Compared to the other contributions that focus on the changing pattern in particular countries (Clements, Nanou and Verney 2014) or on support for specific political actors (Roth, Gros and Nowak-Lehmann D. 2014), we explore whether citizens support for the EU has been affected more by the global or the European dimension of the crisis to take into account the multi-dimensional shape appropriately. That is to say we distinguish between the global economic crisis and the Euro crisis. We argue that only the Euro crisis is likely to have an impact on citizens EU support, whereas the global crisis is too distant to affect peoples' attitudes. Moreover, to get a better understanding of the underlying mechanisms, we investigate the causal link between the Euro crisis and political support. In doing so, we refer to previous studies showing essentially that economic considerations were highly relevant for explaining citizens' support for the EU during the early phases of European integration (Anderson and Reichert 1995; Castles 1998; Eichenberg and Dalton 1993, 2007). Though, within the last decade, the relevance of economic considerations has diminished in the course of time in favor of identity-based approaches (see e.g. Carey 2002; McLaren 2004, 2006, 2010). The interesting question at this point in time is whether and in which way the crisis has changed this pattern. We argue that the crisis has strengthened the explanatory power of economic approaches — bringing thus economic explanations back in (for a similar argument see Serricchio, Tsakatika, and Quaglia 2013). If the crisis led to a revival of economic sources of citizens' EU support, this could have important implications for the future of the EU representing potential complications for further integration.

The article is structured as follows: We first give a more detailed description of previous findings before we derive guiding hypotheses for the analysis. The empirical part of the contribution illustrates first descriptively whether the crisis affects political support and disentangles in a second step the causal link between the crisis and support. As we measure the crisis itself directly via the contextual level as well as through the individual level referring to citizens' perceptions of the crisis, we use multi-level modeling. Finally, we conclude with a discussion of the empirical results and its implications for the future of the EU.

Theory and Hypotheses: How do we Expect the Crisis to Affect EU Support?

It is widely agreed that '[p]ublic attitudes, through mass political behaviour, shape and constrain the process of European integration' (Gabel 1998, 333). Moreover, the general economic voting literature and classical utilitarian approaches would suggest that support decreases in times of crisis (Rattinger and Steinbrecher 2011). However, with regard to the recent developments in the investigation of political support for the EU, we know that economic considerations have been supplemented by identity-based arguments as explanations of citizens' support for the EU when the integration process passed on from an economic to a political union.[1] Hence, we are first and foremost interested in the mere development of political support during the crisis to get first insights whether the current crisis could reverse this pattern again bringing economic factors back in as fundamental explanations of public support for the EU.

However, the two most recent studies conclude that this did not happen during the period of 2007–2010 (Serricchio, Tsakatika, and Quaglia 2013) or that the crisis is a less important determinant of support (Armingeon and Ceka 2013). In our opinion, Serricchio, Tsakatika, and Quaglia (2013) certainly addressed the right problem, but they asked the question too soon. It is less probable that the global crisis affects support for the EU but rather the specific Euro crisis, which started only in the end of 2009 and had its breakthrough in the course of the year 2010 (Illing 2013).[2] In spite of the recent findings pointing in a different direction, we expect the Euro — and not the global — crisis exerting an important impact on citizens' support for the EU. This should be reflected by a decrease in EU support during the Euro crisis.

> Hypothesis 1: The impact of the Euro crisis on EU support is stronger than the impact of the global crisis.

In addition to the general development of EU support, our study is interested in the particular link between the Euro crisis and support to strengthen the rather descriptive argument mentioned above. Therefore, we need to disentangle the crisis and investigate this link at the individual level, the contextual level, and the interaction between both. In the following paragraphs, we shortly summarize the main literature in order to derive our hypotheses for each level of analysis.

At the individual level, we need to distinguish between two different economic perspectives (Loveless and Rohrschneider 2011, 9–10; McLaren 2004, 899–903). On the one hand, 'egocentric utilitarism' suggests that the socioeconomic placement of individuals (education, occupation, or/and income) reflects whether an individual is a winner or a loser of European integration — winners are considered to be rather supportive of the EU (e.g. Anderson and Kaltenthaler 1996; Anderson and Reichert 1995; Gabel 1998; Gabel and Palmer 1995). On the other hand, the 'sociotropic economic' argument states that 'the promised economic benefits of EU membership give rise to expectations on the part of citizens regarding national economic performance' (Anderson and Kaltenthaler 1996, 186). Translating these findings into the current crisis, one can infer that the socioeconomic placement of individuals as well as their perception of the crisis are important explanations for EU support. This brings us to the following assumptions:

> Hypothesis 2a: A negative evaluation of the Euro crisis affects citizens' support for the EU negatively.

> Hypothesis 2b: The better the individual's socio-economic placement, the higher the support for the EU.

'Sociotropic economic explanations' in particular have their counterpart at the contextual level. Empirical findings support the relationship between domestic economic indicators such as the growth rate, intra-European trade, and unemployment on the one hand and public support for the EU on the other hand (Anderson and Kaltenthaler 1996; Anderson and Reichert 1995; Gabel and Palmer 1995). Nevertheless, other scholars challenge these findings illustrating 'that there is no clear relationship between macroeconomic indicators and levels of support for EC membership' (Bosch and Newton 1995, 84). Eichenberg and Dalton (2007) analyze the relationship under altered circumstances concluding that the impact of economic indicators vanished in the post-Maastricht period. The latter findings suggest that macro-economic indicators indeed have an impact on public support for the EU, although this depends on the period of investigation. The current crisis which is following Buti and Carnot (2012) 'the most difficult set of economic and financial circumstances for over half a century' (910) should likewise exert such an impact on citizens' support.

> Hypothesis 3: At the contextual level, the Euro crisis affects citizens' support for the EU directly.

Moreover, it is essential to examine how the two levels interact among each other. The fact that a country is a Eurocountry should be as important for this link as the force of the crisis and its implications in a country. The effect of an individual's perception of the crisis on citizens' support for the EU is assumed to be stronger in Euro countries than in others, since they might be stronger affected by the crisis. In turn, one might argue that Euro countries were and are in general better prepared for the crisis or better equipped with crisis resolution mechanisms (Buti and Carnot 2012, 906).

> Hypothesis 4: The effect of individual perceptions of the crisis on citizens' support for the EU depends on the membership of the country in the Euro zone.

In addition to mere economic explanations of EU support, empirical research suggests a number of other potentially influential factors — especially at the individual level. We account for these indicators such as internal efficacy, political information, sex, and age (Hooghe and Marks 2004; McLaren 2006; Ray 2006) in the form of control variables. We also test the proxy thesis (Anderson 1998; Armingeon and Ceka 2013); identity-based indicators are not available unfortunately.

Data and Methods

The data for the empirical analyses are taken from the Eurobarometer (EB) survey. As the standard EB is conducted between two and five times every year, its advantages for our analyses are clear: We have data for all 27 member states, we have at least two polls every year, and we have very recent data. However, measuring citizens' support for the EU is a difficult matter using the EB. Previous studies have shown that support for the EU is of a multi-dimensional nature (Boomgaarden *et al.* 2011; Tausendpfund 2013). On the one hand, we need indicators to distinguish between specific and diffuse political support (Easton 1965, 1975). On the other hand, we need identical indicators in different surveys. Unfortunately, such indicators are not available for any substantial sequence of polls. Therefore, we use the following indicator of political support for the EU: In general, does the EU conjure up for you a very positive, fairly positive, neutral, fairly negative, or very negative image?[3] It is obvious that this item is not a perfect one, but it is the only one available for the time span under consideration. As it seems to be quite comprehensible for respondents (see the very low share — two per cent — of 'don't know' answers), we use this question as a proxy for citizens' general support for the EU.

The independent variables are to be found at the individual and national level. Based on the theoretical assumptions presented in the preceding chapter, Figure 1 illustrates all assumed effects of the crisis. While H1 concerns the higher ranking assumption that the Euro crisis affects citizens' support for the EU and will be analyzed descriptively, H2a and H2b investigate the subjective relationship at the individual level. As we consider two different mechanisms of the classical utilitarian argument (sociotropic utilitarianism and egocentric utilitarianism), we refer to the following: First of all, to test citizens' perceptions of the crisis, we use the following

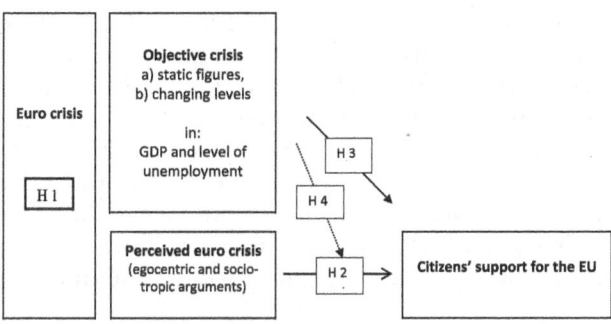

Figure 1. Individual- and contextual-level effects of the Euro Crisis on EU support

statement: 'Some analysts say that the impact of the economic crisis on the job market has already reached its peak and things will recover little by little. Others, on the contrary, say that the worst is still to come.' People could choose between the following statements: 'The impact of the crisis on jobs has already reached its peak' and 'The worst is still to come.' We use the latter statement as an indicator for a negative evaluation of the crisis. Furthermore, to test the effect of the individual perception of the economy, we use three different statements in the survey. The statements are introduced by the following question: 'How would you judge the current situation in each of the following?' On a four-point scale from very bad to very good the respondents evaluate (1) the situation of the national economy, (2) the employment situation in the country, and (3) the financial situation of the own household.

At the contextual level, H3 tests the direct relationship between the crisis and public support for the EU. The measurement of the crisis is a tricky question in this regard. As seen above, general macro-economic indicators, which have been used so far to study EU support, are the growth rate, unemployment, and intra-European trade. The latter disappeared as source of EU support in the post-Maastricht period. Hence, we take into account, the gross domestic product (GDP) per head as a measure for the economic strength and the unemployment rate representing unemployed people as a percentage of the national job market. Data on the GDP and the unemployment rate are taken from Eurostat. In contrast to previous studies, we use not only the static values (the economic situation in October 2012) but also allow for a dynamic perspective taking into account additionally changing values over time. As indicators, we use the unemployment rate and the youth unemployment rate in October 2012, as well as the GDP in 2012 (field work for EB 78.1 was November 2012). For the dynamic perspective, we compute the change of unemployment rate and the GDP between 2009 and 2012. In doing so, we interpret on the one hand a lower GDP as well as a higher share of unemployment in a country as an indicator for the crisis. On the other hand, a decrease in the GDP in the course of the crisis as well as an increase of unemployment implies more strength of the crisis in a country. Furthermore, we include a dummy variable to indicate whether a country was a member of the Eurozone. Finally, Figure 1 depicts in which way H4 tackles the interaction between both the individual and the contextual level.

As pointed out above, we control for potentially influent determinants such as sex, age, and education. Moreover, we take into account internal efficacy ('I understand how the EU works') and political information ('And overall, to what extent do you think that you are well informed or not about European matters?'). To test the proxy thesis, we use satisfaction with national democracy, which is measured by the following survey question: 'On the whole, are you very satisfied, fairly satisfied, not very satisfied or not at all satisfied with the way democracy works in our country?' At the contextual level, we account the duration of membership in the EU in the analyses.

Empirical Analysis

Our empirical analysis starts descriptively by mapping support for the EU in the different countries under consideration, in order to answer the question whether there is a decline of support during the time of the Euro crisis (H1). To describe the development of support for the EU, we use EB 67.2 (April 2007) to EB 78.1 (November 2012). In contrast to Armingeon and Ceka (2013), we illustrate not only the mere differences between 2007 and 2012 but rather present the entire development until 2012. Figure 2 shows the trend in all 27 member states. The gray line is the mean of all member states; the black line is the average of the country. At first glance, we observe considerable differences between the countries. On the one hand, support for the EU in Bulgaria and Romania is always higher than the average of all member states. On the other hand, support in Austria, Finland, and especially in the United Kingdom is below average. It is particularly interesting to note that in Greece, Portugal, and Spain support for the EU is higher than average in the period before the Euro crisis (the vertical line shows the last EB before the crisis — i.e. October/November 2009). Since the end of 2009 — the beginning of the Euro crisis — we observe a persistent decline in support for the EU in these countries (for details on the development of EU support in Greece see Clements, Nanou and Verney 2014). A similar pattern can be observed in Cyprus, the Czech Republic, Ireland, Luxembourg, the Netherlands, Slovakia, and Slovenia.

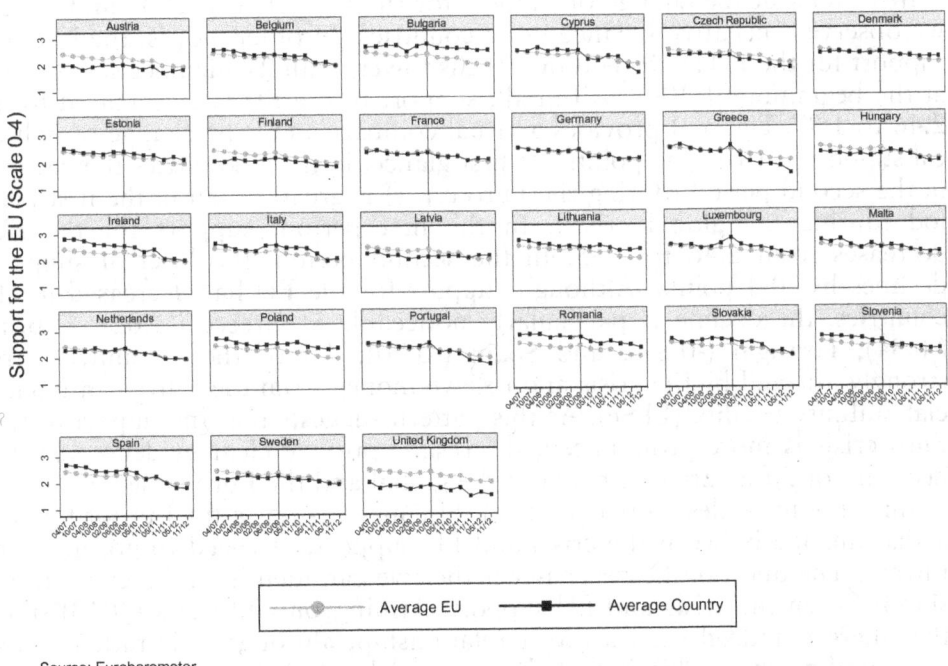

Source: Eurobarometer

Figure 2. Trend of support for the EU from April 2007 to November 2012

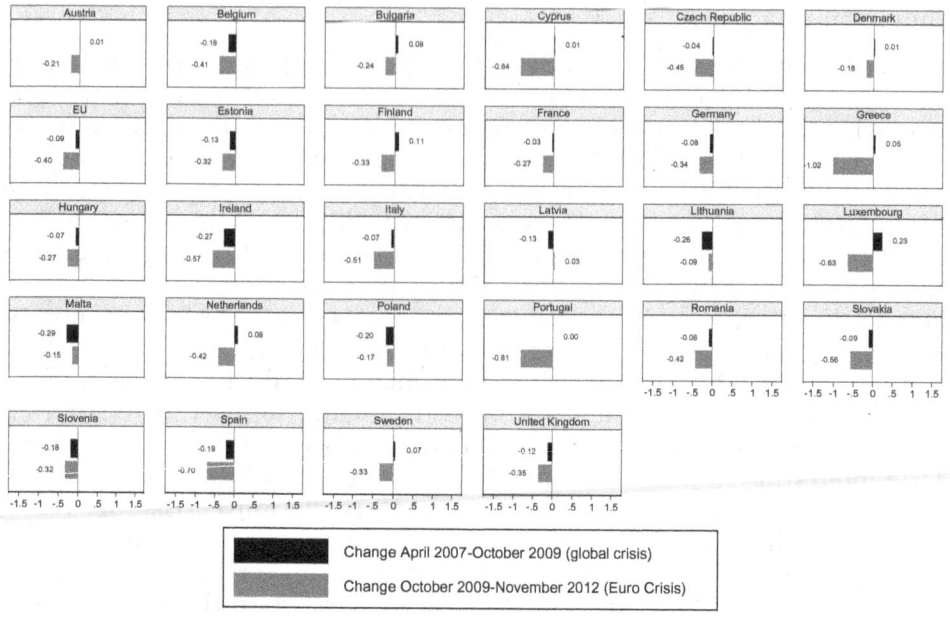

Source: Eurobarometer

Figure 3. Changes of support for the EU from April 2007/October 2009 to November 2012

If we look at the change of support for the EU between 2007 and 2012, we observe a negative balance in all countries. In other words, the level of support for the EU at the end of 2012 is lower in all 27 member states than at the beginning of 2007. All in all, support of the EU has decreased from 2.46 to 1.97. Figure 3 provides a visual comparison of the change of political support at two time points. At first glance, in most countries the decline in the second period (during the Euro crisis) is greater than in the first period (during the global crisis). In the first period, support for the EU decreases from 2.46 to 2.35. In the second period, the level of support declines by -0.4 points. Although support for the EU has decreased in all countries, the decline is particularly noticeable in Greece (-1.02), Cyprus (-0.84), Portugal (-0.81), and Spain (-0.70). All of these countries are strongly affected by the crisis and receive money from the European Financial Stability Facility (EFSF). As this pattern suggests that the impact of the Euro crisis is more pronounced, the results provide clear evidence for the necessity of differentiating between the global and the Euro crisis.

Since the mere descriptive analysis, of course, is not a final proof for the actual linkage between the crisis and EU support, we need to go one step further. The question however is whether we can identify a direct relationship between the crisis and EU support. Armingeon and Ceka (2013) state that there is indeed such a direct relationship, although it is rather weak compared to the evaluation of the national level. To test this, we subject our theory-derived relationships to empirical tests emphasizing the impact of economic factors on support for the EU. Therefore, we estimate the effects of economic indicators on support for the EU using multi-level modeling referring to the most current EB at the time of data analysis (EB 78.1).[4] Moreover, it includes important control variables (as e.g. satisfaction with national democracy). Following the logic of hierarchical modeling, we present a series of models, where each one builds on the preceding one. Starting with the empty model, which excludes independent variables, we can establish the variance to be explained for the individual and the contextual level (i.e. the intraclass correlation). The results of these analyses are displayed in Table 1 (Model 1). The share of cross-national variance on the total variance amounts to six per cent. The estimates in Model 1 also indicate that support of the EU depends on both individual-level as well as contextual-level indicators.

In a first step, we account for individual-level indicators of the Euro crisis (Model 2a, Table 1). The negative coefficient indicates that a negative evaluation of the crisis affects EU support negatively. Thus, it confirms one part of the expected relationship at the individual level (H 2a). In Model 2b, we take into account the economic situation of the respondents. For this purpose, we include the three individual items — the rating of the national economy, of the national job market, and the financial situation of the own household — in the analysis. The estimates indicate that political support for the EU depends on both the individual perception of the

Table 1. Individual models of support for the EU

	Model 1	Model 2a	Model 2b	Model 2c	Model 2d
Individual level					
Constant	.497***	.581***	.425***	.315***	.309***
Crisis		−.129***	−.100***	−.073***	−.075***
National economy			.171***	.114***	.113***
National job market			.092***	.038**	.042***
Own household finance			.104***	.059*	.059*
Gender (Men=1)				−.007	
Age				−.058	
Education				.077	
National democracy				.192***	.191***
Internal efficacy				.087**	.091***
Political information				.056**	.057**
Random effects					
Individual level	.055	.051	.048	.044	.044
Contextual level	.004	.003	.005	.006	.006
ICC	.063	.053	.089	.116	.116
R^2 (Level 1)		.065	.126	.192	.188
N (countries)	22.621 (27)	22.621 (27)	22.621 (27)	22.621 (27)	22.621 (27)

Notes: Multi-level analysis with restricted-maximum-likelihood-estimation. Coefficients are not standardized; all variables are rescaled (lowest value is 0; highest value is 1). Coefficients indicate the change associated with moving from the lowest to the highest value. Significance level: *$p < 0.05$. **$p < 0.01$. ***$p < 0.001$. EU27-weight is used.
Source: Eurobarometer 78.1.

national economic situation as well as on the private financial situation. All three coefficients are positive and significant. Next, we include our individual control variables in the model. The key message of the results in Model 2c in Table 1 is that under control of relevant individual characteristics the effects of the crisis-indicator and the subjective indicators of the economic situation are weaker than in Model 2b but without changing direction and significance.[5] Or to put it simply: the evaluation of the Euro crisis continues to exert an independent effect on EU support.

In the next step, we estimate the contextual-level impact of the Euro crisis on support for the EU. For this purpose, we distinguish between the current economic situation on the one hand and a dynamic perspective on the other hand and estimate the effects of all eight context variables on support for the EU. Initially, we included the indicators separately in the models; i.e. we estimated eight different multi-level models, one model for each indicator (results not shown). Four out of eight contextual indicators are statistically significant: Three indicators of the static perspective (unemployment rate, youth unemployment rate, GDP) and surprisingly only one 'dynamic' indicator (change of GDP 2012–2009) have an effect on political support. We find positive effects of the unemployment rate and negative effects of the GDP. The greater the GDP was in 2012 as well as the change of the GDP between 2009 and 2012 lower the support for the EU. In economically strong states, support for the EU is lower than in 'poor' countries. It is particularly interesting to note that on the one hand, we see a positive relation between the unemployment rate and support for the EU at the contextual level. But on the other hand, we find a negative link between the evaluation of the national job market and support of the EU on the individual level.

In a final step, we merge the three significant contextual-level indicators into one multi-level model (Model 3a, Table 2). For a number of reasons, we only include the youth unemployment rate in our model (e.g. the effect is stronger and the correlation between the youth unemployment rate and the unemployment rate is $r > .95$). As a control variable, we also take into account the duration of membership in the EU. Individual control variables are always included but not shown for reasons of clarity (compared to Model 2d, the results of the individual-level indicators are stable). In doing so, we cannot find any statistically significant results for the youth unemployment rate, the change of the GDP, and the duration of membership in the EU. However, we find a negative effect of the GDP 2012 on support for the EU. To our surprise, it is thus not the change of the economic situation between 2009 and 2012 that has an effect on political support but rather the current economic climate. This conclusion is also supported by Model 3b in Table 2 where only significant indicators are included.

Finally, Model 4a in Table 2 estimates cross-level interactions between the GDP and the core individual variables. Two cross-level interactions are statistically significant; the estimates illustrate that the effect of two individual-level variables depends on the contextual level. The individual effects of the evaluation of the national economy and the national job market on public support for the EU are stronger in countries that are better off in

Table 2. Individual and contextual fixed effects models of support for the EU

	Model 3a	Model 3b	Model 4a	Model 4b
Individual level (core)				
Crisis	−.074***	−.074***	−.066***	−.058***
National economy	.114***	.114***	.082***	.083***
National job market	.043**	.042**	−.026	−.027
Own household finance	.059*	.059*	.057	.060**
Contextual level				
Youth unemployment rate	.043			
GDP 2012	−.268*	−.275**	−.417***	−.446***
ΔGDP 2012–2009	−.025			
Duration of EU-membership	.020			
Member of the Euro area				.034
Cross-level-Interaction				
Crisis × GDP 2012			−.030	
National economy × GDP 2012			.129#	.129*
National job market × GDP 2012			.254***	.258***
Household finance × GDP 2012			.015	
Crisis × Member of the Euro area				−.026**
Random effects				
Individual level	.044	.044	.044	.044
Contextual level	.003	.003	.003	.003
ICC	.059	.064	.062	.061
R^2 (Level 1)	.188	.188	.190	.191
R^2 (Level 2)	.238	.176	.205	.221
N (countries)	22.621 (27)	22.621 (27)	22.621 (27)	22.621 (27)

Notes: Multi-level analysis with restricted-maximum-likelihood-estimation. Coefficients are not standardized; all variables are rescaled (lowest value is 0; highest value is 1). Coefficients indicate the change associated with moving from the lowest to the highest value. Control variables at individual level (model 2d) are included. Significance level: #$p < 0.10$. *$p < 0.05$. **$p < 0.01$. ***$p < 0.001$. EU27-weight is used (for individual variables).
Source: Eurobarometer 78.1.

terms of the economy.[6] In the theoretical part of this paper, we argue that the effect of an individual's perception of the Euro crisis on citizens' support for the EU is stronger in Euro-countries, since they might be more affected by the Euro crisis. In line with our expectations, we detect a statistically significant result: The (negative) effect of the individual perception of the Euro crisis on political support is stronger in Euro-countries (Model 4b, Table 2).

Conclusions and Implications

The aim of this contribution was to investigate the impact of the global and the European dimension of the crisis on citizens' support for the EU. We firstly mapped the development of EU support during the time of the global crises and investigated in a second step the actual linkage between the Euro crisis and EU support. Compared to the rare previous studies on that ongoing topic, our contribution involved a long period of investigation mapping the entire development of EU support and offered the possibility to discern the effects of the global crisis from the Euro crisis. Moreover, we distinguished between individual- and contextual-level indicators to illustrate the Euro crisis appropriately. With regard to the latter and due to the lack of more appropriate panel data, we took into account (in addition to the static perspective) a dynamic operationalization of our indicators. Interestingly, it was not the change of the economic indicators in the course of the crisis but the current economic climate in a country influencing public support for the EU.

Nevertheless, our main finding was that the Euro crisis has undeniably an important impact on citizens' support for the EU. The descriptive overview showed that support for the EU declined in all 27 EU member states from April 2007 to November 2012. However, the sharpest decline occurred during the time of the Euro crisis. Hence, the impact of the Euro crisis on EU support is stronger than the impact of the global crisis, which means that people withdraw their support when the crisis moves from a global and very distant event to a veritable threat to the future of the EU. Thus, we basically confirm the findings presented by Serricchio, Tsakatika and Quaglia (2013), who mapped in particular the impact of the global financial crisis and found no major effects on EU support. As we can detect a clear decline of support, our analysis highlights the relevance of distinguishing between the global and the European dimension of the crisis.

Moreover, our results showed that both levels — the individual level as well as the contextual level — are relevant for explaining public support for the EU. Though, the individual level is crucial in the understanding the link. One important finding in this regard was that the individual evaluation of the Euro crisis played a major role for the explanation of EU support. This enlightens the beforehand described pattern in another interesting direction. Obviously, people need to be affected personally by the crisis in order to withdraw their support. Hence, it is not mainly about national cues leading to a crisis of support as argued by Armingeon and Ceka (2013) but also about classical sociotropic utilitarianism. People are less supportive of the EU because they fear or undergo a personal threat. However, the fact that satisfaction with national democracy, in our study used as control variable, strongly affects EU support fosters the findings presented by these authors.

All in all, the results of this study together with those of Armingeon and Ceka (2013) suggest that the Euro crisis definitely has an impact on citizens' support but at the same time people use national cues to better assess the crisis. Aside from this, the effect of the individual perception of the crisis on EU support depends definitively on the context. First, the effect of the individual perception of the national economy on EU support is stronger in economically powerful countries. Second, the negative effect of the individual perception of the Euro crisis is stronger in EU countries. Hence, one could assume that the considerations of people are driven — once again — very rationally. Obviously, they fear more personal costs due to the crisis and therefore withdraw their support for the EU.

Nevertheless, there is some need to reflect these findings critically in a certain way as the EB data we used features some shortcomings which need to be taken into account in future analyses. First, the operationalization of a multi-dimensional concept such as EU support (Boomgaarden *et al.* 2011) using a one-dimensional indicator is certainly not ideal. However, to grasp this variable in an appropriate way for a large sample of countries and over a longer time period, the EB survey is the only adequate data source. In return, one needs to accept a less satisfactory operationalization. Still, we would advocate for better indicators in cross-cultural surveys. The second shortcoming of our data is the lack of identity-based indicators which on the one hand restricts our findings to some extent. On the other hand this offers some routes for future research. One could check whether the 'bringing economics back in' argument put forward by Serricchio, Tsakatika and Quaglia (2013) holds for the time of the Euro crisis, or whether identity-based theories are really as strong as stated. Finally, the third data problem addresses the lack of longitudinal data with repeated interviews of each respondent to identify attitudinal changes more appropriately. As this kind of data simply does not exist for a larger country sample, our suggestion for future research is of a mere methodological nature: One should strive for better data which would be certainly longitudinal data to map EU support and changes over time in an appropriate way.

Despite these constraints, our findings are still very instructive for the better understanding of the link between the Euro crisis and citizens' EU support. Beside the fact that the Euro crisis indeed has a negative effect on EU support, we can illustrate nicely that in the course of the Euro crisis economic indicators are still essential for the explanation of support. Our findings show that the latter is mainly driven by economic considerations: First of all, EU support is affected by the Euro crisis and not by the more distant global crisis. Second, EU support is affected by the individual perception of the Euro crisis. Finally, this individual perception is in particular striking in stronger Euro countries. Consequently, our findings are in contrast to the literature inspired by post-functionalist perspectives, whereby economic considerations lose their explanatory power of EU support. As a result, the presented empirical evidence can be interpreted as a threat to the future of the EU. If public support which is considered as 'the political foundation for integration' (Gabel 1998, 333) depends on economic considerations, it represents a rather unstable foundation for the future of European integration. Nonetheless, this critical estimation needs to be reflected against the background of additional findings on the mobilization potential of negative attitudes of citizens towards the EU (Hutter and Kerscher 2014).

Notes

1. In general, researchers addressed the issue of national identity as explanation of support for European integration — or rather the lack thereof (e.g. Hooghe and Marks 2005). In this line of reasoning, it has been shown that the perceived threat of the nation state (Carey 2002; McLaren 2004, 2006) and immigration are important explanations of public support for the EU (Boomgaarden and Freire 2009; Braun and Tausendpfund 2013b; Lubbers and Scheepers 2007).
2. Since 2010, Greece, Portugal, Spain, Ireland, and Italy were subjected to financial bailouts and rigorous cuts in state expenditures (Bellucci, Costa Lobo, and Lewis-Beck 2012, 469). Only at this time, people literally experienced the crisis and it is more likely that they responded with a withdrawal of support for the EU. Consequently, to investigate the effects of the crisis on public

support, one needs to map the entire relevant time span from 2007 up to the present, including thus not only the effects of the global crisis but focusing more specifically on the Euro crisis.

3. The respondents were offered five answer categories, ranging from 0 'very negative' to 4 'very positive.' Responses of 'don't know' are excluded of the analyses since the share of 'don't know' answers is low (<two per cent).
4. Multi-level modeling is a hierarchical, regression technique which is required if individual-level variables of a sample are nested within aggregate data as it is in our case: respondents within countries. This method simultaneously and statistically estimates accurately both the influence of contextual- and individual-level factors (e.g. Snijders and Bosker 1999; Steenbergen and Jones 2002).
5. As suggested throughout the literature, we find positive effects of satisfaction with national democracy, internal efficacy, and political information on the one hand and political support on the other. The greater the satisfaction with national democracy, the more likely it is that people support the EU (the same pattern can be found for internal efficacy and political information). As we find no statistical effect for demographic indicators, we exclude the three indicators of the final model (Model 2d, Table 1).
6. Moreover, we tested the different possibilities of interaction between the individual-level indicators for the Euro crisis on the one hand and the 'dynamic' contextual-level indicators (models not shown). However, this dynamic perspective, i.e. the changing values of the economic indicators from 2009 to 2012, shows no statistically significant effect (when applying a level of significance of $p < 0.05$).

References

Anderson, C.J. 1998. When in doubt, use proxies: attitudes toward domestic politics and support for European integration. *Comparative Political Studies* 31, no. 5: 569–601.

Anderson, C.J., and K.C. Kaltenthaler. 1996. The dynamics of public opinion toward European integration, 1973–93. *European Journal of International Relations* 2, no. 2: 175–99.

Anderson, C.J., and S.M. Reichert. 1995. Economic benefits and support for membership in the E.U.: a cross-national analysis. *Journal of Public Policy* 15, no. 3: 231–49.

Armingeon, K., and B. Ceka. 2013. The loss of trust in the European Union during the great recession since 2007: the role of heuristics from the national political system, *European Union Politics* doi:10.1177/1465116513495595

Bauer, M.W., and S. Becker. 2014. The unexpected winner of the crisis: the European Commission's strengthened role in economic governance. *Journal of European Integration*

Bellucci, P., M. Costa Lobo, and M.S. Lewis-Beck. 2012. Economic crisis and elections: the European periphery. *Electoral Studies* 31: 469–71.

Boomgaarden, H.G., and A. Freire. 2009. Religion and Euroscepticism: direct, indirect or no effects? *West European Politics* 32, no. 6: 1240–265.

Boomgaarden, H.G., A.R.T. Schuck, M. Elenbaas, and C.H. de Vreese. 2011. Mapping EU attitudes: conceptual and empirical dimensions of Euroscepticism and EU support. *European Union Politics* 12, no. 2: 241–66.

Bosch, A., and K. Newton. 1995. Economic calculus or familiarity breeds content? In *Public opinion and internationalized governance*, eds. O. Niedermayer and R. Sinnott, 73–104. Oxford: Oxford University Press.

Braun, D., and M. Tausendpfund. 2013a. The impact of the financial crisis on citizens' political support. A multilevel analysis for European countries. In Paper presented at the 41st ECPR Joint Sessions, Mainz, Germany, 11–16 March.

Braun, D., and M. Tausendpfund. 2013b. Immigration as an explanation of public support for European integration: an empirical analysis of EU member states. *Zeitschrift für Vergleichende Politikwissenschaft* 7, no. 3: 205–26.

Buti, M., and N. Carnot. 2012. The EMU debt crisis: early lessons and reform. *Journal of Common Market Studies* 50, no. 6: 899–911.

Carey, S. 2002. Undivided loyalties: is national identity an obstacle to European integration? *European Union Politics* 3, no. 4: 387–413.

Castles, F.G. 1998. Die Bedeutung der Ökonomie für die politische Unterstützung der Europäischen Union. In *Europa der Bürger? Voraussetzungen, Alternativen, Konsequenzen*, eds. T. König, E. Rieger and H. Schmitt, 159–76. Frankfurt: Campus.

Clements, B., K. Nanou, and S. Verney. 2014. 'We no longer love you, but we don't want to leave you': the eurozone crisis and popular euroscepticism in Greece. *Journal of European Integration*.

Down, I., and C.J. Wilson. 2008. From 'permissive consensus' to 'constraining dissensus': a polarizing union? *Acta Politica* 43, no. 1: 26–49.

Easton, D. 1965. *A systems analysis of political life*. New York: John Wiley & Sons.

Easton, D. 1975. A re-assessment of the concept of political support. *British Journal of Political Science* 5, no. 4: 435–57.

Eichenberg, R.C., and R.J. Dalton. 1993. Europeans and the European community: the dynamics of public support for European integration. *International Organization* 47, no. 4: 507–34.

Eichenberg, R.C., and R.J. Dalton. 2007. Post-Maastricht Blues: The transformation of citizen support for European integration, 1973–2004. *Acta Politica* 42: 128–52.

Gabel, M. 1998. Public support for European integration: an empirical test of five theories. *The Journal of Politics* 60, no. 2: 333–74.

Gabel, M., and H.D. Palmer. 1995. Understanding variation in public support for European integration. *European Journal of Political Research* 27, no. 1: 3–19.

Hix, S., and B. Høyland. 2011. *The political system of the European Union*. Houndmills: Palgrave Macmillan.

Hooghe, L., and G. Marks. 2004. Does identity or economic rationality drive public opinion on European integration? *Political Science and Politics* 37: 415–20.

Hooghe, L., and G. Marks. 2005. Calculation, community and cues. *European Union Politics* 6, no. 4: 419–43.

Hooghe, L., and G. Marks. 2009. A postfunctionalist theory of European integration: from permissive consensus to constraining dissensus. *British Journal of Political Science* 39, no. 1: 1–23.

Hutter, S., and A. Kerscher. 2014. Politicizing Europe in hard times: conflicts over Europe in France in a long-term perspective, 1974–2012. *Journal of European Integration*.

Illing, F. 2013. *Die Euro-Krise*. Wiesbaden: Springer VS.

Loveless, M., and R. Rohrschneider. 2011. Public perceptions of the EU as a system of governance. *Living Reviews in European Governance* 6, no. 2: 5–28.

Lubbers, M., and P. Scheepers. 2007. Explanations of political Euro-scepticism at the individual, regional and national levels. *European Societies* 9, no. 4: 643–69.

McLaren, L.M. 2004. Opposition to European integration and fear of loss of national identity: debunking a basic assumption regarding hostility to the integration project. *European Journal of Political Research* 43, no. 6: 895–911.

McLaren, L.M. 2006. *Identity, interests and attitudes to European integration*. Houndmills: Palgrave Macmillan.

McLaren, L.M. 2010. Cause for concern? The impact of immigration on political trust. In *Policy network paper*. London: Policy Network. http://www.policy-network.net/publications_detail.aspx?ID=3889 (accessed 30 December 2013).

Rattinger, H., and M. Steinbrecher. 2011. Economic voting in times of economic crisis. *German Politics* 20, no. 1: 128–45.

Ray, L. 2006. Public opinion, socialization and political communication, In *Handbook of European Union politics*, eds. K.E. Jorgensen, M.A. Pollack and B. Rosamond, 263–81. London: Sage.

Roth, F., D. Gros, and F. Nowak-Lehmann D. 2014. Crisis and citizens' trust in the European Central Bank — panel data evidence for the euro area, 1999–2012. *Journal of European Integration*.

Schäfer, A. 2006. Nach dem permissiven Konsens. Das Demokratiedefizit der Europäischen Union. *Leviathan* 34, no. 3: 350–76.

Scharpf, F.W. 2011. Monetary union, fiscal crisis and pre-emption of democracy. *Zeitschrift für Staats- und Europawissenschaften* 9, no. 2: 163–98.

Serricchio, F., M. Tsakatika, and L. Quaglia. 2013. Euroscepticism and the global financial crisis. *Journal of Common Market Studies* 51, no. 1: 51–64.

Snijders, T.A.B., and R.J. Bosker. 1999. *Multilevel analysis. An introduction to basic and advanced multilevel modeling*. London: Sage.

Steenbergen, M.R., and B.S. Jones. 2002. Modeling multilevel data structures. *American Journal of Political Science* 46, no. 1: 218–37.

Tausendpfund, M. 2013. *Gemeinden als Rettungsanker der EU?* Baden-Baden: Nomos.

Tosun, J., A. Wetzel, and G. Zapryanova. 2014. The EU in crisis: advancing the debate. *Journal of European Integration*.

'We No Longer Love You, But We Don't Want To Leave You': The Eurozone Crisis and Popular Euroscepticism in Greece

BEN CLEMENTS*, KYRIAKI NANOU** & SUSANNAH VERNEY***

*Department of Politics and International Relations, University of Leicester, Leicester, UK;
**School of Politics and International Relations, University of Nottingham, Nottingham, UK;
***Department of International and European Studies, University of Athens, Athens, Greece

ABSTRACT This article analyses whether and how public opinion towards the European Union (EU) in Greece has changed in the context of the current Eurozone crisis. It provides the first detailed treatment of how the crisis has affected citizens' views in a traditionally pro-European member state. It examines whether public opinion has become more Eurosceptic and which societal groups have changed their views and in what direction. It uses data from Eurobarometer surveys conducted before and during the current crisis. Unsurprisingly, the findings show that negative sentiment towards the EU has increased across all social groups in recent years. However, we find a paradox of a decline in general support for the EU and an increase in support for the Euro. In a country seen as traditionally pro-European, Greek public opinion has fallen out of love with the EU, but it clearly does not want to leave the Eurozone or renounce membership altogether.

Introduction

This paper analyses trends in public support for the European Union (EU) in Greece, the Eurozone member most severely affected by the current economic crisis. It provides the first detailed understanding of how citizens' attitudes towards the EU have evolved in response to the ongoing economic crisis and related developments in domestic politics. There has been recurrent speculation about Greece leaving the Eurozone. Domestically, the crisis has caused much political controversy, electoral volatility and civil strife, affecting political parties, voting behaviour and the institutions of governance. According to Eurobarometer data, prior to the crisis, the Greek public was among the most pro-integrationist in the EU. Subsequently, in 2007–11, Greece became the member state with the highest increase in negative attitudes towards EU membership, as noted by Serricchio, Tsakatika and Quaglia (2013). Despite this rather startling shift, there has been little analysis of how Greek public opinion may have changed in response to the crisis. Have particular societal groups changed their views or has there been a more general 'sea-change' in attitudes towards European integration within Greek society? Has discontent with the EU led to a rise in 'hard' Euroscepticism (Szczerbiak and Taggart 2000), implying rejection of the integration project and of national membership? These are questions of critical significance, not only for the future of Greek–EU relations and Greece's status as a long-standing pro-integration member state, but also because of their wider implications for the impact of economic crisis on support for European integration.

Using data from the bi-annual Eurobarometer surveys conducted before and during the crisis, the present article analyses general support for the EU and attitudes towards the single currency. The paper contributes to research into party-based and popular Euroscepticism and the role of the EU issue in the member states of southern Europe (Costa Lobo and Magalhães 2011; Ruiz Jiménez and de Haro 2011; Llamazares and Gramacho 2007; Mavris 2004; Quaglia 2011; Verney 2011a, 2011b) and to recent analysis of public attitudes in the context of the Eurozone crisis (Serricchio et al. 2013). It also contributes to the wider public opinion literature on explaining general support for the EU (Gabel 1998; Hooghe and Marks 2004, 2005; McLaren 2006). Beyond this, the paper aims to deepen our understanding of the impact of the crisis on the EU member states and of how this may affect the future prospects of the integration project itself.

The paper is structured as follows. First, it sets out the wider context of Greece and the Eurozone crisis. Second, it examines how public opinion towards the EU has changed over time in the context of the crisis. Third, it looks more closely at whether and how the opinions of different social groups towards the EU have changed. Fourth, it sets out the multivariate analysis of Greek attitudes towards the EU using the most recently available survey data. Fifth, it presents the main findings from the multivariate analysis. Finally, it concludes the analysis.

Greece and the Eurozone Crisis: The Re-emergence of European Integration as a Contested Issue

The Greek crisis began in October 2009 with the admission by the newly elected Socialist government that Greece was running an unsustainably high budget deficit and public debt. The public revelations concerning the true state of the Greek economy and the manifest reluctance of the EU leadership to provide guarantees against the sovereign default of a Eurozone member triggered a crisis of confidence in the financial markets which rapidly developed into a sovereign debt crisis.

After Greece was definitively excluded from international financial markets in the Spring of 2010, the EU finally intervened, offering a joint EU/IMF loan in May 2010, followed by a second bailout accompanied by private sector sovereign-debt restructuring in March 2012, and then another minor debt 'haircut' in November 2012. The bailouts were granted in exchange for a programme of drastic deficit reduction, imposing severe austerity, and of deep structural reforms, including the reduction of the minimum wage and the rolling back of labour rights. The international creditors were unambiguous about the loss of Greek economic sovereignty. Implementation of the programme was monitored on a regular basis by the "troika", consisting of representatives of the European Commission (EC), the International Monetary Fund (IMF) and the European Central Bank (ECB), who regularly threatened to recommend the withholding of loan instalments if the Greek government did not meet its targets.

For the Greek public, the EU thus became inextricably linked with a fiscal adjustment programme and a loss of sovereignty. As the pain of the deepening crisis and the drastic reduction of state provision were increasingly felt across Greek society, the initial relief of avoiding default and a disorderly departure from the Eurozone and possibly even the EU was increasingly replaced by the feeling that the effects of these measures represented an unfair and indiscriminate punishment, particularly targeting vulnerable population groups such as the young unemployed and elderly pensioners. The EU role in the design and implementation of the Greek adjustment programme meant that disaffection with the latter seemed likely to produce a eurosceptic response.

Such a response could reflect a crisis of 'output legitimacy', given that the EU can no longer guarantee prosperity and growth for its citizens but instead has become involved in the delivery of harsh austerity. The crisis has also brought a crisis of 'input legitimacy'. In the era of the EU/IMF bailouts, citizens in Greece have become increasingly aware that they can no longer influence public policy through traditional forms of political participation, such as voting in national elections, because the main policy directions are laid out in the agreements with the international lenders and cannot be changed. This is in line with Peter Mair's (2011, 15) concluding remarks in his paper discussing the impact of the crisis on political representation in Ireland: that 'this signals the onset of failure of representation and democracy without choices' (see also Krastev 2002).

The realisation that the EU matters a lot could trigger a positive process whereby citizens demand to become more actively involved in debates on the future of the integration process, the content of EU policies, their ideological direction and their impact on questions of equity and solidarity within their societies. However, it could also trigger a negative response, possibly leading even to a popular rejection of European integration itself. In order to see what is actually happening in Greece, let us now turn to the data.

Greece and The EU: The Changing Face of Public Opinion Over Time

Greece is one of the member states traditionally labelled as 'pro-European', and this is evident in relation to public opinion from the time series data presented in Figures 1 and 2. Trend data are shown for public opinion in Greece and for the EU as a whole (reflecting the number of member states at each point in time), based on two long-standing questions which have been asked regularly in Eurobarometer surveys. Notwithstanding some fluctuation of opinion, it is clear that before the crisis, there were generally high levels of support for Greece's EU membership, expressed as agreement with the statements that Greece has benefitted from membership and that membership has been 'a good thing'. When comparing the time series, it is also evident that there has been greater support for membership in Greece than across the EU as a whole.

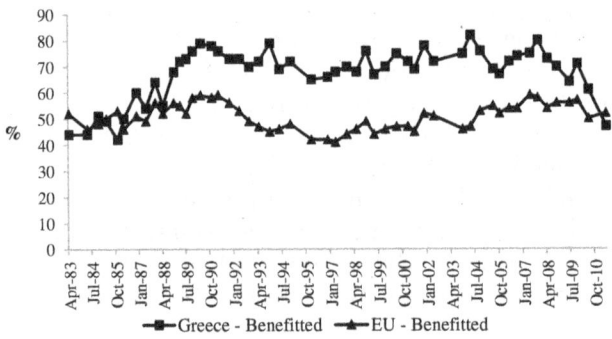

Figure 1. Long-term attitudes towards the EU: Benefitted from membership
Source: Eurobarometer surveys

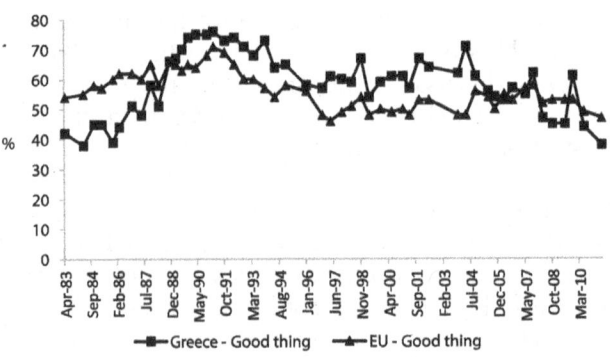

Figure 2. Long-term attitudes towards the EU: Membership is a good thing
Source: Eurobarometer surveys

Next, we turn to the period of crisis and examine the rise in negative sentiment. Figure 3 uses various indicators of public opinion, including the two Eurobarometer questions used in Figures 1 and 2, but this time focusing on the eurosceptic responses, as well as a further three questions designed to measure general attitudes towards the EU. Given that some of these questions have not featured in Eurobarometer surveys over an extended time period, we report data for the period 2003–2012 (or the most recently available data). For each indicator, we report the proportions holding negative views:

- Those who say Greece has not benefitted from EU membership.
- Those who say Greece's membership is a bad thing.
- Those who tend not to trust the EU.
- Those who have a very or fairly negative image of the EU.
- Those who think that the EU is going in the wrong direction.

The trend is very clear. During the first year after the collapse of Lehman Brothers, the general view in Greece was that the international crisis would not really affect the country, while it was felt that participation in the euro offered Greece protection, especially in comparison to the sharp decline suffered by the Swedish kroner. This is reflected in our negative indicators, which all show a small decline in Greek negative sentiment during this period. This is followed by a sharp jump in all cases between Autumn 2009 and Spring 2010 — the period identified earlier in this article as the real beginning of the crisis as far as Greek public opinion was concerned. Subsequently, all indicators show increasing levels of negative sentiment, climbing steadily.

Specifically, in a period of three years, on the three indicators measuring general attitudes towards the EU, the proportion of Greek respondents holding a negative image of the EU almost tripled (from 14% in November 2009 to 49% in November 2012), while those tending not to trust the EU and those believing the EU was going in the wrong direction more than

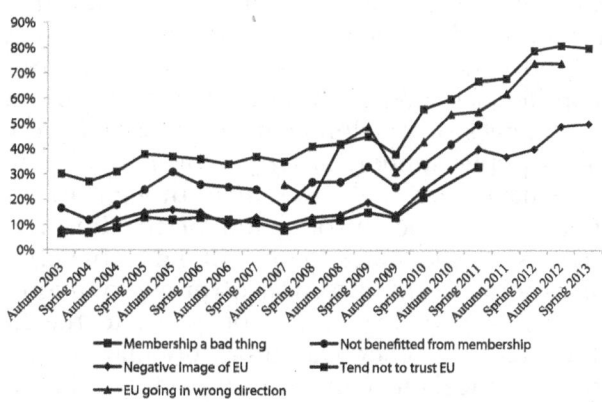

Figure 3. Indicators of negative sentiment in Greece towards the EU
Source: Eurobarometer surveys

doubled (from 38 to 81% and from 31 to 74%, respectively). On the latter two indicators, the overwhelming majority of Eurobarometer's Greek sample now has a negative stance. The two indicators measuring attitudes towards national membership of the EU were somewhat controversially discontinued by Eurobarometer after the Spring 2011 survey. However, in the 18-month period separating the latter from the beginning of the crisis, those regarding EU membership as 'a bad thing' jumped from 13% to 33%. This made Greece in Spring 2011 the EU member state with the highest proportion of respondents giving a negative answer to this question, marginally ahead of the traditionally eurosceptic UK. Meanwhile, between November 2009 and May 2011, those Greek citizens who considered the country had not benefitted from membership doubled from 25 to 50%, the second highest proportion in the EU (this time behind the UK).

Does this mean that three decades after accession, the crisis had turned the Greek population into 'hard' eurosceptics (Szczerbiak and Taggart 2000)? The data do not support such an interpretation. While all our indicators showed a sharp upward trend, they also display significant quantitative differences. In May 2011 (the last occasion on which it is possible to compare the two indicators), while almost three-quarters of the Greek sample agreed the EU was going in the wrong direction, only one-third concurred with the statement that EU membership was 'a bad thing'. It is also worth noting that on the membership question, while in May 2011 Greece had the highest level of negative responses in the EU (33%), the 'hard' Eurosceptics were still outnumbered by those who regarded EU membership as 'a good thing' (38%). This was not the case in the UK, where those with a positive evaluation of EU membership (26%) were significantly fewer than the 'hard' Eurosceptics (32%). What the Eurobarometer data suggest, therefore, is that while the Greek population has clearly lost its former enthusiasm for the EU, it has moved in a Euro-critical rather than a Euro-rejectionist direction.

Perhaps the most striking indication of this is provided by the issue of the single currency, one of the EU's flagship initiatives. During the economic crisis, the very real prospect of 'Grexit' — a probably disorderly Greek departure from the Eurozone — meant that this was the issue on which the country was facing an immediate 'in' or 'out' dilemma. Figure 4 charts longer-term attitudes towards the single currency, covering a period of more than two decades from 1990–2012. The data are based on questions whose wording has altered in successive Eurobarometer surveys to reflect the various stages of development of EMU and the single currency. The figure displays public support in Greece over time. Generally, levels of support in Greece have been high over time, though they have fluctuated, in particular falling after the introduction of the Euro. Support for the euro, though, has *risen again* since the beginning of the crisis, providing an interesting counterpoint to the direction of public opinion evident for the various indicators shown in Figure 3. Compared to the EU average (not shown here), the single currency was more popular in Greece during the 1990s, less popular once the euro was introduced but has once again become more popular since the beginning of the international economic crisis. In the most recent survey for which data are available (Autumn

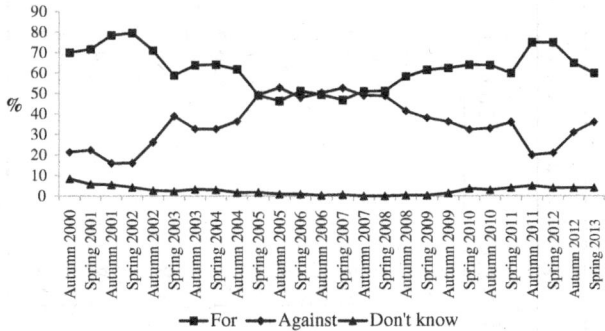

Figure 4. Attitudes towards the single currency
Source: Eurobarometer surveys

2012), 65% of the Greek sample were in favour of the euro compared to 53% across the EU.

The examination of the longitudinal data thus suggests that the majority of Greek public opinion has lost confidence in the EU and disagrees with its current direction, but clearly wants to remain within the Eurozone: an attitude that could be described as 'We no longer love you, but we don't want to leave you'. The next section examines the changing dynamics of opinion across social groups.

Greece and the EU: Changes in Group Attitudes, 2003–2007 and 2007–2011

This section focuses on group attitudes for three Eurobarometer questions at three points in time, using data from surveys conducted in 2003, 2007 and 2011. The questions utilised in this section are the following: whether EU membership is a good thing, a bad thing or neither; whether the country has

Table 1. Overall distribution of opinion in Greece

	2003 (%)	2007 (%)	2011 (%)
Benefitted from membership			
Benefitted	75.0	80.1	47.5
Not benefitted	16.6	17.0	49.9
Don't know	8.4	2.9	2.6
Membership is a good thing			
A good thing	61.9	61.8	37.7
Neither good nor bad	29.7	29.9	33.5
A bad thing	6.7	7.9	27.9
Don't know	1.7	0.5	1.0
Single currency			
For	64.0	50.4	75.5
Against	32.7	49.2	19.6
Don't know	3.3	0.4	4.9

Source: Eurobarometer surveys.

Table 2. Changes in social group attitudes, 2003–2007 and 2007–2011

	Not benefitted		A bad thing		Against single currency	
	Change: 2003–2007	Change: 2007–2011	Change: 2003–2007	Change: 2007–2011	Change: 2003–2007	Change: 2007–2011
Male	0.6	33.5	0.4	26.0	16.3	−25.5
Female	0.2	32.6	2.0	25.3	16.9	−33.5
Aged 15–34	−1.9	29.7	2.0	20.2	10.5	−20.2
Aged 35–54	1.7	36.7	1.1	26.1	20.5	−28.0
Aged 55–64	5.3	31.6	0.0	31.6	19.8	−31.6
Aged 65+	−0.9	33.3	0.9	30.4	18.2	−47.0
15 or under	2.8	35.5	3.2	33.4	19.5	−41.8
16 to 19	0.1	41.0	0.1	16.7	17.0	−26.5
20 and over	−3.8	25.4	−0.6	16.7	16.1	−26.2
Still in education	2.6	15.4	0.7	4.7	10.9	−10.8
Non-manual	−5.9	31.1	0.5	19.9	20.8	−31.5
Manual	8.0	44.1	2.0	35.5	23.8	−34.0
Self-employed	11.1	30.6	2.5	31.0	18.4	−21.1
Other	0.4	31.1	0.9	23.6	12.6	−30.7

Source: Eurobarometer surveys.

benefitted or not from EU membership; and whether for or against a single currency. Table 1 shows the overall distribution of opinion in Greece for these three questions and Table 2 presents changes in opinion for 2003–2007 and 2007–2011 for societal groups classified by sex, age, education and occupational status. Table 2 reports the changes in *negative sentiment*:

- Those who think that membership is a bad thing;
- Those who think their country has not benefitted from membership; and
- Those who are against the single currency.

Looking first at Table 1, we can see that the overall proportion who believe their country has not benefitted barely changed between 2003 and 2007 but then rose substantially between 2007 and 2011 (by 32.9 percentage points). Looking at the breakdown for the various social categories, we can see that, while there was mixed response from groups in the 2003–2007 period, there was a uniformly strong shift in negative sentiment in the latter period. All groups evince large percentage point increases in those who perceive that Greece has 'not benefitted' from membership. Is there a similar pattern for opinion of whether EU membership is a bad thing? Between 2003 and 2007, there is a near-uniform picture of small shifts in a negative direction amongst social groups, with the only exception being those who left education aged 20 years and over (showing a percentage point decrease of just 0.6 percentage points). Between 2007 and 2011, there is a similar uniformly strong shift in a negative direction, with all groups showing sizeable increases in those responding 'a bad thing'. For both of these indicators of negative sentiment, there are large shifts across all social and economic groups; while the extent of the change may vary, the direction does not.

Looking at attitudes towards the single currency, there was a strong shift in a negative direction between 2003 and 2007, again occurring across all social and economic groups. The proportion against the single currency rose from 33.8% in 2003 to around half in 2007 (49.4%). This coincides with the introduction of the euro and can be explained by the latter's association with inflation. However, the opposite occurred between 2007 and 2011, with a substantial decline in negative sentiment to 20.6%. In both periods, the extent of the attitudinal change varies across social and economic groups, but the direction of change is always the same. Of the three indicators, attitudes towards the single currency therefore display the greatest contrast between the two periods captured in Table 2. Even during a period — 2007–2011 — when the public mood was clearly growing dissatisfied with Greece's membership of the EU, support for one of the EU's flagship projects was considerably strengthened and, moreover, outpaced support across the EU as a whole.

Data from the most recently released EB survey (Autumn 2013) confirm strong support for the single currency (62.0% in Greece compared to 52.0% across the EU as a whole). But the negative sentiment towards the EU clearly remains: 54.0% have a negative image of the EU; 72.0% think it is going in the wrong direction; and 77.0% tend not to trust the EU (European Commission 2013). This suggests that the crisis seems to have convinced Greeks that the single currency offers a safe haven in the storm. Thus, in Greece, the crisis has clearly produced a crisis of confidence in the EU; however, this does not extend to rejection of European integration. This interpretation is further underlined by a question only recently included in EB surveys, asking whether member states would be better off outside the EU: in response, a majority in Greece disagreed (57.0%), with 38.0% agreeing and just 5.0% unsure (European Commission 2013).

Greece and the EU: Multivariate Analysis of Public Attitudes

This section introduces the data source and measurement of dependent and independent variables before presenting and discussing the findings from the model estimations.

Data Source and Dependent Variables

The data for this analysis come from three surveys. Firstly, the Autumn 2007 Eurobarometer survey (EB68.1 2007); secondly, the Spring 2011 Eurobarometer survey (EB75.3 2011); and, thirdly, the Spring 2012 Eurobarometer survey (EB77.3 2012). The sample sizes for Greece comprise approximately 1000 respondents in each Eurobarometer survey. The first stage involves multivariate analysis of public attitudes in Greece using the Autumn 2007 survey. The second stage involves analysis of the Spring 2011 and Spring 2012 surveys, due to the availability of key indicators of support. Specifically, the two questions on EU membership were last asked

Table 3. Distribution of opinion for the dependent variables

	Autumn 2007 (%)	Spring 2011[a]/Spring 2012[b] (%)	Change
Benefitted from membership[a]			
Benefitted	80.1	47.5	−32.6
Not benefitted	17.0	49.9	+32.9
Don't know	2.9	2.6	−0.3
Membership is a good thing[a]			
Good thing	61.8	37.7	−24.1
Neither	29.9	27.9	−2.0
Bad thing	7.9	33.5	+25.6
Don't know	0.5	1.0	+0.5
Single currency[b]			
For	50.4	74.8	+24.4
Against	49.2	20.6	−28.6
Don't know	0.4	4.6	+4.2

Source: Eurobarometer surveys. [a]Indicates that the questions were asked in the Spring 2011 survey; [b]Indicates that the question was asked in the Spring 2012 survey.

in the Spring 2011 surveys while the question on support for the single currency was last administered in the Spring 2012 survey. The distribution of opinion for the dependent variables in the 2007 and 2011/12 surveys is shown in Table 3 (indicating the change in percentage points between the two time points).

For all analyses, the dependent variables are measured so that the Eurosceptic responses are scored as 1 and pro-EU or neutral responses are scored as 0:

- Those who say their country has not benefitted from membership are scored as 1 while those who say it has benefitted are scored 0.
- Those who say membership is a bad thing are scored as 1 and those who respond a good thing or neither good nor bad are scored as 0.
- Those who are against the single currency are scored as 1 and those who are in favour of it are scored as 0.

We use binary logistic regression analysis, suitable for dichotomous dependent variables. Missing data are excluded from the analysis.

Independent Variables

The independent variables used here are informed by the main theoretical approaches used in the wider literature on public opinion towards the EU. These approaches relate to economic interests, group identities and political cues (Hooghe and Marks 2004, 2005; McLaren 2006). Survey data permitting, we operationalise a range of independent variables which reflect insights from the economic interests and political cues approaches. Due to the lack of suitable measures for group identities or attachments being available in all EB surveys and since we aim to use equivalent model specifications for the multivariate analyses of the 2007 and 2011 surveys, we do not examine their impact in this paper.

It has been well established that citizens' economic interests and material circumstances are important determinants of their views towards the integration process (Hooghe and Marks 2004, 2005; McLaren 2006). In particular, economic integration — and major projects such as the Single Market and EMU — has varying consequences for citizens in the member states, leading to winners and losers from a country's EU membership. According to existing studies of public attitudes towards the EU, those with higher levels of education or who are in higher-level occupations are more likely to benefit from economic integration (Gabel 1998; Hooghe 2007; McLaren 2006), including particular policies such as the single currency.

As well as 'objective' indicators of socio-economic location 'subjective' assessments of personal and national economic conditions have also been shown to be consequential for attitudes on EU-related issues (Anderson 1998; Gabel and Whitten 1997; Hooghe and Marks 2005). Positive appraisals of past or future economic performance or conditions are thought to underpin support for the EU and its policies. As de Vreese *et al.* observe: 'the "subjective utilitarian model" suggests that European integration is supported if perceptions and future evaluations of the economy are positive' (2008, 513).

We use both objective and subjective indicators of socio-economic circumstances. The former is measured, first, by the age at which an individual finished their education (measured as a series of dummy variables: aged 15 and under; 16–19 years; 20 and over; still in education). It is measured, second, by occupational status (dummies for self-employed, in manual employment, in non-manual employment or not currently working — a student, retired, unemployed or a home person). We use retrospective assessment of the national economy as our subjective indicator of socio-economic circumstances. Higher scores represent more positive assessments.

While it may be a powerful determining factor, public opinion towards the EU is not only influenced by individuals' economic interests. Indeed earlier 'accounts of attitudes towards European integration resemble the old adage of "where you stand determines where you sit", and are almost exclusively concerned with economic utilitarianism' (McLaren 2006, 31). However, public opinion is also shaped by the domestic political context of member states. Increasingly, research into public opinion and the EU has found that citizens rely on cues and proxies rooted in domestic politics to form opinions about the integration process (Anderson 1998; Sánchez-Cuenca 2000). Indeed, because of the complex and multifaceted nature of multilevel governance within the EU, 'one would expect domestic politics to shape public views on European integration' (Hooghe and Marks 2005, 425). While, unfortunately, measures of party support are not available in the surveys used here, we can employ measures of frequency of political discussion or level of interest in politics. We also examine trust in governing institutions — specifically, whether respondents tend to trust or tend not to trust the national parliament and government. Finally, in order to reduce the chances of omitted variable bias, all models employ socio-demographic controls for gender (scored as 1 if male and 0 if female) and age (a continuous variable). A summary of the independent variables is provided in the Appendix.

Results and Discussion

The binary logistic regression results for the 2007 survey are shown in Table 4 and for the 2011/12 surveys in Table 5. In contrast to the earlier analysis of change in social group attitudes, this section reports two sets of cross-sectional analyses. The same model specification is used for the three dependent variables, to permit comparison of the effects of the independent variables across models and time points. First, looking at the results reported in Table 4 for the 2007 survey it is clear that gender has a consistent impact in all three models. Compared to women, men are less likely to think Greece does not benefit from membership or is a bad thing, and less likely to be against the single currency. Age is only significant in the third model (single currency), where older people are less likely to be against the Euro. In terms of the objective indicators of socio-economic circumstances,

Table 4. Binary logistic regression estimations (EB Autumn 2007)

	Not benefitted from membership			Membership is a bad thing			Against single currency		
	B	S.E.	Exp(B)	B	S.E.	Exp(B)	B	S.E.	Exp(B)
Sex	−0.51**	0.20	0.60	−0.46***	0.16	0.63	−0.40***	0.15	0.67
Age	0.01	0.01	1.01	0.01	0.01	1.01	0.01**	0.01	1.01
Left education: Aged 16–19	−0.45*	0.26	0.64	−0.12	0.21	0.89	−0.55***	0.20	0.57
Left education: Aged 20+	−0.59*	0.32	0.55	−0.24	0.25	0.79	−0.60***	0.23	0.55
Still in education	0.06	0.46	1.06	−0.52	0.38	0.60	−0.68*	0.35	0.51
Occupation: Self-employed	0.07	0.31	1.07	−0.05	0.25	0.95	0.10	0.23	1.10
Occupation: Manual	0.50	0.32	1.65	0.23	0.25	1.26	0.56**	0.24	1.75
Occupation: Non-manual	−0.13	0.37	0.87	0.07	0.27	1.08	−0.20	0.25	0.82
Discuss politics	0.10	0.13	1.10	−0.12	0.11	0.89	−0.20**	0.10	0.82
Life satisfaction	−0.49***	0.13	0.61	−0.34***	0.11	0.71	−0.24**	0.10	0.78
National economy	−0.58***	0.15	0.56	−0.54***	0.11	0.58	−0.40***	0.11	0.67
Trust government	−0.84***	0.27	0.43	−0.73***	0.20	0.48	0.08	0.19	1.09
Trust parliament	−0.48**	0.24	0.62	−0.77***	0.18	0.46	−0.50***	0.18	0.60
Constant	1.21*	0.67	3.36	2.37***	0.53	10.72	1.99***	0.50	7.30
Weighted N	959			982			984		
Nagelkerke R^2	0.22			0.26			0.17		

Notes: *** $p \leq .01$;
** $p \leq .05$;
* $p \leq .10$.
Omitted reference categories: left education aged 15 or under; not in work.

Table 5. Binary logistic regression estimations (EB Spring 2011[a] and EB Spring 2012[b])

	Not benefitted from membership[a]			Membership is a bad thing[a]			Against single currency[b]		
	B	S.E.	Exp(B)	B	S.E.	Exp(B)	B	S.E.	Exp(B)
Sex	−0.15	0.15	0.86	0.00	0.16	1.00	−0.04	0.17	0.96
Age	0.00	0.01	1.00	0.00	0.01	1.00	−0.02***	0.01	0.98
Left education: Aged 16–19	−0.17	0.21	0.84	−0.34	0.20	0.71	−0.71***	0.23	0.49
Left education: Aged 20+	−0.89***	0.24	0.41	−0.87***	0.25	0.42	−1.37***	0.28	0.25
Still in education	−0.98***	0.37	0.38	−1.20***	0.42	0.30	−1.55***	0.42	0.21
Occupation: Self-employed	−0.08	0.22	0.92	0.25	0.22	1.29	−0.19	0.24	0.83
Occupation: Manual	−0.14	0.24	0.87	−0.06**	0.25	0.94	−0.25	0.29	0.78
Occupation: Non-manual	0.71**	0.28	2.04	0.59	0.26	1.80	−0.02	0.27	0.98
Discuss politics	−0.04	0.07	0.96	0.09	0.08	1.10	0.00	0.09	1.00
Life satisfaction	−0.20**	0.09	0.82	−0.33***	0.09	0.72	0.01	0.10	1.01
National economy	−0.53***	0.16	0.59	−0.39**	0.18	0.68	−0.19	0.23	0.82
Trust government	−0.84**	0.32	0.43	−1.34***	0.38	0.26	0.18**	0.38	1.20
Trust parliament	−1.06***	0.31	0.35	−0.26	0.34	0.77	−1.08	0.51	0.34
Constant	2.09***	0.50	8.12	0.71	0.51	2.04	0.85	0.56	2.34
Weighted N	964			979			928		
Nagelkerke R^2	0.23			0.20			0.06		

Notes: *** $p \leq .01$;
** $p \leq .05$;
* $p \leq .10$.
Omitted reference categories: left education aged 15 or under; not in work. [a]Indicates that the data come from the Spring 2011 survey; [b]Indicates that the data come from the Spring 2012 survey.

the results are rather patchy, with both education and occupation having more effect in the model of attitudes towards the single currency. Here, those who left education aged 16–19 years or 20 and over, as well as those still in education, are less likely to be against the Euro compared to those who left education aged 15 or under. In relation to occupational status, those in manual employment are more likely to be against the Euro compared to those not currently in work. However, the occupational status dummies have no effects in the first two models (not benefit from membership and membership is a bad thing).

Turning to the attitudinal variables in Table 4, hese have collectively larger impact and the directions of the relationships are generally the same across the different specifications of the dependent variables. Higher life satisfaction has consistent effects: it is negatively related to thinking Greece has not benefitted from membership, believing membership is a bad thing and being against the single currency. Frequency of discussion of politics similarly has a consistent and negatively signed relationship with the three dependent variables. Greater discussion of politics leads to less likelihood of holding anti-EU views and being opposed to the Euro. Economic perceptions also have significant effects in all three models: positive economic appraisals of the national economy are negatively related to anti-EU attitudes and being opposed to the Euro. It appears then that the wider economic context is shaping the attitudes of Greek citizens towards both membership of the EU and their country's involvement in the Euro. Finally, it is clear that political attitudes rooted in the domestic context — which can act as 'cues' or 'proxies' are shaping public opinion on membership and the single currency. Specifically, those who tend to trust national political institutions — the government and parliament — are less likely to hold unfavourable assessments of EU membership and to be against the Euro. These findings confirm insights from the political cues approach.

Turning to the results for the Spring 2011 and Spring 2012 surveys reported in Table 5, we can see that there is a mixed performance for the socio-demographic and socio-economic variables. In particular, education has stronger effects in Table 5 than in Table 4 and is a more potent explanatory factor than is occupational status. Generally, those who left aged 20 years and over, or who are still in some form of education, are less likely to hold negative views of membership and the Euro compared to those who finished education at an earlier age. This is also the case for those who finished education aged 16–18 years, but only for opinion towards the single currency. The occupational status variables have no significant impact in the model of attitudes towards the Euro. In the models of general support for membership, manual workers are more likely to think that membership is a bad thing and those in non-manual employment are more likely to think that the country has not benefitted from being in the EU, but these are otherwise isolated effects as occupational status performs poorly overall. Age again has a significant effect on opinion towards the single currency in 2012, with older people less likely to be opposed.

As with the results from Table 4, all of the attitudinal variables — with the exception of subjective economic perceptions — have consistent and significant effects on general support for the EU. Evaluations of the national economy are only significant in the first model, relating to views as to whether Greece has benefitted from its membership. Again, positive retrospective assessments of the national economic situation are negatively related to unfavourable views of the EU. In contrast to Table 4, however, this variable has no significant impact in the other two models. Next, general life satisfaction again is related to less likelihood of holding negative views of the EU, as was evident in Table 4. With the exception of trust in government in the model assessing attitudes towards the single currency, the measures of trust in political institutions have significant effects in all models, again supporting the political 'cues' approach to explaining public support for European integration. Those who tend to trust either parliament or the government is less likely to hold unfavourable views of EU membership and the Euro.

Taken together, the findings for evaluations of national political institutions support one set of findings from the political 'cues' approach (Anderson 1998; Sánchez-Cuenca 2000). Specifically, we find that positive attitudes towards the national parliament and government are less likely to be related to opposition to the EU and single currency, rather than the opposite relationship, whereby some previous studies have found that negative views of domestic institutions are related to greater support for the EU and its institutions (Sánchez-Cuenca 2000). Also, there are similar effects for subjective economic perceptions across models, which are again in keeping with established findings from the wider literature. That is, positive appraisals of the national economy are less likely to be related to negative evaluations of the EU and the Euro (Gabel and Whitten 1997). Finally, in relation to objective economic interests, although the results are less impressive and consistent overall, when they are significant we find that those groups whom we would expect to be more secure in their economic circumstances — precisely those groups thought to have the human capital to take advantage of the opportunities offered by membership and key elements, such as the Single Market and its economic freedoms — are less likely to be unfavourable towards the EU and the Euro (Gabel 1998). The results here for individuals' economic circumstances and public attitudes towards the EU are interesting in the light of Roth *et al.*'s findings that, amongst the four member states at the centre of the crisis — Greece, Spain, Portugal and Ireland — there has been a more pronounced fall than across the European Area-12 — in public trust in the ECB, which has been driven by increasing unemployment rates (n.d.).

Conclusion

For the majority of Greek citizens, the EU was always positively associated with democracy, economic prosperity and a move away from the inherent weaknesses of national politics. The handling of the Eurozone crisis has changed this. The empirical analyses reported in this paper shed important new light on the response of Greek public opinion in the context of the current crisis. In particular, the detailed single-country focus (the 'microscopic' approach) complements broader cross-national research (the 'telescopic' approach) on public opinion towards the EU in the context of the crisis, which also finds changes in political support across member states (Braun and Tausendpfund n.d.). The traditional picture of Greece as a 'pro-European' member state, a characteristic it shared with other southern European countries, has changed during the period of economic crisis. The longitudinal evidence examined here show that negative evaluations of the EU increased sharply between 2007 and 2011 in contrast to the steady high levels of pro-European sentiment during the previous two decades. Our breakdown of opinion by social groups shows that this shift in negative opinion is a 'sea change' affecting society as a whole, with all social groups sharing in it.

The fact that public opinion in Greece has turned more Eurosceptic is hardly surprising. What is surprising though is that the decline in general EU support is accompanied by increase in support for the euro. Support for the single currency has increased between 2007 and 2011 and is now higher in Greece than the EU as a whole. This is also confirmed by the most recently released EB survey (Autumn 2013). What can account for the coexistence of these contradictory opinions? We argue that this picture is closely linked to the wider debate about the change from a 'permissive consensus' to a 'constraining dissensus; and the fact that European integration has become more politicised in the member states (Hooghe and Marks, 2009). Increase in public disenchantment with the EU is often seen as indication of a rejection of European integration and an obstacle to further integration (Tosun et al. n.d.). We argue that the picture in Greece supports a different interpretation to that of 'constraining dissensus'. Instead of Greek citizens wanting less Europe, their critical attitudes represent a move away from the norm of consensus governance and depoliticisation of the content of EU policies to one of conflict and politicisation. The majority of Greek people seem to adopt a pragmatic approach where they are aware that being in the Euro and the EU is the realistic alternative despite the pain of austerity policies domestically. However, they are also signalling their discontent with the lack of effective solutions from Europe in terms of outputs.

Future research should investigate the links between the positions of political parties and the opinions of their supporters. This is particularly important given the changing political and electoral landscape in Greece — including the increasing prominence of minor parties with Eurosceptic platforms – within the context of the unfolding Eurozone crisis. Such research should be accompanied by an analysis of how the EU issue in the context of the crisis has changed in Greece in terms of its salience for and the positioning of, the mainstream and non-mainstream parties, as Hutter and Kerscher have shown for France (n.d.) where there has been greater politicisation of the European integration issue.

References

Anderson, C.J. 1998. When in doubt, use proxies: attitudes toward domestic policies and support for European integration. *Comparative Political Studies* 31, no. 5: 569–601.

Braun, D., and M. Tausendpfund. n.d. The impact of the Eurozone crisis on citizens' support for the European Union. *Journal of European Integration*, special issue.

Costa Lobo, M., and P.C. Magalhães. 2011. Room for manoeuvre: Euroscepticism in the Portuguese parties and electorate 1976–2005. *South European Society and Politics* 16, no. 1: 81–104.

de Vreese, C.H., H.G. Boomgaarden, and H.A. Semetko. 2008. Hard and soft: public support for Turkish membership in the EU. *European Union Politics* 9, no. 4: 511–30.

European Commission. 2013. *Standard Eurobarometer 80. Autumn 2013. Public Opinion in the European Union*, http://ec.europa.eu/public_opinion/archives/eb/eb80/eb80_anx_en.pdf.

European Commission, Brussels: Eurobarometer 75.3. May 2011. TNS OPINION & SOCIAL, Brussels [Producer]; GESIS, Cologne [Publisher]: ZA5481, dataset v1.0.0, doi:10.4232/1.10768.

European Commission: Eurobarometer 68.1. 2007. TNS Opinion & Social, Brussels [Producer]. GESIS Data Archive, Cologne. ZA4565 data file version 4.0.1, doi:10.4232/1.10988

European Commission: Eurobarometer 77.3. 2012. TNS Opinion & Social, Brussels [Producer]. GESIS Data Archive, Cologne. ZA5612 Data file Version 1.0.0, doi:10.4232/1.11558.

Gabel, M. 1998. *Interests and integration: market liberalization, public opinion, and European Union*. Ann Arbor: University of Michigan Press.

Gabel, M., and G.D. Whitten. 1997. Economic conditions. *Economic Perceptions and Public Support for European integration, Political Behavior* 19, no. 1: 81–96.

Hooghe, L. 2007. What drives Euroskepticism? Party-public cueing, ideology and strategic opportunity *European Union Politics* 8, no. 1: 5–12.

Hooghe, L., and G. Marks. 2004. Does identity or economic rationality drive public opinion on European integration? *PS: Political Science & Politics* 37, no. 3: 415–20.

Hooghe, L., and G. Marks. 2005. Calculation, Community and cues: public opinion on European integration. *European Union Politics* 6, no. 4: 419–43.

Hooghe, L., and G. Marks. 2009. A postfunctionalist theory of European integration: from permissive consensus to constraining dissensus. *British Journal of Political Science* 39, no. 1: 1–23.

Hutter, S., and A. Kerscher. n.d. Politicizing Europe in hard times: conflicts over Europe in the 2012 French election campaign in a long-term perspective. *Journal of European Integration*, special issue.

Krastev, I. 2002. The Balkans: democracy without choices. *Journal of Democracy* 13, no. 3: 39–53.

Llamazares, I., and P. Gramacho. 2007. Eurosceptics among Euroenthusiasts: an analysis of Southern European public opinions. *Acta Politica* 42, no. 2–3: 211–32.

Mair, P. 2011. Bini Smaghi vs. the parties: representative government and institutional constraints, Florence: EUI Working Papers, RSCAS 2011/22.

Mavris, Y.E. 2004. From accession to the euro: the evolution of Greek public attitudes towards European integration, 1981–2001. In *Greece in the European Union*, eds. D.G. Dimitrakopoulos and A.G. Passas, 113–38. London: Routledge.

McLaren, L.M. 2006. *Identity, interests and attitudes to European integration*. Basingstoke: Palgrave.

Quaglia, L. 2011. 'The Ebb and Flow' of Euroscepticism in Italy. *South European Society and Politics* 16, no. 1: 31–50.

Roth, F., D. Gros, and F. Nowak-Lehmann. n.d. Crisis and citizens' trust in the European Central Bank — panel data evidence for the Euro area, 1999 to 2012. *Journal of European Integration*, special issue.

Ruiz Jiménez, A.M., and A. de Haro. 2011. Spain: Euroscepticism in a pro-European country? *South European Society and Politics* 16, no. 1: 105–31.

Sánchez-Cuenca, I. 2000. The political basis of support for European integration. *European Union Politics* 1, no. 2: 147–71.

Serricchio, F., M. Tsakatika, and L. Quaglia. 2013. Euroscepticism and the global financial crisis. *JCMS: Journal of Common Market Studies* 51, no. 1: 51–64.

Szczerbiak, A., and P. Taggart 2000. Opposing Europe: party systems and opposition to the Union, the Euro and Europeanisation, University of Sussex OERN Working Paper No. 1.

Tosun, J., A. Wetzel, and G. Zaypryanova. n.d. The EU in crisis: advancing the debate. *Journal of European Integration*, special issue.

Verney, S. 2011a. Euroscepticism in Southern Europe: a diachronic perspective. *South European Society and Politics* 16, no. 1: 1–29.

Verney, S. 2011b. An exceptional case? Party and popular Euroscepticism in Greece, 1959–2009. *South European Society and Politics* 16, no. 1: 51–79.

Appendix. Independent variables

Variable	Measurement
Sex	Dummy variable (1 = male, 0 if female).
Age	Continuous variable (15 years and upwards).
Education	Measured as the age a respondent finished full-time education. Dummy variables: aged 15 and under, 16–18 years, 19 and over, still in education. Those who left education aged 15 and under are the reference category.
Occupation	Dummy variables: self-employed, manual occupation, non-manual occupation, other (retired, student, unemployed and house person). The 'other' group forms the reference category.
Satisfaction with life	Scale ranging from 1 to 4. Higher values represent greater life satisfaction.
Economic perceptions	Retrospective evaluations of the national economy. Scale scored from 1 to 4. Higher scores represent more positive evaluations.
Trust in national government	Dummy variable scored 1 = tend to trust and 0 = tend not to trust.
Trust in national parliament	Dummy variable scored 1 = tend to trust and 0 = tend not to trust.
Political interest/ discussion	Scale scored from 1 to 4. Higher scores represent more frequent discussion of politics (EB68.1 2007, EB77.3 2012) or greater interest in politics (EB75.3 2011).

Politicizing Europe in Hard Times: Conflicts over Europe in France in a Long-term Perspective, 1974–2012

SWEN HUTTER & ALENA KERSCHER

Geschwister-Scholl-Institute for Political Science, University of Munich, Munich, Germany

ABSTRACT This article examines whether and how the Euro crisis has affected the long-term trends of politicization of Europe in France. Has the crisis fueled the extent of politicization? Do we observe shifts in specific aspects of Europe being politicized? Are the patterns of opposition changing? To answer these questions, the authors compare the electoral campaign in 2012 with all French campaigns since 1974. Additionally, France is put in a broader comparative perspective. Politicization is conceptualized as three interrelated dimensions: issue salience, actor expansion, and polarization. Methodologically, the article is based on a relational content analysis of newspaper articles. The findings show that the Euro crisis boosted the level of politicization, and economic policies, as well as justification frames became more important. However, the degree of polarization was higher in election campaigns that focused more on constitutional conflicts over membership and were dominated by concerns with national identity and sovereignty.

Introduction

The spotlight has been on the *politics* dimension in European integration studies since the mid-2000s. In this context, the concept of politicization has become key to understanding recent transformations (see de Wilde 2011). This is most prominent in Hooghe and Marks' (2009) programmatic article that puts politicization center stage of a new post-functionalist theory of European integration. More specifically, Hooghe and Marks argue that Europe has become politicized in electoral and referendum campaigns, and that we witness a shift from 'permissive consensus' to a period characterized by 'constraining dissensus' in the post-Maastricht era. Similarly, Kriesi *et al.* (2008, 2012) show that conflicts over European integration have become more salient in party competition in Western Europe since the 1990s. This is part and parcel of a broader transformation of political conflict, which is caused by the ongoing opening-up of economic, cultural, and political borders. In contrast with these arguments, other authors argue that European integration clearly has the potential to change domestic politics, but underscore that the issue has not yet been politicized by political parties (e.g. Green-Pedersen 2012; Van Der Eijk and Franklin 2004).

The current Euro crisis tends to refute the 'skeptics' since European affairs have become more visible in the public sphere, and citizens are reminded, almost on a daily basis, of the enormous interdependencies among European economies and societies. Furthermore, earlier economic crises have been major drivers of politicization and political realignments (e.g. Gourevitch 1984). Thus, many observers see the current crisis as yet another major event fueling the politicization of Europe, and bringing public contestation into the world of European decision-making (e.g. Kriesi and Grande 2012; Statham and Trenz 2012b). In the words of Statham and Trenz (2012b): 'The Eurozone crisis has an extraordinarily high potential for generating a deep and on-going politicization of the EU within national domestic politics across the region' (18f.).

By studying party contestation, this article adds to the previous contributions of this special issue that looked at public opinion only. These studies indicated a growing anti-European sentiment among citizens as reflected in increasingly negative evaluations of EU membership or distrust towards European institutions (see Braun and Tausendpfund *this volume*; Clements *et al. this volume*; Roth *et al. this volume*). However, shifts in public opinion are only latent potentials as long as they are not mobilized by collective political actors and reflected in citizens' behavior. That is why this article looks at how political parties publicly contest European integration in election campaigns. Obviously, the Euro crisis is a crucial moment in the history of European integration (see Tosun *et al. this volume*), but we still lack sufficient information both on the magnitude of politicization induced by the crisis, as well as on the way the crisis has changed the existing conflicts over Europe.

More precisely, we contribute to the debate by studying how the Euro crisis has affected the long-term trends of politicization in France. While Schimmelfennig (*this volume*) is certainly right that the crisis has boosted politicization, we argue that more detailed studies are needed which focus not just on the extent, but also on the kind of politicization induced by the crisis. This will allow us to draw more precise conclusions about how citizens' changing preferences and party contestation amidst the crisis may affect the future of European integration. This is because not all kinds of politicization may negatively influence further integration only.

This article takes a first important step by providing such an in-depth analysis for the French case. France is a paradigmatic case both because of its key role in the European integration project and because of earlier episodes of politicization. First, besides Germany, France is seen as the motor behind the integration process in general and a key player in the Eurozone more specifically. Thus, increasing politicization in France may influence the political climate in the EU and future steps of integration more than if this happens in smaller and more peripheral states (de Wilde and Zürn 2012, 149). A good example is increasing politicization related to the EU accession of Turkey in France (and Germany), which negatively affected the negotiation process (see, e.g. Koenig et al. 2006). Second, Eurosceptic mobilization in France shows the typical pattern of the inverted U-curve: This is because of economically based opposition from the far left and identity- or sovereignty-based opposition from the far right.

Empirically, we study the public debate among political parties as it unfolds during national election campaigns through relational content analysis of newspaper articles. Studying politicization during the heyday of domestic mobilization sets high stakes, as European issues have to compete with other domestic issues during the campaign. At the same time, it enables us to directly compare the mobilizing power of European integration with other issues (Green-Pedersen 2012, 121f.; Hutter and Grande forthcoming). Most commentators on the French election in the Spring of 2012, which resulted in the victory of the Socialist contender François Hollande over the incumbent Nicolas Sarkozy, emphasized that European issues played a significant role (e.g. Clift 2013; Drake 2013; Hewlett 2012; Lequesne 2012). This article puts the 'snapshots' provided by the cited studies in a long-term perspective, which takes into account the years since the supposed end of the 'permissive consensus' by comparing the latest campaign in 2012 with all campaigns since 1974.

This article is structured as follows. The next section presents the way in which we conceptualize politicization. Thereafter, we present the hypotheses. Here, we draw on general ideas about what drives politicization and on the findings for earlier episodes of politicization in France. Next, the methods and data are introduced, which is followed by the empirical findings. We conclude with a summary and by coming back to the post-functionalist argument. More precisely, we emphasize what our results suggest in view of Hooghe and Marks's (2009) claim that politicization has a 'constraining' effect on the elites involved in European decision-making.

A Multi-dimensional Concept of Politicization

We adopt a broad understanding of politicization and take seriously its multi-dimensional character (see also de Wilde 2011). More precisely, we follow Hutter and Grande (forthcoming) by conceptualizing politicization as three interrelated dimensions: issue salience, actor expansion, and polarization.

The first dimension takes into account that only topics that are frequently raised by political actors in public debates can be considered politicized. Thus, *salience* refers to the visibility of a given issue in public debates. If an issue is not debated in public, it can be politicized only to a very limited extent if at all. This mirrors recent proposals by Green-Pedersen (2012) and by Guinaudeau and Persico (2013), who suggest looking at politicization through the lens of salience. The second dimension is the *expansion of the actors* involved in a public debate. With respect to European integration, this dimension assesses the degree to which the dominant executive actors are joined by other actors in the public debate. The assumption is that, as long as only executive politicians publicly debate European integration, the issue is not fully politicized (see Statham and Trenz 2012a, 79ff.). This article focuses on election campaigns, in which political parties compete for votes. Therefore, the expansion of the scope of actors refers to the degree to which not only party-affiliated actors in government but also party actors without a government function emphasize European issues (e.g. opposition leaders or spokespersons in parliament). Finally, the third dimension of politicization refers to the degree of *polarization*, i.e. the intensity of conflict over an issue among the various actors. Thus, to speak of a highly politicized constellation, actors need to put forward differing positions and we must find strong opposing camps.

To get an *overall* measure for the level of politicization, we combine the three dimensions with the help of an index. Following Hutter and Grande (forthcoming), this index of politicization emphasizes the key importance of salience by multiplying it with the sum of the other two dimensions: politicization = salience × (actor expansion + polarization). As in any index, the proposed measure clearly hides some of the nuanced findings based on the three individual dimensions. However, the index helps us in not overemphasizing high levels of actor expansion and polarization when the salience is low because the two dimensions are actually not visible to the public in this case.

Politicizing Europe in the French Context

France is a paradigmatic case with respect to the key driving forces behind the politicization of Europe. In the following, we illustrate this by referring to the literature and earlier episodes of politicization in France. Generally speaking, the literature focuses on two sets of variables to explain differing levels and forms of politicization over time and across contexts. First, authors highlight that the increasing *level and scope of integration* is a key force that drives the politicization process. As de Wilde and Zürn (2012) argue, 'the rising politicization of European integration is *primarily* a reaction to the increasing authority of the EU over time' (140). The more European institutions exercise authority over citizens, the more they become the object and addressee in political controversies. Hooghe and Marks (2009) add that the effects of these authority shifts have been amplified because they are embedded in a broader breakdown of national boundaries and because of peoples' fairly stable (and, for a large part, exclusively national) identities (see also Kriesi *et al.* 2008, 2012).

Second, the role of *political actors and their mobilization strategies* is stressed. While the processes described so far may give rise to potentials and focal points for contestation, actors need to mobilize these tensions so that they become politically manifest. Thus, as Hooghe and Marks (2009) aptly state, 'As European integration has grown in scope and depth, it has proved ripe for politicization. But there is nothing inevitable about this. Whether an issue enters mass politics depends not on its intrinsic importance, but on whether a political party picks it up' (13). The question then is which parties are most likely to politicize Europe. Here, the literature emphasizes radical parties — particularly those on the right (see Gómez-Reino and Llamazares 2013).

More precisely, three party strategies have been stressed in this context: 'position taking,' 'selective emphasis,' and 'framing.' To put it simply, the literature indicates that radical right-wing parties have been successful in politicizing Europe because they challenge the pro-European consensus of mainstream parties, put the issue high on the agenda, and emphasize its consequences for national sovereignty and identity. By doing so, they have been able to map European issues onto a second non-economic conflict dimension in West European political spaces, which cross-cuts the traditional economic left/right divide.

Previous episodes of politicization in France illustrate these points. Set in motion by the rise of the populist right, the 'redefinition of cultural conflicts as well as the emergence of the issue of European integration on the political agenda has produced far-reaching changes in the structure of oppositions in the French party system' (Bornschier and Lachat 2009, 361). More importantly, it has given rise to a tri-polar conflict constellation, composed of the left, the moderate right, and the populist right (e.g. Grunberg and Schweisguth 2003). The Front National (as the main radical right-wing challenger) has become the strongest opponent of integration and heavily relies on cultural-identitarian arguments in its discourse. The Front National belongs to the key cases where the radical right party and its voters are the most Eurosceptic in the country, and there is a statistically significant party-voter linkage with respect to European issues (Gómez-Reino and Llamazares 2013).

In addition, the French case demonstrates that politicization comes in waves that follow critical events and thresholds of the integration process. Major steps of integration, such as treaty reforms and enlargement rounds, serve as focal points of controversies, since they both accentuate the tensions induced by integration and constitute opportunities for challengers to raise their critique. In France, the conflicts over the ratification of the Maastricht treaty and the European Constitution were most important. Not by chance, Guinaudeau and Persico (2013) observe a very high salience of Europe in the party manifestos in France during the 1990s and no pronounced decline thereafter.

However, the French story is more complex than this because it is characterized by Eurosceptic mobilization both on the right and on the left. This can be traced back to the strength of the traditional class cleavage and the resulting fragmentation of the party system. Moreover, the politicization is not just driven by radical actors but also by conflicts within mainstream parties. A recent example for conflicts on the right is the split of the anti-European *Debout la République* (DLR) from the Union for a Popular Movement (UMP) in 2008. In the case of the debate over the European Constitution, the radical left and right were most critical, but conflict within the Socialist party was decisive for the overall level of politicization (Statham and Trenz 2012a).

The French case also illustrates that conflicts over Europe are not just about questions of identity and national sovereignty (mainly raised by the right) but also about the economic and social consequences of integration (mainly raised by the left). For example, Kriesi (2007) shows that the positions of French parties on European integration barely correlate with their positioning on other key issues mapping onto the cultural dimension. This casts doubt on the assumption that Europe is part of this cultural dimension in France. By de-composing the issue of European integration, Guinaudeau and Persico (2013) support this hunch since French political parties very often emphasize *economic* aspects when they talk about Europe in their manifestos. This focus on social issues and questions of solidarity is also visible when looking at how the dissenting Socialists justified their opposition to the Constitution (Statham and Trenz 2012a, 134).

Based on the general expectations and earlier episodes of politicization, we propose two hypotheses. Generally speaking, we conceive the Euro crisis and the measures taken to cope with it as constituting yet another critical event and threshold within the integration process (Tosun *et al. this volume*). As indicated above, such thresholds have been key moments of politicization. They accentuate the tensions induced by integration and draw public attention to European affairs. Furthermore, the way the crisis and the management of it unfold has given rise to many focal points for contention. Amongst others, European leaders have met not just for a few but for many 'critical' European summits and have adopted a range of measures to cope with the crisis. In a comparative perspective, the increase in politicization is expected to be more pronounced in Eurozone member states, countries economically hit by the crisis, and key states within the European decision-making arena. All this holds for the French case.[1]

Our expectation that the crisis fuels the politicization process is quite straightforward, but has it also affected the conflict constellation? Statham and Trenz (2012b) argue that it is crucial to understand that the new wave of politicization is 'driven by redistributive conflicts both within and across member states, and this is how it has expressed itself through public contestation' (18f). Likewise, Serricchio *et al.* (2013) expect that economic considerations have a stronger effect on individual attitudes towards Europe in times of crisis (see also Braun and Tausenpfund, *this volume*). Following this argument, we expect that the economic nature of the crisis may well accentuate a trend that has already been visible in France. As stated, France is a paradigmatic case with respect to both types of Euroscepticism: economic- and identity-based. Thus, we expect that conflicts over economic issues, as well as framing strategies referring to the economic and social consequences of Europe, may become more important in times of crisis. Since the focus on economics is not exceptional in the French context, we do not expect pronounced changes regarding the patterns of opposition among political parties. Concerning the party constellation, the situation should be similar to the debate over the European Constitution; the moderate right in government is challenged by the Socialists in opposition, as well as by radical parties from both left and right. Thus, the left is expected to follow its earlier critique based on economic and social justifications while the populist right is expected to be the only political force that fundamentally opposes the European integration project by justifying its critique with reference to national sovereignty and identity.

In summary, we formulate the following two hypotheses:

Hypothesis 1. Because of the current Euro crisis, European integration is expected to have become more politicized in the 2012 French election campaign when compared to previous campaigns.

Hypothesis 2. Because of the current Euro crisis, economic issues and framing strategies are expected to have become more salient, but we expect no pronounced differences in the patterns of opposition in the 2012 French election campaign when compared to previous campaigns.

Media Data and the Core Sentence Approach

Methodologically, this article adopts the approach used by Kriesi *et al.* (2008, 2012) to study the transformation of political conflict in Western Europe.[2] Regarding the source, we think that *media data* are especially well suited for our purpose as they provide information about all three dimensions of politicization already introduced. As Statham and Trenz (2012a) state, 'Politicization requires the expansion of debates from closed elite-dominated policy arenas to wider publics, and here the mass media plays an important role by placing contesting political actors in front of a public' (3). Media data allow us to study systematically how the various parties compete with each other, who is actually speaking as a party representative, as well as which thematic aspects related to European integration are debated and how parties justify their positions.

More precisely, we focus on debates among French political parties during the campaigns for the six presidential elections in the period 1974–2012. The period of observation is the two months before the first round of each election. The content analysis rests on all articles (except commentaries) published in *Le Monde* that report on the electoral contest in particular or on national politics more generally. Out of all the articles related to national politics, we then identified those articles that cover a 'European integration issue' — broadly defined as ranging from general orientations and constitutive issues to policy issues.

In a second step, we coded the articles with the help of the so-called *core sentence approach*. In this type of quantitative content analysis, the unit of analysis is not the whole article but the 'core sentence,' which consists of the most basic pieces of information of a grammatical sentence. More precisely, we focus on relations between two actors (at least one being a party actor) with a thematic reference to European integration (*actor–actor sentences*) as well as on relations between an actor and a European issue (*actor–issue sentences*). The direction of the relationship between the two is quantified using a scale from −1 to +1 with three intermediary positions. With respect to actor–issue sentences, we also coded the *frames* used by the actors to justify their position towards a given European issue.

The labor-intensive manual coding of the newspaper articles resulted in 2872 core sentences related to European integration with a share of 82.9% actor–issue statements and 17.1% actor–actor sentences. Furthermore, we can draw on 2077 coded frames in the following analyses.

The three components of politicization are operationalized as follows: salience is measured by the share of sentences on European integration as a percentage of all sentences related to any issue. For the expansion of actors, we look at the share of non-executive actor statements as a percentage of all sentences on European integration. The indicator for polarization of party positions is based on Taylor and Hermann's index for ideological polarization and ranges from 0 (not polarized at all) to 1 (most polarized). In a final step, we combine the indicators in an index as described above. Obviously, such an index raises the question of how to interpret these values. Following Green-Pedersen (2012), we compare the politicization of Europe with a broader set of issues. More precisely, we calculated a *benchmark* by relying on the data of the Kriesi *et al.* project (2008, 2012). This data are based on the same coding strategy as the one used in this article, but it covers 12 issues (e.g. welfare, budget, or cultural liberalism). To ease interpretation, the following graphs show the mean and maximum values for all 12 issues, as well as for immigration as yet another new key issue of party contestation in France.

Empirical Results

To begin with, we test our hypothesis that the crisis has increased the extent of politicization in French elections. For this purpose, Figure 1 shows how the level of politicization, as measured by our index, has developed from 1974 to 2012. This measure indicates a clear upward trend in the long-run, and we observe by far the highest level in the latest election. In other words, the campaign amidst the crisis is characterized by a boost in the extent of politicization. Our benchmark based on all types of issues has been met only in 2007 and 2012. Furthermore, in 2012, Europe was even more politicized than immigration ever was. This supports our first hypothesis and confirms the claims of those who saw the latest election as being fought in the 'shadow of the crisis' (e.g. Clift 2013; Drake 2013; Hewlett 2012; Lequesne 2012).

That Europe was highly politicized in the 2012 French campaign is underscored both when looking back at the last two French elections and when putting France in a comparative perspective. In 2002, Jean-Marie Le

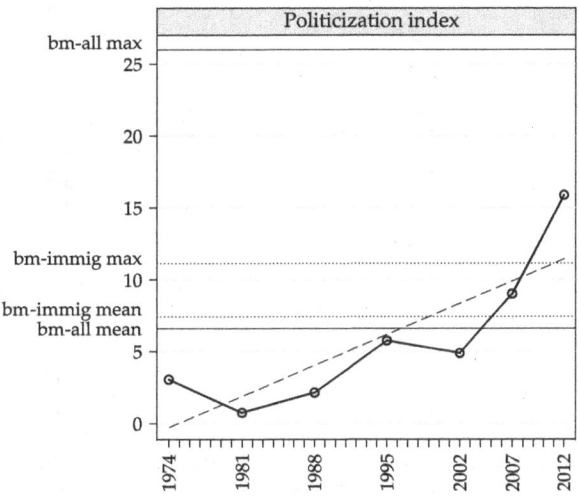

Figure 1. Politicization index by year, France 1974–2012
Note: The figure shows the value of the politicization index by election. The gray-dashed line shows the linear trend, while the additional horizontal lines show the average and maximum index for a set of 12 issues (solid lines) and immigration (dotted lines).

Pen made it to the second ballot and tried to mobilize voters by using anti-Europeanism and fears about the future of 'French identity.' The 2007 campaign, by contrast, was still amidst the discussions about how to proceed after the no-vote in the referendum on the European Constitution. Thus, both campaigns saw major European questions on the agenda, but these issues did not boost politicization as much as the current Euro crisis. In their comparative study for the pre-crisis period, Hutter and Grande (forthcoming) observed only two campaigns with a higher level of politicization in a sample of 49 elections in 5 West European countries (i.e. Austria, Britain, Germany, France, and Switzerland). This was in Britain in 1997 and in Switzerland in 1999. Again, this highlights that the 2012 campaign in France is a case of high politicization.

Figure 2 shows the development based on the three indicators used to construct the index. In general, all three measures show that Europe has become increasingly politicized since the 1970s, and that the 2012 election campaign is an exemplary case for this trend. However, the three measures point also to interesting differences. Generally speaking, Europe is a fairly salient issue in French electoral campaigns, but it tends to be both relatively executive-dominated and not as polarized as other issues (this most obvious when comparing Europe with immigration).[3] These differences become very noticeable in 2012. The crisis has brought about a more salient debate over Europe. It is not related to such a strong increase in the share of non-executive actors and in the degree of polarization. Thus, while all indicators point to a politicized situation in 2012, the campaign is clearly not as exceptional with respect to the second and third politicization dimensions.

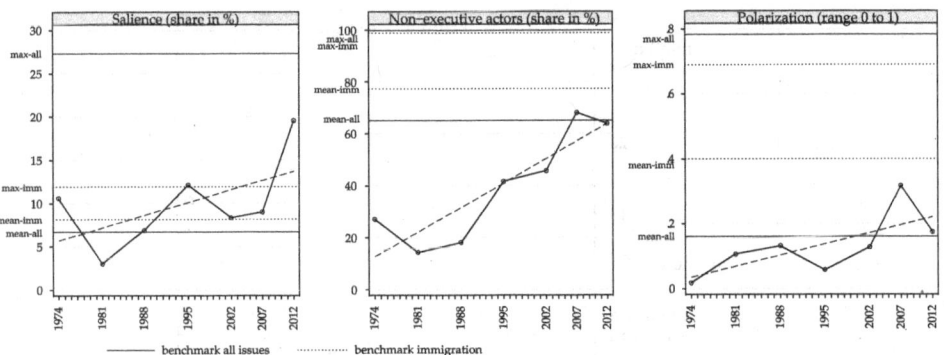

Figure 2. The three politicization measures by year
Note: The figure shows the values of salience (percentage of all core sentences), actor expansion (percentage of non-executive actors), and polarization (range 0–1) by election. The gray-dashed lines show the linear trends, while the additional horizontal lines show the average and maximum value for a set of 12 issues (solid lines) and immigration (dotted lines). The correlation coefficients between the three variables are 0.32 for salience-actors, 0.44 for salience-polarization, and 0.56 for actor-polarization.

Again, it is interesting to compare 2012 with 2007 when Europe was less salient, but far more polarized. A detailed look at the 2007 campaign shows that this was due to the combined effect of struggles over the failed Constitution and over Turkish accession. Thus, the European issues raised in 2012 were less polarizing than those of 2007 when key questions related to both widening and deepening ranked high on the agenda. This is underscored when comparing the French campaign in 2012 with the pre-crisis elections in the five West European countries. Whereas the French 2012 campaign is the third most salient campaign, it ranks only eighth and eleventh regarding actor expansion and polarization. Higher polarization was mainly observed in campaigns that centered on membership conflicts (be it related to a country's own accession or to EU membership of another state) (Hutter and Grande forthcoming).

The previous findings support the hypothesis that Europe has become more politicized in the course of the crisis, but we do not yet know whether and how the crisis has changed the way conflicts over Europe are fought. To test our second hypothesis, Table 1 presents more detailed results on the issues, frames, and political parties found when we focus on the statements related to European integration. To ease interpretation, we divided the period in three phases: pre-Maastricht (until 1992), post-Maastricht (until 2007), and Euro crisis (2012).

Let us briefly explain how we categorized the many coded issues and frames for the analyses. Regarding *issues* of European integration, we distinguish four categories: (a) general orientations, (b) deepening and intervention in economic policy fields, (c) deepening and intervention in non-economic policy fields, and (d) widening. The typology combines information on the nature of European issues and the more substantive contents being discussed. Regarding *frames*, we adopt Helbling *et al.*'s (2010) typology and distinguish between 'utilitarian frames' and 'cultural

Table 1. Issues, frames, and actors by period, France 1974–2012 (in %)

		1974–1988	1995–2007	2012
Issues	General orientations	18.2 (0.01)	18.3 (0.20)	5.6 (0.36)
	Deepening and intervention in economic policy fields	**34.7 (0.11)**	**31.8 (0.11)**	**73.9 (0.20)**
	Deepening and intervention in non-economic policy fields	38.9 (0.06)	46.5 (0.20)	20.5 (0.07)
	Widening	8.2 (0.00)	3.5 (0.30)	0.0 (-)
Frames	Cultural	9.1	27.9	11.2
	Economic	**19.4**	**28.3**	**37.2**
	Political efficiency	40.0	14.5	34.9
	Other utilitarian	31.6	29.3	16.7
Party families	Challenger parties	**3.2**	**20.2**	**31.4**
	Radical left: Front de Gauche, PCF	1.6	8.5	9.8
	Greens: Les Verts	0.0	4.0	4.3
	Radical Right: FN	1.6	7.7	8.0
	Others: DLR	0.0	0.0	9.3
	Mainstream parties	**96.8**	**79.8**	**68.2**
	Social democrats: PS	18.8	31.6	27.7
	Liberals: MoDem	18.9	9.8	3.5
	Conservatives: UMP	59.2	38.5	37.5
	N (core sentences/frames)	810/573	1666/1246	396/258

Note: The table presents the share of issue, framing, and party families in percent of all core sentences and frames, respectively. The figure in brackets shows the degree of polarization per issue. The most important figures with respect to our second hypotheses are highlighted in bold. The list of party families is supplemented with important examples for a given category in 2012.

frames.' The first type consists of arguments referring to particular interests, as well as to efficiency and cost-benefit calculations. Most importantly for this article, economic considerations belong to this type. The second type of frame refers to ideas and values that are considered by the actors to be inherent to a particular community.

The results in Table 1 confirm the first part of our second hypotheses since *economic considerations* are on the rise during the Euro crisis. *First*, the trend towards economic policy fields may seem unsurprising due to the nature of the crisis, but the magnitude of the changes certainly is. In 2012, more than 70% of statements reported focus on economic aspects. By contrast, general orientations towards integration and proposals on how to reform the EU system more generally have become far less salient, and topics related to enlargement completely disappeared from the debate. A detailed look at the economic issues being debated in 2012 underscores the impact of the crisis. Almost all statements under the label 'economic deepening and intervention' refer to measures related to solving the crisis in the Eurozone (for details, see Figure 3). *Second*, the figures in brackets show

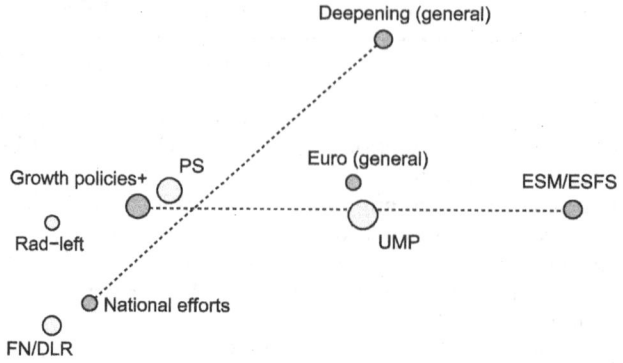

Figure 3. The political space of the Euro debate, France 2012
Notes: The figure presents the results of a weighted MDS procedure (Stress-1 = 0.29). The size of the circles indicates the share of the respective issue or actor category in percent of all core sentences used for the analyses. The analyses were done for parties with more than 20 observations and for issue categories with at least five statements by more than one party: the radical left (rad-left), the Socialist Party (PS), the Union for a Popular Movement (UMP), as well as the cluster of Front National and Arise the Republic (FN/DLR).

the polarization scores by issue category. This indicates that issues focused on economic integration are more polarizing in 2012 than before. Since these issues are most salient, they are responsible for the ongoing polarization of European integration in France. However, as suggested, the polarization of these economic issues did not reach the high levels recorded for the struggles over Turkish accession and the Lisbon Treaty in 2007. *Third*, the shift towards economics can also be seen when looking at the frames used by the parties to justify their positions. Although economic and other utilitarian frames were always more important than cultural-identitarian ones, the latest campaign differs to the post-Maastricht phase. Unsurprisingly, there is a close linkage between economic issues and frames — for example, when Nicolas Sarkozy pleads for the 'Buy European Act' to support the prosperity of European companies. However, populist right-wing parties were successful in framing economic issues in a cultural way in the past (see Helbling *et al.* 2010). Therefore, it is very significant to note that even the Front National shifted away from a culturally based critique.

In addition, the findings in Table 1 show that challengers from the left and from the right have gained in visibility in the post-Maastricht period. In 2012, we need to add the 'others' category to the share of radical parties because it covers statements by DLR, the Eurosceptic split-off from the UMP. The party drew considerable attention in the public debate, as it vehemently raised more general questions of European integration by suggesting withdrawal from the EU and other far-reaching institutional reforms in order to guarantee greater national sovereignty. This contrasts with all other parties — even with the Front National — that predominantly focused on more specific measures related to solving the crisis.

Finally, we use multi-dimensional scaling (MDS) to uncover the patterns of opposition in 2012. MDS is a flexible method and allows for a representation of (dis-)similarities between pairs of objects. We focus on the representation of parties and issues in a common space. This gives us a condensed view on the actors' positions. To disentangle the economic issues, we regrouped them in five sub-categories: Euro (in general), national efforts, ESM/ESFS, Growth+, and deepening (Figure 3).[4]

First, we observe a *two-dimensional structure*, which mirrors the patterns found for earlier periods in France. The dominant 'horizontal' dimension is due to conflicts about the right economic policies to cope with the crisis, whereas the secondary 'vertical' dimension is about more fundamental questions of membership and sovereignty. More specifically, the first dimension highlights the conflict between the moderate and radical left on the one side and the moderate right on the other. The left strongly criticizes the measures already decided upon (especially the ESM) and demands shifts towards more growth-oriented and interventionist measures. The moderate right-wing UMP, by contrast, defends the measures already taken, for which it was one of the main promoters on the European level. However, the UMP's central position indicates that the French political right is not utterly against protectionist and interventionist policies (Hewlett 2012, 419).

The second dimension is less important, as indicated by the salience of the respective issues. The conflict centers on questions about deepening (in general) and, to a smaller degree, about how much the countries hit by the crisis should bear the costs themselves. As expected, this dimension is due to the positioning of right-wing Eurosceptic parties (this time, the Front National and DLR), which vehemently oppose further deepening and demand the maintenance of national sovereignty. While the radical left is also fairly critical regarding deepening, this was not a salient issue for them. Thus, the second dimension underscores the conflict between the radical right and the mainstream parties from left and right.

Finally, the close integration of the two spatial dimensions needs to be emphasized. This mirrors that we did not witness a strong increase in the polarization of party positions. The integration of the dimensions is mainly because the right-wing Eurosceptics shared the left's opposition to the current rescue measures and because no factions within the mainstream parties questioned the Euro/EMU per se. This contrasts with earlier campaigns when there was quite a high share of dissenting voices within the Socialists and the RPR/UMP. Furthermore, even the radical challengers form left and right focused more on the current measures adopted than a fundamental critique of the European project.

Conclusions

While we can only speculate about what the crisis implies for the future of European democracies (e.g. Streeck 2013), we can already describe how it has affected the long-term trends of politicization of Europe. By doing so, we move closer to understanding the mechanisms that may translate the increasing anti-European sentiment among EU citizens into the world of European decision-making. In this article, we took an important step in this direction by answering the questions of whether and how the crisis affected the politicization of Europe in France, i.e. in a key member of the Eurozone.

Methodologically, we relied on a relational content analysis of newspapers to study the debates as they unfolded during all election campaigns from 1974 to 2012. This allowed us to study systematically how the political parties compete with each other over Europe, who is actually speaking as a party representative. As well as which thematic aspects are emphasized and how the actors justify their positions.

Overall, our results confirm that the crisis led to an increasing politicization in the French electoral arena (see Clift 2013; Drake 2013; Hewlett 2012; Lequesne 2012). Thus, the incumbent Nicolas Sarkozy set the stage for the whole campaign when he announced his candidacy by emphasizing that France 'cannot act as if the crisis did not exist [...] as if Europe did not exist [...] as if the world did not exist.' (cited in Drake 2013, 125). The crisis fueled politicization, but it did not fundamentally change the way conflicts over Europe are fought. Moreover, the crisis mainly boosted the salience of European issues.

The degree of polarization, by contrast, was clearly higher in 2007 when key questions related to deepening and Turkish accession were on the agenda. In 2012, economic issues and justification frames prevailed. This was less polarizing than a debate focused on identity- and sovereignty-based claims. The mainstream parties fought essentially about the right policy solutions to cope with the crisis, whereas it was almost exclusively the radical challengers from the right who addressed more fundamental questions related to the European project and opened up a second conflict dimension. However, it is significant to note that even the Front National shifted away from a predominantly cultural discourse.

We share Schimmelfennig's (*this volume*) view that post-functionalists have so far failed to show how such politicization decisively affected the policies and institutional reforms adopted during the crisis. Yet, we would like to add that more evidence on the extent and especially the kind of politicization induced by the crisis are needed to definitely answer whether and how politicization affects the future of European integration. Politicization may not per se lead to ever tighter constraints on transfers of political authority to the EU and the accession of new member states. The specific mobilization strategies adopted by political parties may be crucial in this regard. Our results are instructive: The French 2012 campaign was very focused on economic policies and justifications. This led to a salient but less polarizing constellation as compared to previous campaigns in France and other European countries that focused on constitutive conflicts over membership and that were more dominated by concerns about national identity and sovereignty. This is the type of 'identity politics' Hooghe and Mark's (2009) emphasized when they speculated about the negative consequences of politicization for further integration. Our results rather point in the direction suggested by Börzel and Risse (2009, 219f.): politicization could also be beneficial for the future of European integration if political actors reframe European issues along the economic left-right cleavage and start debating the direction of European *policies* instead of focusing on integration and constitutionalization as such.

In this article, we only made a first cut at this complex question and more comparative evidence is needed because the extent and kind of politicization may depend on a number of contextual factors (e.g. the party system, the integration level, or the severity of the crisis). For example, the German election campaign in 2013 points to a deliberate depoliticization by the mainstream parties even if Germany saw the rise of a new Eurosceptic challenger, i.e. the new Alternative for Germany party. This seems to be no feasible strategy for political parties in those Eurozone member states that are economically hardest hit by the crisis and whose economic policy-making capacity is most heavily constrained by European and international policy measures. Furthermore, we need to wait and see because a more identity-based critique of integration may break through when the debate shifts from crisis management to more general questions about the future setup of the European Union.

Acknowledgements

This article is based on research conducted in a larger project on 'The Politicization of Europe'. The project was financed by the German Research Council (DFG) from 2010 to 2014. We thank Simon Bornschier, Isabelle Guinaudeau, Edgar Grande, and Hanspeter Kriesi for their valuable comments.

Notes

1. Although France is a creditor country and did not have to adopt austerity programs, its economic conditions were judged to be worrisome by many commentators at the time of the election (e.g. *The Economist* 31 March 2012).
2. For a more detailed discussion of the methods and data, we refer the reader to the methodological chapters of the two volumes and an online appendix for this article published on http://www.mwpweb.eu/SwenHutter/publications.html.
3. The trends for our salience measure mirror those based on party manifestos (e.g. Guinaudeau and Persico 2013, 153). However, the differences between the three dimensions of politicization highlight that we should not just focus on salience.
4. The issue category *Euro* (*general*) covers general statements about the Euro and 'solving the Euro crisis' (10.0% of all coded statements); *National efforts* covers statements about more efforts by the 'debtor' countries or calls for certain countries to leave the Eurozone (10.6%); *ESM/ESFS* covers the two main measures adopted at the time of the election campaign (15.0%); *Growth +* covers all statements for or against more support from Europe to the countries hit by the crisis or for more protectionist measures (e.g. Hollande's call for more growth-oriented measures) (27.2%); *Deepening* (*general*) covers statements for/against more fundamental reforms of EU institutions, and statements related to national sovereignty or the withdrawal from the EU (22.4%).

References

Bornschier, S., and R. Lachat. 2009. The evolution of the French political space and party system. *West European Politics* 32, no. 2: 360–383.

Börzel, T.A., and T. Risse. 2009. Revisiting the nature of the beast — politicization, European identity, and postfunctionalism. A comment on Hooghe and Marks. *British Journal of Politic Science* 39, no. 1: 217–220.

Clift, B. 2013. Le Changement? French socialism, the 2012 presidential election and the politics of economic credibility amidst the Eurozone crisis. *Parliamentary Affairs* 66, no. 1: 106–123.

De Wilde, P. 2011. No polity for old politics? A framework for analyzing the politicization of European integration. *Journal of European Integration* 33, no. 5: 559–575.

De Wilde, P., and M. Zürn. 2012. Can the politicization of European integration be reversed? *JCMS: Journal of Common Market Studies* 50, no. 1: 137–153.

Drake, H. 2013. Everywhere and nowhere: Europe and the world in the French 2012 elections. *Parliamentary Affairs* 66, no. 1: 124–141.

Gómez-Reino, M., and I. Llamazares. 2013. the populist radical right and European integration: a comparative analysis of party–voter links. *West European Politics* 36, no. 4: 789–816.

Gourevitch, P.A. 1984. Breaking with orthodoxy: the politics of economic policy responses to the Depression of the 1930s. *International Organization* 38, no. 1: 95–129.

Green-Pedersen, C. 2012. A giant fast asleep? Party incentives and the politicisation of European integration. *Political Studies* 60, no. 1: 115–130.

Grunberg, G., and E. Schweisguth. 2003. French political space: two, three or four blocs? *French Politics* 1, no. 3: 331–347.

Guinaudeau, I., and S. Persico. 2013. EU politicization through the lens of salience: How the EU enters the French, British and German electoral agenda (1986–2009). *French Politics* 11, no. 2: 143–168.

Helbling, M., D. Hoeglinger, and B. Wüest. 2010. How political parties frame European integration. *European Journal of Political Research* 49, no. 4: 495–521.

Hewlett, N. 2012. Voting in the shadow of the crisis: the French presidential and parliamentary elections of 2012. *Modern & Contemporary France* 20, no. 4: 403–420.

Hooghe, L., and G. Marks. 2009. A postfunctionalist theory of European integration: from permissive consensus to constraining dissensus. *British Journal of Political Science* 39, no. 1: 1–23.

Hutter, S., and E. Grande. Forthcoming. Politicizing Europe in the national electoral arena: a comparative analysis of five West European countries, 1970–2010. *Journal of Common Market Studies*.

Koenig, T., S. Mihelj, J. Downey, and M. Gencel Bek. 2006. Media framings of the issue of Turkish accession to the EU. *Innovation: The European Journal of Social Science Research* 19, no. 2: 149–169.

Kriesi, H. 2007. The role of European integration in national election campaigns. *European Union Politics* 8: 83–108.

Kriesi, H., and E. Grande. 2012. The Euro-crisis: a boost to politicization of European integration? Paper prepared for the EUDO 2012 Dissemination Conference on 'The Euro Crisis and the State of European Democracy', Florence.

Kriesi, H., E. Grande, M. Dolezal, M. Helbling, D. Hoeglinger, S. Hutter, and B. Wuest. 2012. *Political conflict in Western Europe*. Cambridge: Cambridge University Press.

Kriesi, H., E. Grande, R. Lachat, M. Dolezal, S. Bornschier, and T. Frey. 2008. *West European politics in the age of globalization*. Cambridge: Cambridge University Press.

Lequesne, ed. 2012. *La Campagne Présidentielle francaise de 2012 au Prisme de l'Externe*. Dossier du CERI. Paris: CERI — CNRS. http://www.sciencespo.fr/ceri/fr/content/la-campagne-presidentielle-francaise-de-2012-au-prisme-de-lexterne (accessed 12 July 2013).

Serricchio, F., M. Tsakatika, and L. Quaglia. 2013. Euroscepticism and the global financial crisis. *JCMS: Journal of Common Market Studies* 51, no. 1: 51–64.

Statham, P., and H.-J. Trenz. 2012a. *The politicization of Europe: contesting the constitution in the mass media*. London: Routledge.

Statham, P., and H.-J. Trenz. 2012b. The politicization of the European Union: from constitutional dreams to Euro-Zone crisis nightmares. Paper prepared for the 3rd International Conference on Democracy as Idea and Practice, Oslo, 12–13 January 2012.

Streeck, W. 2013. The crisis in context: democratic capitalism and its contradictions. In *Politics in the age of austerity*, eds. Armin Schäfer and Wolfgang Streeck, 262–286. Cambridge: Polity Press.

Van Der Eijk, C., and M.N. Franklin. 2004. Potential for contestation on European matters at national elections in Europe. In *European Integration and Political Conflict*, eds. Gary Marks and Marco R. Steenbergen, 32–50. Cambridge: Cambridge University Press.

'Beggars can't be Choosers': The European Crisis and Chinese Direct Investment in the European Union

SOPHIE MEUNIER

Woodrow Wilson School of Public and International Affairs, Princeton University, Princeton, NJ, USA

ABSTRACT Virtually non-existent five years ago, Chinese foreign direct investment (FDI) into Europe has surged spectacularly in recent years in an international context of declining FDI globally. While the stock of Chinese FDI in Europe is still minuscule, the flows show the rapidly growing interest of Chinese companies in being present in Europe, both through greenfield investment and through mergers and acquisitions. This surge of Chinese FDI occurred concomitantly to the explosion of the sovereign debt crisis in Europe and the general economic downturn in many countries of the European Union (EU). This paper asks whether the European crisis contributed to the surge of Chinese FDI in Europe. In particular, did this surge occur as a result of an explicit strategy formulated by governments in EU Member States in order to dig their countries out of the crisis? The main argument is that the crisis has provided Chinese investors with two types of bargains: economic bargains due to depressed prices and a greater number of assets for sale, and political bargains due to the lessened political resistance to deals that may have been objectionable in flusher times.

Introduction

China has emerged as a major investor globally over the past decade. Its investments in sovereign debt, portfolio and foreign direct investments (FDI) have flown throughout the globe, from massive positions in US treasuries to ubiquitous ownership and exploitation of African and Australian mines. When it comes specifically to FDI, the numbers are staggering: the stock of outbound FDI held by China doubled between 2008 and 2011 to reach $364 billion in 2011. The growth continued in 2012, with an additional $62 billion invested abroad by Chinese companies in an international context where global FDI flows declined (OECD 2013a). In 2012, China became the third largest direct investor in the world in flows, after the US and Japan (excluding tax heavens).

Chinese FDI is now flowing to Europe as well. Virtually non-existent five years ago, Chinese investment into Europe has surged spectacularly in recent years (Burgoon, Jacoby, and Meunier 2014). From Sweden to Germany, from Greece to Hungary, private and public Chinese investors have built factories, participated in infrastructure projects, and purchased iconic European companies. They have learned how to vinify French Bordeaux and Burgundy, how to talk the language of German Mittelstand companies, and how to handle Greek dockworkers.

To be sure, China is still a minor investor in Europe in terms of stocks of investment, and the size of Chinese investment is very modest compared to the size of Chinese trade with Europe. But the flows tell a different story, with investments that tripled from 2006 to 2009, tripled again by 2011 to $10 billion and reached $12 billion in 2012 (Hanemann 2013; Hanemann and Rosen 2012). According to official EU figures, Chinese investment flows into Europe grew by 155 per cent between 2009 and 2011 (EUROSTAT 2013). China is indeed becoming an important player in Europe. In 2012, China was the third largest foreign investor in Germany in terms of the number of projects, after the United States and Switzerland (Germany Trade and Invest 2013). By some estimates, Europe was the first destination for Chinese outbound FDI in 2012, representing up to 33 per cent of all Chinese investments abroad (A Capital Dragon Index 2013; The Economist 2013).

This surge occurred concomitantly to the sovereign debt crisis in Europe and the general economic downturn in many countries of the European Union (EU). Did the economic and financial crisis contribute to the surge of Chinese FDI in Europe? Building on the main theories of policy change positing that exogenous shocks facilitate instances of far-reaching policy change (Tosun *et al.* this issue), this paper analyses whether this surge occurred as a result of a policy change — and more specifically an explicit strategy formulated by governments in EU Member States in order to dig their countries out of the crisis.

The central argument is that the supply of Chinese capital ready to be invested abroad would have probably soared no matter what, as the combined result of China's accumulation of foreign reserves, official government policy ordering its firms to 'go global' and economic need to move up the value chain by acquiring foreign know-how and technology. What the economic crisis in Europe has affected is the European demand for Chinese investment. The crisis has created two types of bargains for Chinese investors. Economically, the crisis has created 'bargain basement' deals throughout Europe, which Chinese firms have been eager to snap up. Politically, Chinese FDI has been able to increase fast because the crisis has triggered a policy change in many European countries by lessening political resistance to FDI at the domestic level ('beggars can't be choosers') and by leading short term to prevail over long-term calculations in cash strapped and high unemployment European countries, helped by the disunited nature of EU governance in practice over FDI policy.

The paper first presents trends and patterns of foreign investment in the EU in recent years, notably from China. Section Two analyses the internal Chinese rationales for investing in the EU, independently of the crisis. The third section explores the economic mechanisms through which the European crisis has enabled the surge of Chinese investment: the combination of depressed prices and a greater number of assets for sale in response to the sovereign debt crisis has created opportunities for foreign acquisitions at 'bargain basement' prices. Section Four analyses the political mechanisms through which the economic crisis has lessened political resistance in Europe. One conclusion is that the crisis precipitated an evolution that probably would have happened, albeit less fast and widely.

Recent Patterns of FDI in Europe

The financial crisis born in the United States in 2008 followed by the sovereign debt crisis in the Eurozone led to a global decline of FDI worldwide, as potential investors lost confidence in the face of economic uncertainty and capital dried up, therefore contributing to the economic downturn. It is against this backdrop of declining FDI worldwide, and especially in the EU, that Chinese FDI started to rise, making the contrast more spectacular.

The Explosion of FDI Worldwide and in Europe Until the Financial Crisis

FDI is recognized as a key driver of global economic integration, which overall promotes economic growth for both the home and the host economies (even if it has costs as well). For the home economy, FDI opens up new markets, enables access to resources and allocates production efficiently, leading to a maximization of profits. For the host economy, this influx of foreign capital improves national economic performance because it leads to job creation in the short term and spillover of technology and know-how in the long term (Lipsey and Sjoholm 2004; Pandya 2013). Even if countries sometimes restrict the inflow of foreign capital under some circumstances (for instance related to national security or culture), they mostly compete to attract FDI through a variety of incentives because the benefits of hosting FDI are usually superior to its costs.

According to the standard definition accepted by policy-makers and academics, direct investment is a class of investment where the investor acquires at least 10 per cent of the voting power of an enterprise, which establishes 'lasting interest' and control over the affiliated company's operations — in contrast to portfolio investment where investors do not generally expect to influence the management of the enterprise (International Monetary Fund 1993; OECD 2008a).

FDI comes in two major forms of mode of entry into the host economy: cross-border Mergers and Acquisitions (M&A), whereby the investor acquires existing assets abroad, either through mergers or full takeovers and 'greenfield investment', whereby the investor creates new facilities from the ground up in the host country (for instance a new factory, assembly plant or distribution centre).

Two important developments occurred during the 1990s. First, countries implemented major changes to their national regulatory environments, making foreign investment easier and more welcome. Second, the number of Bilateral Investment Treaties (BITs) decupled between 1980 and 1999, jumping from 181 to 1856 (UNCTAD 2000). As a result, that period saw an explosion of FDI worldwide. European countries were major actors of this explosion, both at the sending and receiving end. By 1999, companies based in the European Union accounted for two-thirds of all investment outflows, and extra-EU FDI surpassed intra-EU FDI for the first time in 1997. As for inflows, the EU was also the world's biggest recipient of FDI. After a slump in the early 2000s, the trends resumed, with global FDI reaching its peak in 2007 at around $2 trillion. Then, it all abruptly stopped and declined as a result of the American financial crisis.

FDI in Europe after the American and European Crises

The financial crisis that emerged in the United States in September 2008 led to a sharp decline in global FDI activity over the next four years. FDI flows started to recover slightly in the world by 2010 but declined again after 2011— FDI inflows declined by 18.3 per cent between 2011 and 2012, as shown in Figure 1. In 2012, FDI flows to developed economies plummeted, in the words of UNCTAD, falling back to levels seen 10 years ago (UNCTAD 2013). This decline was especially pronounced in the EU, where FDI inflows plunged by 41 per cent in 2012, which accounted for two-thirds of the global FDI decline. Europe remains today the world's

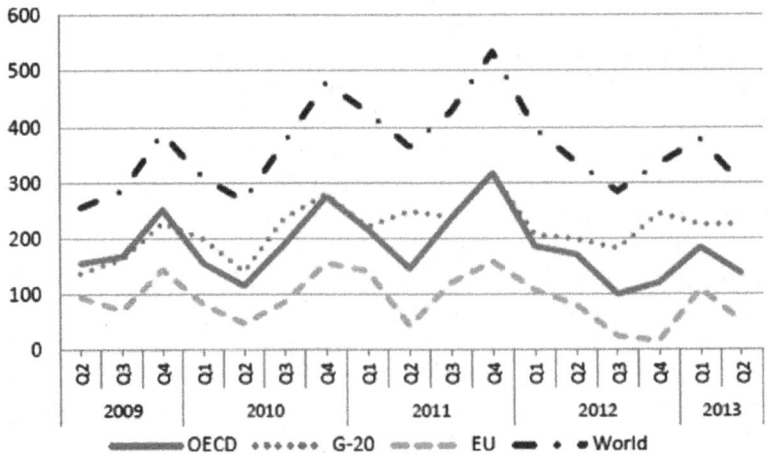

Figure 1. 2012 FDI inflows ($ billion)
Source: Author's calculations, based on OECD 2013a.

largest destination for global FDI, but its share is now down to 22 per cent.

The majority of EU countries underwent significant drops in FDI flows as a result of the joint sovereign debt crisis and general economic downturn in the region. Some European countries, such as Belgium and Germany, saw large declines in FDI inflows in 2011 (UNCTAD 2013). In the Southern European countries hit by the crisis, the FDI flows were more than halved from 2011 to 2012; Italy even experienced sizable divestment (UNCTAD 2013).

The Surge of Chinese FDI in the EU

It is against this backdrop of declining FDI in the EU that Chinese FDI started to rise. Annual Chinese outward foreign direct investment (OFDI) flows to Europe grew from less than $1 billion per year from 2004 to 2008 to roughly $3 billion in 2009 and 2010. In 2011, flows tripled again to almost $10 billion. In 2012, they reached $12 billion. The number of annual investments with a value of more than $1 million grew from less than a 10 decade ago to 50 in 2007 and almost 100 in 2010 and 2011 (Hanemann and Rosen 2012). In 2011, China became the 7th foreign investor in the EU in number of deals (Ernst & Young 2013).

The geographical distribution of Chinese OFDI in the EU is very diverse, as shown in Figure 2, but its top three locations are also the largest three European economies: France, Germany and the UK. The contrast was particularly striking in Germany, where global FDI had severely declined during the period but where Chinese FDI was booming. By 2012, China had become the third largest investor in Germany when measured by number of projects (after the United States and Switzerland), according to Germany Trade and Invest, the national investment promotion agency. About 800 Chinese companies are now present in the Lander of North Rhine-Westphalia, the first German state in terms of foreign capital, where Chinese investment now accounts for almost one-third of FDI inflows (Tuo 2013).

The sectoral distribution of Chinese OFDI in the EU is also very diverse, with investment in a wide range of sectors with a particular focus on utilities, coal-oil-gas, automotive, chemicals, industrial machinery and consumer services (Hanemann 2013).

For the European countries hosting that investment, even if it is one among many, China is becoming a non-negligible investor — Chinese telecom giant Huawei now employs more than 8000 workers in the EU for instance. For China, the EU now represents, by some estimates, the first destination for its OFDI in the world (A Capital Dragon Index 2013).

To what extent did the economic crisis in Europe precipitate, facilitate or on the contrary hinder this surge of Chinese FDI into Europe? The remainder of the paper explores three complementary explanations for the surge: first, internal Chinese motives for investing in Europe, irrespective of the crisis; second, economic 'bargain' mechanisms as a direct result of the crisis and third, political 'bargains' implicitly struck by national governments desperate for solutions out of the crisis.

	Country	Investment Value ($ million)	Number of Greenfield Projects	Number of Acquisitions	Total Number of Deals
1	France	5,722	46	24	70
2	United Kingdom	3,684	69	26	95
3	Germany	2,543	113	33	146
4	Sweden	2,251	14	6	20
5	Hungary	2,065	14	4	18
6	Netherlands	1,164	32	15	47
7	Belgium	847	12	3	15
8	Greece	714	5	0	5
9	Italy	554	31	16	47
10	Austria	391	6	5	11
11	Romania	299	13	1	14
12	Poland	190	15	1	16
13	Spain	187	22	1	23
14	Czech Republic	76	10	1	11
15	Finland	48	1	4	5
16	Portugal	47	5	0	5
17	Bulgaria	47	6	1	7
18	Luxembourg	46	1	1	2
19	Ireland	44	6	1	7
20	Denmark	30	6	1	7
21	Latvia	3.8	1	0	1
22	Cyprus	3	0	1	0

Figure 2. China's FDI in the EU 27 2000–2011 (in $ million and number of deals)
Source: (Hanemann and Rosen 2012).

Internal Chinese Motives for Investing in Europe

The first explanation for this surge of Chinese FDI in Europe at the time of the crisis is actually not related to the crisis at all. Chinese investors, responding to their own strategic and commercial agenda, had their own motives for trying to penetrate the European market independently of the crisis.

The 'Going Global' Policy and the Explosion of Chinese FDI in the World

Chinese outbound investment is a relatively recent phenomenon, since at the time of its opening policy in 1979 China had virtually no OFDI. The impulse for Chinese outbound investment came directly from the Chinese government who, in 2000, urged its companies, both private and state-owned enterprises, to 'go global' and followed up this admonition in the following decade in three successive five-year plans with a variety of policy measures designed to facilitate Chinese investment abroad (OECD 2008b).

As a result, Chinese OFDI exploded in the world. By 2010, China had become the world's fifth largest exporter of OFDI by flows — after the US, Germany, France and Hong Kong. In 2011, Chinese companies had amassed $364 billion in stock of outbound investment (Hanemann and Rosen 2012). China has also become the largest outbound investor among emerging economies, ahead of Russia; indeed, it accounts for about a third of all OFDI from emerging economies.

The geographical composition of Chinese OFDI evolved over time. Initially, it concentrated almost exclusively on developing countries and focused mostly on natural resources and raw materials — Chinese companies invested in Asia, in Latin America and in oil and mines throughout the African continent (Brautigam 2011). Then, Chinese companies began to invest in natural resources in developed economies, such as Australia and Canada. Finally, in 2008, as their national economy had matured and they were trying to move up the value chain, Chinese companies started to invest in the United States and the European Union (Shambaugh 2013).

Internal Chinese Rationales for Investing in the EU

In addition to heeding the exhortation of their government to 'go out', Chinese companies had many commercial motives for investing in Europe starting in the late 2000s, irrespectively of the crisis (Burgoon, Jacoby, and Meunier 2014; Knapp and Meunier 2012). Among these commercial motives were the following:

Acquiring technology. Chinese companies are looking for advanced technology across a wide array of sectors. It is indeed much quicker and cheaper (and legal) to acquire technology by purchasing an existing company that possesses this technology than by trying to develop it from scratch. Technology is essential for China to improve productivity and move up the global value chain.

Learning know-how. Wage inflation, labour shortages and a rapidly ageing population are putting pressure on a developing Chinese economy. Chinese companies are investing in European companies to gain the managerial know-how to build multinational companies. Investment is, in part, about purchasing human talent.

Building brands. China is in desperate need of global brands. According to a survey conducted by Millward Brown, 83 per cent of consumers beyond China's borders can't recall a single Chinese brand. Consumer-facing companies such as Haier, Lenovo and Tsingtao Beer have relatively short histories operating in international markets but have made significant strides forward on this front. Buying Volvo was a quick way for Chinese automaker Geely to build its own brand reputation rather than to develop it from scratch. Many Chinese companies are trying to replicate this model. This trend is particularly visible in the apparel sector, where Chinese companies (mainland and Hong Kong-based) are purchasing reputable, though struggling, European fashion brands, such as French shoemaker Robert Clergerie and British apparel company Aquascutum, with the goal of using their good names and turning them into global empires.

Servicing Chinese companies abroad. As Chinese state-owned banks help provide M&A consulting services and finance Chinese companies expanding abroad, the banks themselves are also going global. They follow their clients. Industrial and Commercial Bank of China has 244 institutions in 34 countries worldwide. The bank is also planning to offer wealth management services as Chinese companies grow abroad.

Circumventing trade barriers. Like Japanese companies did in the 1980s, Chinese companies are investing in Europe (and the US) to avoid potential trade barriers, such as duties, tariffs and subsidies. Currently, raw earth materials and solar panels have been the focal point of a brewing trade war between China and the EU. Chinese companies are seeking European target companies to invest especially in the solar sector in anticipation of future trade barriers, should a negative verdict be reached by the EU Commission or in the WTO.

Divergent Patterns of Chinese FDI in the EU and the US

The growth of Chinese OFDI in the EU and the US initially occurred simultaneously, which is not surprising since the rationales for investing were similar and the target companies of M&A activity often substitutable: acquisitions in either Europe or the US could satisfy Chinese companies' desire for brand, know-how and technology, among others (Hanemann 2013).

What is notable, however, is that the patterns of Chinese OFDI in the EU and the US started to diverge in 2011, as shown in Figure 3. Since 2011, the EU has attracted twice as much Chinese OFDI as the US. Europe has been by far the preferred destination for non-resources Chinese investments: in 2012 Europe accounted for 61 per cent of all non-resources M&A deals by Chinese companies and 86 per cent of all industrial transactions (A Capital Dragon Index 2013). This trend is likely to continue: Chinese companies already investing in the European setting have expressed commitments and plans to invest more in the near future. In a January 2013 survey of some 74 Chinese companies already investing in

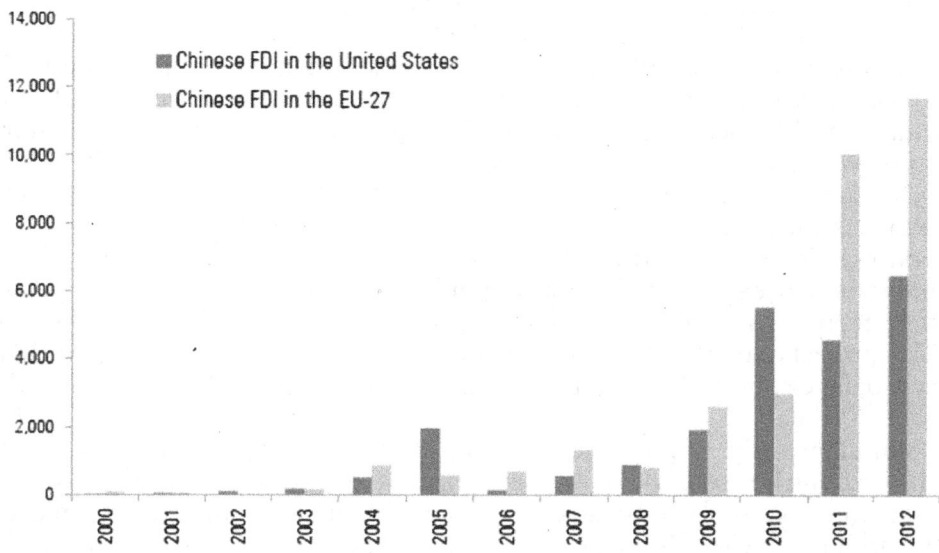

Figure 3. Annual Chinese FDI flows to the United States and European Union 2000–2012 (in $ million)
Source: (Hanemann 2013).

Europe, 86 per cent expressed plans to 'invest higher amounts than their current investments' (European Union Chamber of Commerce in China 2013).

Major Chinese investments (over $1 billion) concluded in Europe over the past two years include a massive investment by China's Three Gorges into Energias de Portugal, Bright Foods' purchase of the British Weetabix and the development of a Huawei logistics centre in Hungary.

The size of the surge of Chinese OFDI and the magnitude of the divergence between Chinese OFDI going to the EU and to the US need to be kept in perspective, however. They are both still minuscule relatively to the total stock of FDI hosted by both regions, and a handful of massive deals can tip the balance. However, even at this small scale, the divergence is real. It can indeed be explained, this paper argues, by the economic crisis in Europe, which has provided Chinese investors with two kinds of bargains: economic and political.

Economic Mechanisms: The European Crisis and 'Bargain Basement' Prices

The second explanation for the surge of Chinese FDI into Europe is that the economic crisis has provided Chinese investors with a multitude of economic bargains, which few other investors have been well positioned to take advantage of. This section first analyses the economic mechanisms that have produced bargains and then questions whether China indeed seized these bargains at all.

The Crisis and 'Bargain Basement' Deals in Europe

To put it simply, the European economic crisis created the opportunity for 'bargain basement' deals because of the simultaneous combination of lower demand and higher supply: fewer buyers were willing to invest while more assets were up for sale.

Demand for European assets plummeted because of low growth prospects in the short term, leading to a decreased valuation in many EU countries. This was particularly visible in real estate assets, especially in countries that experienced a housing bubble (i.e. Spain and Ireland). Moreover, there was a lack of available European capital willing to invest in risky projects due to financial institutions hoarding cash to safeguard their own balance sheets (especially French and German banks), depressing the prices further.

Simultaneously, supply increased as more assets were put up for sale while countries embarked on privatization programmes of state-owned assets in response to constraints to reduce deficits and public debt imposed by bailout agencies (European Council, European Central Bank, and IMF). Greece was put on a particularly stringent privatization plan with the goal of raising $64 billion (50 billion euros) as part of a reform programme agreed with international lenders (see Clements *et al.* this issue). Assets for sale include ports (e.g. Piraeus, Thessaloniki), railways (TrainOSE), airports (Athens International Airport, 26 smaller airports) and so forth. Similarly, Portugal had to implement a strict privatization programme of state-owned companies in sectors such as airlines, energy, insurance and broadcasting. Additionally, more assets became available for sale throughout Europe as austerity measures led to bankruptcies.

Moreover, many investment opportunities became available in the infrastructure sector, as indebted governments could not pour money into infrastructure projects needing to be replaced or modernized.

Why Chinese Companies could take Advantage of these Bargains

Several reasons explain why Chinese investors were well positioned to take advantage of these bargains. First, China had the means to do so. China has accumulated the largest foreign exchange reserves in the world, estimated around $3.4 trillion, resulting from trade surpluses coming from its export-driven economy (Rabinovitch 2013). These gigantic reserves must be used and placed somewhere.

Second, China could take advantage of these bargains because it realized with the 2008 financial crisis in the US that it needed to diversify in a variety of ways. An estimated two-thirds of its reserves are held in dollar-denominated assets — China is the largest foreign owner of US government debt. That makes China vulnerable to, as well as invested in, the health of the US economy. The American financial crisis prompted a move towards diversifying Chinese reserves both away from the dollar and into different kinds of assets. That meant diversifying from the US to Europe (and from the dollar to the euro) and diversifying away from government securities into other instruments, including portfolio investments and FDI

(Hanemann and Rosen 2012). As a result, China has now a vested interest in ensuring that European economies remain stable.

Finally, real assets could simply be a good investment that brings higher returns than government debt. Because of the actions taken by central banks in response to the American financial crisis and then the European crisis, the yields on government bonds in the US and Europe have been very low. China expects higher returns from investing in real assets — such as companies, ports and utilities — than from government-issued financial instruments. It kills two birds with one stone since it also helps China advance the strategic goals underlying the 'go global' policy.

Did Chinese Investors Really Snap up Bargains?

While Chinese FDI into Europe has surged since the outbreak of the European crisis, it is a leap to conclude that bargain hunting has been the opportunistic drive behind this surge. To be sure, anecdotes abound of how the crisis has enabled China to scoop up bargains in Europe: for instance, Zhu Weixiang, general manager of Zhejiang Xuebao Fashion Co, a leading Chinese fur coat maker poised to acquire a fur coat factory in Turin, declared to the press that 'the debt crisis in Italy has given us an ideal investment opportunity' (Yiqi, Liu, and Chunyan 2013). Yet, many of the 'bargain basement deals' were passed over by China; many of the assets purchased by China were not bargains; and the overall state of each European economy is not a good predictor of Chinese investment there.

First, China did not jump on the opportunity to acquire these supposed bargains. Many assets put up for sale by indebted governments have had trouble attracting foreign investors at all, in spite of heavy investment promotion campaigns especially in the direction of China. Greece has raised only about 1.6 billion euros (out of a promised 50) since the first bailout package in May 2010. So far, it has not found bidders for the majority of its privatization portfolio, including infrastructure (e.g. Hellenic Motorways, TrainOSE, regional airports), land development (e.g. public buildings in Athens, seafront property, thermal springs) and corporate (e.g. casinos, Hellenic Post). The same is true for real estate assets in the countries where property prices had fallen most dramatically, such as Ireland, Spain and Greece. In Spain, where housing prices dropped 27 per cent between June 2007 and June 2013, Chinese buyers are only starting to purchase property now that the real estate prices seem to have bottomed out and stabilized (Passino 2013).

Moreover, many of the assets purchased by China were not acquired at bargain prices. Yes, Chinese companies have made some cheap acquisitions because these assets would not find another acquirer, such as the heavily indebted Hungarian company Borsodchem purchased by the Chinese Wanhua in 2011 or the Italian yacht maker Ferretti purchased by the Chinese bulldozer manufacturing company Shandong in 2012. But a review of successful or failed Chinese acquisitions in Europe since the outbreak of the crisis reveals a pattern of paying full price or even overpaying for the assets. For instance, in the sale of a 50 per cent stake in Yoplait, the world's second biggest yogurt brand, the Chinese Bright Food had overbid the eventual acquirer General Mills by an estimated 100 million euros. In the acquisition of a 21.35 per cent stake in Energias de Portugal, the Chinese Three Gorges Corporation was the highest of four international bidders. A similar pattern of paying a premium price, rather than a bargain price, for acquisitions in Europe is found in the real estate sector, where Chinese buyers have been heavily investing in expensive properties in London and Paris, two markets which never collapsed even after the outbreak of the euro crisis.

Overall, the state of each European economy is not a good predictor of the volume of Chinese investment there, as shown in Figure 4. There is no significant relationship between the volume of Chinese FDI and the state of economic crisis in individual countries. Decisions to invest in a country could be affected by information about economic conditions with a lag, but this would run against the argument of opportunistic investing, since by definition opportunity does not wait and has to be seized on immediately.

In summary, some Chinese FDI in Europe since the crisis can be explained by the existence of economic bargains. Chinese companies seized these bargains because, unlike other investors, they were in a position to do so, and because they calculated that these were good investments for undervalued assets. But in many cases Chinese investors did not take the bargain bait because they understood, like other potential investors, the risks associated with policy uncertainty given the precarious economic situation in Europe and they were trying to minimize their risk exposure.

Political Mechanisms: The European Crisis and Lessened Political Resistance

The existence of economic bargains is therefore not enough to explain why Chinese investment surged into Europe. An additional explanation is that the economic crisis prompted policy change both at the national and at the EU levels by lessening political resistance and making Chinese FDI less controversial and more palatable than would have been the case in flusher times.

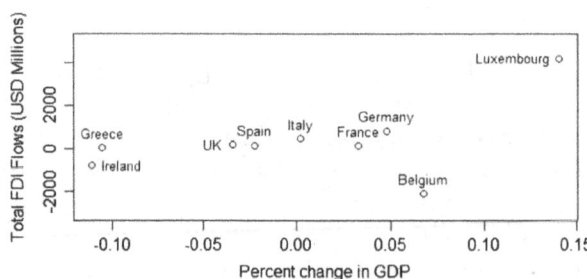

Figure 4. GDP change vs. Chinese FDI flows 2008–2011
Source: Author's calculations, based on OECD (2013a).

Political Bargains at the National Level

As a result of the crisis, European countries have stepped up efforts to actively portray themselves as attractive destinations for foreign capital. In particular they are competing against each other through a variety of means to promote themselves as 'China's gateway to Europe' and to attract Chinese investment — including investment promotion, simplified investment procedures, a shower of incentives and national political deals. These active strategies represent evidence that the economic and financial crisis has helped to bring about policy change at the national level that facilitates Chinese investment.

Investment promotion. Countries have recently established investment promotion agencies in China to encourage Chinese investment in their own country: for instance, 'Invest in France,' 'Germany Trade and Invest', 'UK Trade and Investment', 'IDA Ireland' and 'AICEP (Portugal)' all have a physical presence in China. They are waging elaborate Public Relations campaigns to portray their country in the best light — from infrastructure to education, from their climate to their health care system, from the beauty of their landscape to the regulatory ease with which businesses can get established. In addition to promoting the advantages of their country, these agencies offer support to enterprises looking to invest — for instance, information or assistance with administrative procedures. According to the European Chamber of Commerce in China, countries doing the best job with their investment promotion have been 'disproportionately successful in attracting ODI from China' (European Union Chamber of Commerce in China 2013, 17).

National politicians have also recently taken on the task of promoting Chinese investment in their country. For instance, Greek Prime Minister Antonis Samaras, accompanied by a trade and investment delegation of 87 Greek business leaders, went to China in May 2013 to promote the attractiveness of Greece to Chinese investors. In light of the importance of appraisals of the national economy for public opinion (Clements *et al.* this issue) and ensuring re-election, this move by Greek policy-makers can be interpreted as a rational one. Similarly, in France, a country which has invented the term 'economic patriotism' and has often throughout history scrutinized foreign investors for fear of undermining national identity, President Francois Hollande said during his April 2013 trip to China that France was ready to welcome more Chinese investment and during a July 2013 meeting with 40 Chinese business leaders in Paris that France would remove all obstacles to Chinese investment. This statement ties in with empirical studies showing how salient economic aspects had become in the 2012 French national elections (see Hutter and Kerscher this issue). British Prime Minister David Cameron is openly courting Chinese investors, including China's sovereign wealth fund the Chinese Investment Corporation, to invest in the building of a 'super-sewer' under London (Sakoui and Pickard 2013).

A simplified investment process. European countries are also courting Chinese investment by promising an easier and quicker investment process. This includes removing perceived regulatory obstacles and concluding special 'fast track' deals for Chinese investment, even if the EU investment environment is already perceived by Chinese investors as open and welcoming, especially compared to the US and Australia, for instance (European Union Chamber of Commerce in China 2013, 19).

EU countries are, overall, among the least regulatory restrictive for FDI in the world, based on measures of equity restrictions, screening and approval requirements, restrictions on key foreign personnel and other operational restrictions. According to the OECD which has developed the FDI Restrictiveness Index since 2003, 20 out of the 25 countries least restrictive towards FDI in 2012 were EU members (OECD 2013b). More restrictions can always be lifted, however, and as Figure 5 shows, countries which lowered further regulatory obstacles to FDI between 2006 and 2013 include Austria, Belgium, the Czech Republic, Denmark, Estonia, Finland, Germany, Greece, Hungary, Ireland, Italy, Latvia, the Netherlands, Poland, Slovenia, Spain, Sweden and the United Kingdom.

Some countries are promising China even easier access by proposing to 'fast-track' certain investments. This can be achieved by removing regulatory obstacles on a bilateral basis. Greece, for instance, signed a series of memoranda with China during Prime Minister Samaras' visit to China in May 2013 to make Chinese investment in Greece even faster and easier. They included a 'cooperation protocol' between Greece's privatization agency, the Hellenic Republic Asset Development Fund and the China Development Bank, as well as a 'cooperation agreement' between the Greek investment promotion agency 'Invest in Greece' and the China Development Bank (ANA 2013).

Some countries have even created joint investment funds with China to facilitate Chinese investment ventures. In April 2012, China announced that it would set up a $500 million investment cooperation fund with Central and Eastern European countries. In May 2012, Belgium launched the EUR50 million 'Belgium-China Mirror Fund' dedicated to facilitate Chinese investment into Belgium. In September 2012, France created a EUR 150 million euro Sino-French investment fund (Tonnelier 2012).

A shower of incentives. National and local governments in Europe are trying to attract foreign investors through a variety of incentives. Some of these incentives are geared towards all foreign investors, while other incentives may seem particularly attractive to China.

A first type of incentives are financial and fiscal. In order to promote foreign investment in particular regions, sectors or skill levels, countries are offering: cash incentives (e.g. Spain offers 'non-returnable subsidies' for investment in depressed regions); reduced interest loans (e.g. Germany offers an 'entrepreneur loan' of up to EUR 25 million to investors); tax relief (e.g. Portugal created in May 2013 a 20 per cent tax deduction on investments of up to EUR 5 million); tax credits (e.g. France introduced in January 2013 a new 'tax credit for competitiveness and employment' which

	2012	2006
Austria	0.106	0.149
Belgium	0.040	0.042
Czech Republic	0.055	0.066
Denmark	0.072	0.077
Estonia	0.022	0.026
Finland	0.019	0.055
France	0.045	0.045
Germany	0.023	0.030
Greece	0.039	0.058
Hungary	0.049	0.061
Ireland	0.043	0.050
Italy	0.050	0.052
Latvia	0.065	0.067
Lithuania	0.041	0.041
Luxembourg	0.004	0.004
Netherlands	0.015	0.020
Poland	0.072	0.076
Portugal	0.007	0.007
Slovak Republic	0.049	0.049
Slovenia	0.007	0.013
Spain	0.021	0.036
Sweden	0.059	0.079
United Kingdom	0.061	0.077

Figure 5. FDI regulatory restrictiveness for EU countries
Source: (OECD 2013b).

amounts to a reduction in social contributions); tax exemption (e.g. in April 2013 Greece passed a law including tax exemptions in certain 'strategic investments') and so forth.

A second type of incentives are operational, providing the investor with national and local government help in a variety of areas, such as: labour (e.g. Germany helps foreign investors with recruitment support, training support, wage subsidies and on-the-job training); R&D grants loans, tax credits and silent partnerships (e.g. in April 2013, the United Kingdom updated its tax-credit scheme for investment in R&D) and technology (e.g. incentives to create and acquire Intellectual Property in Ireland through an IP regime which provides a tax write-off for broadly defined IP acquisitions).

A third type of incentives, which have spread throughout Europe since the outbreak of the economic crisis, are related to rules of citizenship and residency. Unlike the previous two categories of incentives, they are not directed to companies, but to individuals themselves. The trend in the EU is striking. In December 2012, Hungary adopted the 'Hungarian investment immigration law' granting residency to those investing at least EUR 250,000 in government bonds. In January 2013, Portugal instituted the 'Golden Residence Permit' which enables foreigners to acquire residency status in Portugal if they transfer at least EUR 1 million in capital, or create 10 new jobs in Portugal, or purchase property worth at least EUR 500,000. In May 2013, Cyprus started to grant citizenship to foreigners with direct investments in Cyprus of at least EUR 5 million. In September 2013, Spain passed a law granting residency status to non-EU investors in Spanish property of at least EUR 500,000. That enables Chinese buyers to kill two birds with one stone, as summarized by a Chinese property consultant: 'Most Chinese investors want to buy a property in Barcelona because not only are they getting a good investment, but there is now the opportunity to acquire Spanish residency at the same time. What's more, the market is particularly attractive given the historic low prices'(Steed 2013).

National political bargains. At the highest political level, national governments could also potentially make foreign policy promises to China in order to attract its FDI. They could offer greater support for Chinese policies at the international level — such as supporting the lifting of the arms embargo imposed by the EU after the Tiananmen incident in 1989. They could also promise less interference in Chinese domestic politics, especially on issues of human rights and Tibetan independence.

These national political bargains are mostly implicit, but sometimes they can be explicit: 'Referring to geopolitical issues, Mr Li Keqiang noted that China is Greece's ally in the Cyprus issue and asked for Athens' help in improving China's relations with the European Union, especially in light of Greece's upcoming stint in the EU presidency in the first half of 2014' (ANA 2013).

Political Bargains at the European Level

The economic crisis in Europe has also lowered the potential political resistance to Chinese investments at the EU level and slowed down the transition to a new supranational regime for FDI in the EU (Meunier 2013b; Meunier 2014).

Before the crisis, the EU had introduced a major reform of its FDI policy (both outbound and inbound), first in the European constitutional treaty, and later in the Lisbon Treaty (Meunier 2013b). FDI is now a supranational competence and investment decisions should, theoretically, be taken collectively at the EU level. In theory, the move to a 'single voice' in FDI policy was supposed to strengthen the hand of European countries when negotiating investment deals with third countries. In the specific case of China, it was expected to increase the EU's bargaining leverage in negotiating market access for European investments in China.

Since the implementation of the Lisbon Treaty in December 2009, however, the new policy has been taking a very long time to be implemented — in large part because the economic crisis has highlighted the importance of an influx of foreign capital and revealed that, for EU Member States, the biggest competitors in attracting FDI were the other EU Member States. The only progress being made now is on the outbound front, when it comes to negotiating BIT. Indeed, as evidence of the importance taken by the issue of Chinese FDI in Europe, the first BIT to be negotiated on behalf of the whole EU will be with China: in May 2013 the Commission asked the Council for a mandate which it received in October 2013. The negotiations, which are expected to take a long time, will be launched soon. But there is no political appetite at the moment for implementing a common policy on inbound investment — a time of crisis is not a time to implement restrictions on foreign investment (Meunier 2013b).

All in all, the analysis of political bargains vis-a-vis Chinese investment revealed that the economic and financial crisis prompted European policymakers to change policy in order to facilitate Chinese FDI at the national level, which is in line with theories of policy change (Tosun *et al.* this issue). At the EU level, however, policy change has been moderate. The relative persistence of national regulatory arrangements can be attributed to the absence of political will for harmonized investment policies due to regulatory competition among the individual member states. The existence of regulatory competition, in turn, can be related to an increased politicization of economic considerations and the vote-maximizing behaviour of rational policy-makers, which supports key arguments of postfunctionalism as an approach to understanding European integration (for an overview, see Schimmelfennig this issue).

Conclusion

That the surge of Chinese direct investment into Europe coincided with the outbreak of the economic crisis is not disputed. The central question of this paper concerns causality: was Chinese FDI able to increase in Europe as a direct consequence of the crisis? The answer provided was threefold. First,

Chinese companies were driven by internal motives for investing in Europe and would have attempted to do so even in the absence of an economic crisis in Europe. Second, the crisis offered Chinese investors the opportunity to find economic bargains in Europe, but bargain-hunting is not the main pattern of Chinese investment into Europe over the past three years. Third, what the crisis directly did contribute to was to lower, and even wipe out, political resistance to Chinese investment. However, investment-related policy change predominantly took place in the individual member states. At the EU level, moderate policy change only could be observed since the individual member states compete against each other for attracting Chinese FDI and therefore are reluctant to shift to an EU-wide harmonization of investment policies.

China has sometimes acted opportunistically in Europe as a result of the crisis but it has not been arrogantly plundering European natural or industrial jewels. Even if profit maximizing is only one of the goals of Chinese investors, whose government orders them to 'go abroad' to conquer new markets and bring back technology, Chinese companies are not willing to jump in into any investment only because it is available — instead, they look for the right opportunity and invest further only if their first investment has been successful. If anything, Chinese potential buyers may have held out from investing in the countries most severely hit by the crisis for fear that the markets had not bottomed out yet. Opportunity has not been judged independently from risk. Moreover, China has been careful not to provoke any political backlash in Europe. The new trend in Chinese OFDI in Europe is a shift towards minority investments, a new trend 'confirmed by statements of senior Chinese government and business leaders supporting minority investments as a more prudent, accepted and efficient approach toward outbound investments' (A Capital Dragon Index 2013).

The economic crisis transformed the time horizon of European politics. In hard times, beggars can't be choosers. European policy-makers clearly prioritized short-term concerns (e.g. unemployment) over long-term concerns (e.g. cultural identity, national security). Here lies a major difference between the EU and the United States. Chinese foreign investment in the US, from telecoms to bacon products, has been scrutinized over the issue of national security, both because it is an institutional requirement and because the US perceives China to be its main security competitor over the next decades. By contrast, the FDI policies of most EU countries are not dictated by the primacy of national security. A few countries, such as France, have identified 'strategic sectors' which require some kind of vetting of foreign investment, but the majority of Member States have no particular screening mechanism or vetting restrictions on FDI — and to most of them, a rising China is only a distant threat of no immediate relevance, while the economic crisis represents clear and present danger.

In sum, the findings of this paper suggest that the economic and financial crisis represents an obstacle to European integration since it drives individual member states to compete against each other for attracting FDI in the hope of reducing the economic hardships they are experiencing. As evidenced by other contributors to this special issue (see Clements *et al.*

and Hutter and Kerscher), economic factors have become a crucial dimension of political competition. As a result, vote-seeking national and local policy-makers are interested in improving the domestic macroeconomic situation rather than pushing for EU-wide investment policies that would effectively disable member states' ability to engage in regulatory arbitrage. The politicization of regulatory politics regarding FDI thus can be interpreted as providing support for the logic of postfunctionalism as a tool for explaining European integration thus qualifying the findings of Schimmelfennig (this issue).

References

A Capital Dragon Index. 2013. *2012 full year*. A Capital Dragon Index, http://www.acapital.hk/dragonindex/Overview (accessed 25 May 2013).

ANA. 2013, May 17. Agreements signed by China and Greece. Athens News Agency, http://www.hri.org/news/greek/ana/2013/13-05-17.ana.html#01 (accessed 5 February 2014).

Brautigam, D. 2011. *The Dragon's gift: the real story of China in Africa*. Oxford: Oxford University Press.

Burgoon, B., W. Jacoby, and S. Meunier. 2014. The politics of hosting Chinese investment in Europe.

Ernst & Young. 2013. Coping with the crisis, the European way. *Europe Attractiveness Survey*, http://www.ey.com/GL/en/Issues/Business-environment/2013-European-attractiveness-survey (accessed 5 February 2014).

European Union Chamber of Commerce in China. 2013. *Chinese outbound investment in the European Union*, http://www.rolandberger.com/media/pdf/Roland_Berger_Chinese_outbound_investment_in_the_European_Union_20130131.pdf, http://www.europeanchamber.com.cn/en/publications-chinese-outbound-investment-eu-european-union (accessed 5 February 2014).

EUROSTAT. 2013. Top ten countries as extra EU-27 partners for FDI positions, http://epp.eurostat.ec.europa.eu/statistics_explained/index.php?title=File:Top_ten_countries_as_extra_EU-27_partners_for_FDI_positions,_EU-27,_end_2009-2011_(EUR_1_000_million).png&filetimestamp=20130722084750 (accessed 5 February 2014).

Germany Trade and Invest. 2013, May 7. *USA tops Germany's investor lists*. Germany Trade and Invest, http://www.gtai.de/GTAI/Navigation/EN/_Meta/press,did=809646.html (accessed 24 May 2013).

Hanemann, T. 2013, February 25. *Chinese investment: Europe vs. the United States*, http://rhg.com/notes/chinese-investment-europe-vs-the-united-states (accessed 24 May 2013).

Hanemann, T., and D. Rosen. 2012. *China invests in Europe: patterns, impacts and policy implications*. New York, NY: The Rhodium Group. http://rhg.com/wp-content/uploads/2012/06/RHG_ChinaInvestsInEurope_June2012.pdf (accessed 5 February 2014).

International Monetary Fund. 1993. *Balance of payments manual (BPM5)*. Washington DC: International Monetary Fund. https://www.imf.org/external/pubs/ft/bopman/bopman.pdf (accessed 5 February 2014).

Knapp, J., and S. Meunier. 2012, July 31. Coming to America: top ten factors driving Chinese foreign direct investment. *The Huffington Post*.

Lipsey, R., and F. Sjoholm. 2004, May. Host country impacts of inward FDI: why such different answers? *Working Paper No. 192*. Stockholm: European Institute of Japanese Studies, Stockholm School of Economics. http://swopec.hhs.se/eijswp/papers/eijswp0192.pdf (accessed 5 February 2014).

Meunier, S. 2013. Integration by stealth: how the European Union became competent over foreign direct investment. *Working Paper*, Princeton University, Princeton, NJ.

Meunier, S. 2014. Divide and conquer: how China can exploit the multiplicity of investment rules in the EU. *Journal of European Public Policy*.

OECD. 2008a. *OECD benchmark for foreign direct investment fourth edition*. Paris: OECD. http://www.oecd.org/daf/inv/investmentstatisticsandanalysis/40193734.pdf (accessed 5 February 2014).

OECD. 2008b. *OECD investment policy reviews: China 2008*. Paris: OECD. http://www.oecd.org/investment/investmentfordevelopment/41792683.pdf (accessed 5 February 2014).

OECD. 2013a, April. *FDI in figures*. OECD, http://www.oecd.org/daf/inv/FDI%20in%20figures.pdf (accessed 23 May 2013).
OECD. 2013b. *FDI regulatory restrictiveness index 2012*, http://www.oecd.org/investment/fdiindex.htm (accessed 16 September 2013).
Pandya, S. 2013. *Trading spaces: foreign direct investment regulation 1970–2000*. New York, NY: Cambridge University Press.
Passino, C. 2013, August 7. Plans to grant investor residency could revive Spain's real estate market. *Forbes*.
Rabinovitch, S. 2013, April 11. China's forex reserves reach $3.4tn. *Financial Times*.
Sakoui, A., and J. Pickard. 2013, May 26. UK officials court Chinese investors for super-sewer. *Financial Times*.
Shambaugh, D. 2013. *China goes global: the partial power*. New York, NY: Oxford University Press.
Steed, A. 2013, May 21. Residency law gives the Spanish market a boost. *The Telegraph*.
The Economist. 2013, April 20. Overseas investment: nice to see you, EU. *The Economist*.
Tonnelier, A. 2012, September 6. La France et la Chine créent un fonds d'investissement [France and China create an investment fund]. *Le Monde*.
Tuo, Y. 2013, May 28. Growing hub for Chinese firms in Germany. *China Daily*.
UNCTAD. 2000. *World investment report 2000: cross-border mergers and acquisitions and development*. New York and Geneva: UNCTAD.
UNCTAD. 2013. *World investment report 2013: global value chains*. New York and Geneva: UNCTAD, http://unctad.org/en/PublicationsLibrary/webdiaeia2013d1_en.pdf
Yiqi, Y., C. Liu, and Z. Chunyan. 2013, June 2013. China boosts its presence in Europe. *China Daily*.

Crisis and Citizens' Trust in the European Central Bank — Panel Data Evidence for the Euro Area, 1999–2012

FELIX ROTH*,**, DANIEL GROS** & FELICITAS NOWAK-LEHMANN D.*

*Faculty of Economics and Business Administration, University of Göttingen, Göttingen, Germany;
**Centre for European Policy Studies, Brussels, Belgium

ABSTRACT Throughout the crisis, citizens' trust in the European Central Bank has significantly declined throughout the Euro area (EA-12). Although a decline in the core countries of the EA-12 has been distinct, a more pronounced decline has been taking place in the peripheral countries of the EA-12. Taking panel data and using a fixed effects DFGLS estimation for an EA-12 country sample over the time period of 1999–2012 with a total of 305 observations, this paper detects a negative and significant relationship between unemployment and trust in times of crisis. The robustness analysis of the paper confirms that this decrease in trust is strongly driven by the significant increase in unemployment rates in the four peripheral countries Spain, Ireland, Greece and Portugal.

Introduction

The bankruptcy of Lehman Brothers in September 2008 triggered a crisis of trust (Guiso 2010; Sapienza and Zingales 2012) and of confidence (Tonkiss 2009). It has acted as the starting point of a financial and economic crisis for most advanced economies worldwide, including advanced economies in the Euro area (EA) (European Economic Advisory Group 2010). Within the EA, the financial and economic crisis culminated in a sovereign debt crisis from 2010 onwards (De Grauwe 2010). The breeding ground of the financial crisis was mostly created by a lack of regulation within the institutional framework of the financial system in the US as well as in Europe (Acharya et al. 2009; De Grauwe 2009; Financial Crisis Inquiry Commission 2011; Stiglitz 2009). Since central banks are commonly identified as the major guardians of the financial system (Healy 2001, 22), the financial and economic crisis will most likely have negatively affected citizens' trust in central banks. Indeed, it has been shown that citizens' trust in national central banks (Gros and Roth 2009; Wälti 2012) and in the European Central Bank (ECB) (Ehrmann, Soudan, and Stracca 2013; Jones 2009; Roth 2009a; Wälti 2012) has reached all-time lows in January/February 2009 and May 2010. Based on these findings, it seems worthwhile to analyse the precise channels that have caused this loss of citizens' trust in central banks.

In this respect, this paper will focus on the EA and citizens' trust in the ECB over a 13-year time period (from 1999 to 2012). The paper will be structured in the following manner. It will first embed the concept of citizens' trust in the ECB within the overall concept of systemic trust and will elaborate what might be the consequences of an enduring loss of citizens' trust in the ECB. In the next step, the paper will try to identify those factors that most likely led to the loss of citizens' trust in the ECB. Based upon these theoretical assumptions, the paper will elaborate on the measurement of the data, the model specification and the research design. A description of the trend in citizens' trust will be followed by a discussion about methodological issues, a presentation of the econometric results and a discussion of our results in the context of previous empirical findings — as well as the underlying theoretical assumptions. The conclusion will summarize the main findings.

Theoretical Links

The Consequences of an Enduring Loss of Citizens Trust in the ECB

Trust can be conceptualized into three forms: thick, interpersonal and systemic or institutional trust (Khodyakov 2007; Roth 2009b). As this paper will analyse citizens' trust in the ECB, it will take the concept of systemic trust as its starting point. A prominent (and for our paper suitable) elaboration of systemic trust is given within the sociological discipline by Luhmann (2000) and Giddens (1996). Both authors stress the importance of systemic trust in today's modern complex societies (Giddens 1996, 165; Luhmann 2000, 26). For Luhmann systemic trust is necessary to reduce the complexity of modern societies in order to stabilize its very foundations (Luhmann 2000, 72). Giddens characterizes systemic trust as necessary to secure the functioning of modern societies and warns that decreasing levels of systemic trust have in some cases the potential to break apart institutional arrangements (Giddens 1996, 166). Concerning the later argument, political scientists such as Kaltenthaler, Anderson, and Miller

(2010) focus on trust in (policy-making) institutions. Alongside Kosfeld *et al.* (2005, 673), Kaltenthaler, Anderson, and Miller (2010, 1262) argue that a certain level of citizens' trust in a policy-making institution is crucial for the legitimacy of that institution.

How do these arguments apply to the concept of trust in the ECB and what are the consequences of an enduring loss of citizens' trust in the ECB? As the ECB is a (policy-making) institution, it can be argued that a certain level of citizens' trust in the ECB seems to be crucial to maintain its legitimacy. In addition, as the ECB is an *independent* institution that is not democratically elected (as highlighted in Article 130 TFEU of the Treaty of Lisbon (2010)), the legitimacy argument applies to an even greater extent than to other policy-making institutions. In this respect, a high level of citizens' trust in the ECB can be characterized as a proxy for a high approval rating among citizens which ultimately secures the independence of the ECB. It follows from the above argumentation that a loss of trust will make the ECB vulnerable to political influence, as citizens will most likely pressure politicians to minimize the ECB's independence (Kaltenthaler, Anderson, and Miller 2010, 1261). This reasoning is shared by the ECB policy-makers. Via publicly available communications (ECB 2010), an interview with the then president Wim Duisenberg (Wenkel 2008) and other interviews with experts (Kaltenthaler, Anderson, and Miller 2010, 1267), ECB policy-makers confirm that they depend on citizens' trust in the ECB to resist pressures from politicians and secure their independence.

As we have argued that a loss of trust in the ECB will endanger the ECB's independence, we still have to clarify why this granted independence is important for the ECB. Concerning the importance of the independence of central banks, a general and a crisis embedded argument should be mentioned. In the context of the general argument, a detailed literature survey by Eijfinger and de Haan (1996) evaluating the pre-existing theoretical and empirical literature comes to the conclusion that the independence of central banks will be associated with lower inflation rates. Lower inflation rates will entail fewer costs to long-term economic growth (Eijfinger and de Haan 1996, 54). In the context of the crisis embedded argument, the ECB's decision to become the lender of last resort in the government bond market (De Grauwe 2013, 520) was pivotal in stabilizing the Eurozone in times of crisis (De Grauwe and Ji 2013a, 2013b, 2). However, as the broadening of the ECB's mandate has resulted in strong opposition (De Grauwe 2013, 522; Fratzscher 2013; Giavazzi *et al.* 2013), it seems reasonable to argue that the ECB's granted independence has played a significant role in its continuing effort to stabilize the Eurozone in times of crisis.

Possible Drivers of Citizens Trust in the ECB

Although citizens' perceptions might influence their systemic trust (Banducci, Karp, and Loedel 2009, 572), this paper focuses on the impact of three macro-economic variables: (i) unemployment, (ii) inflation and (iii) growth of GDP per capita when trying to identify those factors that led to a loss of citizens' trust in the ECB. This undertaking seems to be reasonable as it is soundly rooted in economic theory when considering the literature on popularity functions (Bellucci and Lewis-Beck 2011, 192–94; Nannestad and Paldam 1994, 215–16) and the pre-existing literature on trust in the ECB (Fischer and Hahn 2008). As however, the most recent economic literature linking institutional trust to business cycles stresses the important role of unemployment for explaining systemic trust (Stevenson and Wolfers 2011) and as it is the unemployment rate which has increased significantly, in particular in the periphery countries of the EA, throughout the crisis (and not the inflation rate — which has been muted by the ECB), this paper will primarily focus on the unemployment coefficient when depicting its econometric results.

Measurement of Data, Model Specification and Research Design

Measurement of Data

Measures for trust in the ECB were based upon the biannual standard Eurobarometer (EB) surveys from spring 1999 (EB51) to autumn 2012 (EB78).[1] Respondents were asked the following question: 'I would like to ask you a question about how much trust you have in certain institutions. For each of the following European bodies, please tell me if you tend to trust it or not to trust it'. Respondents were then presented with a range of institutions. Possible answers included the following three categories: 'Tend to trust it', 'Tend not to trust it' and 'Don't know'. Applying a concept as introduced by Gärtner (1997, 488–89), we utilize a 'net trust' measure, which is obtained by subtracting the percentage of those who trust from those who do not trust.[2] In order to match our trust data to our macro-economic data, a procedure proposed by Wälti (2012, 597) is applied.[3] Monthly data on unemployment, inflation (change of HICP) and sovereign bond yield rates were retrieved from Eurostat. The values for unemployment were adjusted seasonally. Quarterly data on GDP and population size were taken from Eurostat's data.[4,5] The quarterly data were interpolated to gain monthly observations in order to utilize the monthly matching approach.[6]

Model Specification

Within our baseline model, an unbalanced panel, net trust in the ECB is estimated as a function of unemployment, inflation, growth of GDP per capita and other important control variables. As this paper is interested in explaining the 'within variation' throughout the crisis period, a fixed-effects estimation approach is utilized. The baseline model for our estimation, which holds in the long term when all adjustments have come to an end, reads as follows:

$$\text{Trust\_ECB}_{it} = \alpha_i + \beta \, \text{Unemployment}_{it} + \chi \, \text{Inflation}_{it} + \delta \, \text{Growth}_{it} + \varphi \, Z_{it} + w_{it} \tag{1}$$

where i characterizes each country and t represents each time period. Trust_ECB$_{it}$ is the net trust amount in the ECB for country i during period t. Unemployment$_{it}$, Inflation$_{it}$, Growth$_{it}$, and Z_{it} are accordingly unemployment, inflation, growth of GDP per capita and important control variables such as indicators of financial stress like e.g. sovereign bond yields. α_i depicts a country-specific constant term and w_{it} is the error term. As we utilize an Feasible Generalized Least Square (FGLS) estimation approach, time dummies are not included within our baseline estimation as they are mutually exclusive with FGLS.

Research Design

Our baseline econometric analysis will estimate Equation (1) with the aid of an EA-12 country sample (Austria, Belgium, Finland, France, Germany, Greece, Ireland, Italy, Luxembourg, the Netherlands, Portugal and Spain) over the 13-year time period from 1999 to 2012.[7] With 29 time periods (t = 29) and 12 countries (n = 12) and thus with a ratio of t/n of 2.4, estimation of Equation (1) will be performed via time series econometrics. As we identify the events associated with the bankruptcy of Lehman Brothers in September 2008 as the start of the crisis, a pre-crisis period (3-4/1999–3-5/2008) will be differentiated from a crisis period (10-11/2008–11/2012) within the descriptive and econometric analysis. In addition, throughout the analysis a *core* country sample, the EA-8 (Austria, Belgium, Finland, France, Germany, Italy, Luxembourg and the Netherlands), will be differentiated from a *periphery* country sample, the EA-4 (Greece, Ireland, Portugal and Spain).

Descriptive Statistics

Table 1 shows the levels of net trust in the ECB before the crisis (3-5/2008) and in the fourth year of the crisis (11/2012) and the values for the changes in net trust (11/2012-3-5/2008) for all EA-12 countries, as well as an EA-12, EA-4 and EA-8 country sample.[8] Table 1 clarifies that in the EA-12 net trust in the ECB has declined significantly throughout the crisis no less than by 45 percentage points. Whereas a majority of citizens still trusted the ECB before the crisis (+29 per cent), in the fourth year of the crisis a majority distrusted the ECB (−16 per cent). However, with 34 percentage points (from 27 to −7 per cent), the decline is less pronounced in the EA-8 compared to a decline of 84 percentage points (from +34 to −50 per cent) in the EA-4. This significant difference in the aggregate trends can be explained by analysing the values for the individual countries. Whereas the four periphery countries Spain, Ireland, Greece and Portugal have faced a significant decline in trust in the ECB with values of −98, −67, −65 and −52 percentage points, respectively, core countries such as Austria and France only faced a moderate decline by −17 and −14 percentage points, respectively. Overall, comparing the decline in trust in the ECB to other European institutions such as the EC and European Parliament (EP) over the same time frame, the decline in trust in the ECB is the more significant

Table 1. Net trust levels and changes in net trust in the EA-12, EA-4, EA-8 and individual EA-12 countries (2008–2012)

Country	Levels 3-5/2008	Levels 11/2012	Changes 11/2012–3-5/2008
EA-12	29	−16	−45
EA-4	34	−50	−84
EA-8	27	−7	−34
Spain	40	−58	−98
Ireland	47	−20	−67
Greece	1	−64	−65
Portugal	39	−13	−52
Germany	35	−13	−48
Belgium	42	−6	−48
Netherlands	70	24	−46
Italy	21	−11	−32
Finland	49	24	−25
Luxembourg	42	24	−18
France	10	−7	−17
Austria	20	6	−14

Notes: EA-12, EA-4 and EA-8 are population weighted. As the table displays levels in net values, all level values below 0 indicate that a majority of respondents mistrust the ECB.
Sources: Standard EBs 69 and 78.

in all EA-12 countries (see here Roth, Nowak-Lehmann D., and Otter 2013, 8–9).[9]

Given that Table 1 only depicts a before-after comparison for two points in time (3-5/2008 and 11/2012), Figure 1 compares the 13-year time trends (from 1999 to 2012) for the EA-12 country sample with the ones from the EA-4 and EA-8 (for the time trends of all individual EA-12 countries see Figure A1 in the Appendix). Four interesting findings emerge. First, in the EA-12 trust significantly declined throughout the crisis period (10-11/2008 to 11/2012) in comparison to the pre-crisis period (3-4/1999–3-5/2008, with mean levels declining by 24 percentage points from 25 to 1 per cent) and departed from its long-term trend (with standard deviations tripling). Second, the decline was more pronounced in the EA-4 with a drop in mean levels of 34 percentage points in comparison to 22 percentage points in the EA-8 and standard deviations quadrupling in the EA-4 but only doubling in the EA-8. Third, whereas the EA-4 and EA-8 trends are highly correlated throughout the pre-crisis period and even in the direct aftermath of the financial crisis until 5/2010, from 5/2010 [the start of the sovereign debt crisis onwards (De Grauwe 2010)], the decline in the EA-4 continued steadily reaching a level of −50 per cent in 11/2012, in comparison to a level of −7 per cent for the EA-8. Fourth, taking aside the short time period from 1-2/2009 until 6-7/2009, a majority of citizens mistrusted the ECB in the EA-12 and EA-8 from 11/2011 onwards. In the EA-4, a majority of citizens already mistrusted the ECB from 11-12/2010 onwards. However, whereas the majority of distrust in the EA-8 is still narrow with a net value

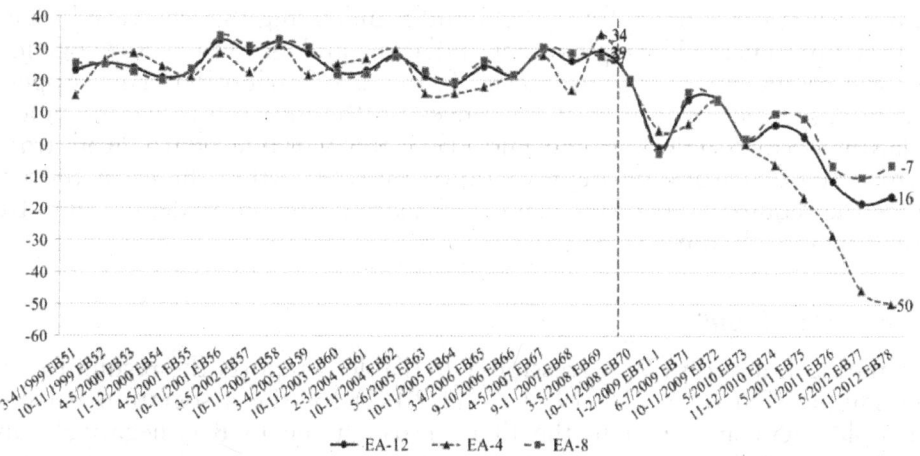

Figure 1. Net trust in the ECB in per cent, EA12, EA4 and EA8, 1999–2012
Notes: As the figure depicts net values, all values below 0 indicate that a majority of respondents mistrust the ECB. For the aggregation of the EA-12, EA-4 and EA-8, population weights were applied. The dotted line represents the incidence of the bankruptcy of Lehman Brothers in September 2008.
Sources: Standard EBs 51-78 and Special EB 71.1.

of −7 per cent in 11/2012 (in Austria, Finland, the Netherlands and Luxembourg a majority of citizens actually still trusted the ECB — see Table 1), already a large majority mistrusted the ECB in 11/2012 in the EA-4 with a net value of −50 per cent (in Greece and Spain, in total values, 81 and 75 per cent of citizens, respectively, mistrusted the ECB in contrast to only 17 per cent of citizens in both countries who still trusted the ECB).

Econometric Analysis

Discussion on the Estimation Procedure

We estimated Equation (1) by means of dynamic ordinary least squares (DOLS), a method that permits to fully control for endogeneity of the regressors (Stock and Watson 1993; Wooldridge 2009).[10] In order to correct for autocorrelation,[11] we apply a FGLS procedure.[12] Both applications lead to the following Equation (2):[13]

$$\text{Trust\_ECB}^*_{it} = \alpha_i + \beta_1 \text{Unemployment}^*_{it} + \chi_1 \text{Inflation}^*_{it} + \delta_1 \text{Growth}^*_{it} + \varphi_1 Z^*_{it}$$
$$+ \sum_{p=-1}^{p=+1} \beta_{2p} \Delta \text{Unemployment}^*_{it-p} + \sum_{p=-1}^{p=+1} \chi_{2p} \Delta \text{Inflation}^*_{it-p}$$
$$+ \sum_{p=-1}^{p=+1} \delta_{2p} \Delta \text{Growth}^*_{it-p} + \sum_{p=-1}^{p=+1} \varphi_{2p} \Delta Z^*_{it-p} + u_{it}$$

(2)

with α_i being the country fixed effect and Δ indicating that the variables are in first differences. Unemployment, inflation and growth turn exogenous and the coefficients β_1, χ_1, δ_1 and φ_1 follow a t-distribution. This property permits us to derive statistical inferences on the impact of unemployment, inflation and growth.[14] * indicates that the variables have been transformed (purged from autoregressive processes) and that the error term u_{it} fulfils the requirements of the classical linear regression model (i.e. it is free from autocorrelation).

Econometric Results

Estimating Equation (2), regression 1 in Table 2 reports the results for the full sample (FS) (from 3-4/1999 to 11/2012) for the association between unemployment and trust in the ECB. Trust in the ECB is negatively and significantly (99 per cent level) associated with unemployment (−4.9). Given that we would expect a structural break caused by the crisis,[15] regressions 2 and 3 in Table 2 report the results for a pre-crisis (BC) sample (from 3-4/1999 to 3-5/2008) and a crisis (C) sample (from 10-11/2008 to 11/2012). In the pre-crisis period, one detects no significant relationship between trust and unemployment in regression 2. In the crisis sample (regression 3), trust in the ECB is strongly negatively (−5.5) and highly significantly (99 per cent level) related to unemployment. With a coefficient of this size, one can conclude that in times of crisis a 1 percentage point increase in unemployment is related to a decrease in 5.5 in net trust in the ECB. Furthermore, it becomes evident that the significant association for unemployment in the FS is strongly driven by the crisis period.

Table 2. Unemployment and net trust in the ECB, fixed-effects DFGLS estimations, EA12

	1	2	3
Dependent variable	Trust ECB	Trust ECB	Trust ECB
Period	FS	BC	C
Unemployment	−4.9***	1.0	−5.5***
	(0.79)	(0.95)	(0.84)
Inflation	Yes	Yes	Yes
Growth	Yes	Yes	Yes
Durbin–Watson statistic	2.40	2.25	2.10
Adjusted R^2	0.79	0.73	0.86
Country fixed effects	Yes	Yes	Yes
Control for endogeneity	Yes	Yes	Yes
Elimination of first-order autocorrelation	Yes	Yes	Yes
Observations	305	200	105
Number of countries	12	12	12

Notes: FS = Full Sample; BC = Before Crisis; C = Crisis; ECB = European Central Bank.
***$p < 0.01$.
Standard errors are in parentheses.

Sensitivity of Results

As the highly significant (99 per cent level) and strong relationship (−5.5) between unemployment and trust in times of crisis would bear important policy implications (due to the fact that unemployment rates have increased significantly in the periphery countries), Table 3 conducts a sensitivity analysis on this relationship. Row 1 in Table 3 depicts the coefficient of unemployment from regression 3 in Table 2. Rows 2–5 exclude Spain, Ireland, Greece and Portugal. After the consecutive exclusion of Spain and Ireland (row 3), the relationship decreases in size (−2.9) and significance (below the 90 per cent level). Once all four countries are excluded, the overall size of the coefficient remains at −2.9 but with a standard error of 3.14 loses in significance (row 5). This indicates that the strong negative (−5.5) and highly significant (99 per cent level) relationship between unemployment and trust is largely driven by the EA-4 countries. In Spain, Greece, Ireland and Portugal a significant increase in unemployment rates throughout the crisis (16.6, 17.5, 10 and 7.5 percentage points from 3-5/2008 to 11/2012) are associated with a decline in trust of 98, 65, 67 and 52 percentage points (see results in Figure A2 and Table 1 respectively).[16]

Table 3. Sensitivity analysis between unemployment and trust in times of crisis

Row	Specification change	C. Un.	St. Err.	Obs.	Cou.	Ad.-R^2
Baseline regression						
1	No change	−5.5***	0.84	105	12	0.86
Exclusion of outliers						
2	Spain	−5.6***	1.15	96	11	0.85
3	Spain + Ireland	−2.9	1.97	87	10	0.85
4	Spain + Ireland + Greece	−3.0	2.12	81	9	0.83
5	EA-4	−2.9	3.14	72	8	0.83
Restructuring of time sample						
6	9-11/2007–11/2012	−6.2***	0.99	129	12	0.84
7	10-11/2008–5/2012	−4.9***	0.82	94	12	0.86
8	10-11/2008–11/2011	−4.4***	0.94	83	12	0.86
9	10-11/2008–5/2011	−4.4***	1.00	72	12	0.86
10	10-11/2008–11-12/2010	−4.2**	1.68	60	12	0.84
Inclusion of additional variables						
11	Sov. bond yields	−5.4***	1.03	105	12	0.87
12	Sov. bond yields — 5/2011	−3.9***	1.41	72	12	0.86
13	Sov. bond yields — 11-12/2010	−3.4*	1.98	60	12	0.83
Various alterations						
14	Excluding Special EB 71.1	−5.2***	0.90	93	12	0.87
15	Including TD	−4.3***	0.66	105	12	0.88

Notes: C. Un. = Coefficient on Unemployment; St. Err. = Standard Error; Obs. = Observations; Cou. = Countries; Ad.-R^2 = Adjusted-R^2; TD = Time Dummy.
***$p < 0.01$.
**$p < 0.05$.
*$p < 0.10$.

Rows 6–10 analyse the robustness of the unemployment coefficient when altering the time periods utilized. Since the beginning of the financial and economic crisis can be located as early as 2007 (Stiglitz 2012, 1), row 6 analyses a crisis sample starting from 9-11/2007. The unemployment coefficient slightly increases in size (−6.2). Excluding one period at a time and commencing with the observation in 11/2012 in rows 7–10, the coefficient remains robust throughout the crisis although steadily declines in size. We can be sure that our econometric analysis has not omitted any important variables, having found that our time series are cointegrated. However, to take up concerns over missing variables, row 11 includes the additional variable sovereign bond yields as most recent empirical results have stressed their importance for trust in the ECB (Wälti 2012). After the inclusion of sovereign bond yields, the coefficient of unemployment (−5.4) remains robust.[17] In row 12, we keep the additional variable sovereign bond yields and shorten the time frame from 10-11/2008 to 5/2011. The coefficient of unemployment still remains highly significant (99 per cent level) but declines in size to −3.9. However, by analysing a time frame from 10-11/2008 to 11-12/2010 in row 13, the relationship between unemployment and trust loses significance (90 per cent level) and strength (−3.4). Hence, it appears reasonable to conclude that the highly significant and negative relationship between unemployment and trust in the ECB is driven by the time period from 5/2011 onwards (the 2nd year of the sovereign debt crisis).

Rows 14 and 15 perform two additional robustness tests. By excluding the Special EB71.1 in row 14, the results remain robust (−5.2). The inclusion of time-fixed effects instead of utilizing the FGLS approach in row 15 produces a slightly smaller coefficient (−4.3) but yields a poor Durbin–Watson statistic.

Discussion of Results

Discussion of Results Compared to Previous Empirical Findings

Besides a cross-sectional empirical study (Kaltenthaler, Anderson, and Miller 2010), a macro-economic panel analysis (Fischer and Hahn 2008) — both of which focus exclusively on the pre-crisis period, and a publication and working papers that conduct micro-based analyses (Bursian and Furth 2011; Ehrmann, Soudan, and Stracca 2013; Farfaque, Hayaty, and Mihailov 2012), the only macro-based empirical evidence for the crisis period that can be directly compared to our results are the findings by Wälti (2012). With these findings, our empirical analysis comes to an ambivalent conclusion. On the one hand, it confirms the conclusion by Wälti (2012) that in the aftermath of the financial crisis from 10-11/2008 until 11-12/2010 unemployment was only weakly related to trust in the ECB.[18] On the other hand, we contradict this finding once analysing a longer crisis time period. Utilizing a crisis time period from 10-11/2008 to 11/2012, we find a strong negative relationship between unemployment and trust from 5/2011 onwards. This relationship is strongly driven by the four periphery countries Spain, Ireland, Greece and Portugal, in which a significant increase in unemployment rates is related to a significant decline in trust in the ECB.[19]

In this respect, it should be noted that the significant increase in unemployment rates in the EA-4 has not only affected trust in the ECB but also trust in the EC, EP and national institutions (see also Ehrmann, Soudan, and Stracca 2013; Roth, Nowak-Lehmann D., and Otter 2013).[20]

Discussion of Our Results in Light of the Underlying Theoretical Assumptions

Drawing upon the theoretical links, the empirical evidence showing that a majority of citizens in the EA-12 started to mistrust the ECB from 11/2011 onwards (in the EA-4 from 11-12/2010 onwards) should be worrying for the decision-makers of the ECB because it endangers the legitimacy of the ECB and thus ultimately its independence (Kaltenthaler, Anderson, and Miller 2010, 1262).[21] Given the low approval rating, it becomes more likely that the ECB will become vulnerable to political influence (Torres 2013) and that citizens will start to pressure politicians to minimize the ECB's independence (Kaltenthaler, Anderson, and Miller 2010, 1267). Following the general argument, as the independence of central banks is associated with lower inflation rates (Eijfinger and de Haan 1996) and as lower inflation rates are associated with long-term economic growth (Eijfinger and de Haan 1996, 54), the loss of the ECB's independence would most likely harm long-term economic growth. Following the crisis embedded argument, the ECB's independence permitted it to broaden its mandate to assure financial stability even against strong opposition (De Grauwe 2013, 522; Fratzscher 2013; Giavazzi *et al.* 2013). And as this broadened mandate continues to stabilize the Eurozone in times of crisis (De Grauwe and Ji 2013a, 2013b, 2), a loss of the ECB's independence would most likely endanger the stability of the Eurozone.

One might now still want to reflect upon the fact, whether the significant decline in trust in the ECB poses an obstacle or an opportunity for further EU/EA integration (Tosun, Wetzel, and Zapryanova 2014). The answer to this question remains ambivalent. On the one hand, the loss of trust in the ECB across all EA-12 countries endangers the legitimacy of the ECB, an institution which has become one of the central actors in securing the stability of the Eurozone. On the other hand, some of the urging policy measures within the EA, amongst others reducing the high unemployment rates in the EA-4, can most likely only be resolved by collective action and will thus trigger a process of deeper political integration within the EA. As such, the current crisis could be identified as a clear opportunity for a further deepening of the EU/EA Integration process. The empirical evidence that a majority of EA-12 citizens' support the Euro in times of crisis (Roth, Jonung, and Nowak-Lehmann 2012; for the Greek case see also Clements, Nanou, and Verney 2014) should be viewed as an ideal pre-requisite for the implementation of a process of deeper political integration within the EA.[22]

Conclusion

This article has examined the trends and determinants of net trust in the ECB, focusing on unemployment and a particular focus on the crisis period from 10-11/2008 to 11/2012. Five findings deserve to be highlighted.

First, throughout the crisis net trust in the ECB has declined significantly in the EA-12 and has departed from its long-term trends. However, whereas this decline in trust has been distinct in the EA-8, the decline in the EA-4 has been even more pronounced.

Second, from 11/2011 onwards, a majority of citizens started to mistrust the ECB in the EA-12 and EA-8. In the EA-4, this trend already started from 11-12/2010 with large majorities mistrusting the ECB in 11/2012.

Third, with a majority of citizens mistrusting the ECB from 11/2011 onwards, the ECB's legitimacy might be endangered. With its legitimacy potentially endangered, it will prove more difficult for the policy-makers of the ECB to resist pressures from politicians to minimize their independence. Concerning the general argument, a loss of the ECB's independence would endanger price stability and therefore harm long-term economic growth. Concerning the crisis embedded argument, a loss of the ECB's independence would endanger the ECB's new mandate to assure financial stability and stabilize the Eurozone in times of crisis.

Fourth, taking panel data and using a fixed effects DFGLS estimation for a EA-12 country sample over the time period of 1999–2012, this paper detects a strong and significant negative relationship between unemployment and trust in times of crisis. This relationship remains robust to a range of alterations and is strongly driven by the significant increase in unemployment rates in the EA-4 and from 5/2011 onwards.

Fifth, a reduction of the high unemployment rates in the EA-4 seems to be necessary in order to regain trust in the ECB in those countries. And this issue may determine the future of Eurozone integration and systemic trust.

Acknowledgements

Felix Roth wants to thank the Verein für Socialpolitik for scheduling the special session 'Trusting Banks in a Financial Crisis' at its annual conference on 8 September 2010 in Kiel, which gave him the opportunity to present a preliminary version of the paper. He would like to thank the seminar participants of that session for their valuable comments. In addition, the authors would like to thank the participants of the 14th Göttinger Workshop 'Internationale Wirtschaftsbeziehungen' at the University of Göttingen in February 2012, the fourth IFABS Conference in Valencia in June 2012, and the seventh Annual International Symposium on Economic Theory, Policy and Applications in Athens in July 2012. The authors are grateful to Lars Jonung, the guest editor team from the Mannheim Centre for European Social Research Jale Tosun, Anne Wetzel and Galina Zapryanova, as well as two anonymous referees for their valuable comments. Two preliminary working paper versions of this paper were published as CEPS Working Document 334 on 26 July 2010 and as CEGE Discussion Paper 124 at the University of Göttingen in May 2011.

Notes

1. Standard EB surveys include about 1000 respondents per EU country. The interviews are performed face-to-face in the home of the respondents. For each standard EB survey, new and independent samples are derived. To guarantee the polling of a representative sample of the population, the sampling design is multi-stage and random. The raw data are available on CD-ROM from Gesis ZA Data Service for Standard EBs 51-62 (Gesis 2005a, 2005b) and were received on request from Gesis ZA Data Service for Standard EBs 63-69 (Gesis 2009). Data for the Standard EBs 70-78 and Special EB 71.1 were taken from the European Commission's (EC) tables of results (2009a, 2009b, 2009c, 2010a, 2010b, 2011a, 2011b, 2012a, 2012b). Following Jones (2009) and Ehrmann, Soudan, and Stracca (2013), the observations from the Special EB 71.1 in 1-2/2009 were taken into consideration. For a detailed reasoning, see Roth, Nowak-Lehmann D., and Otter (2013, 4). The elimination of data from EB71.1 does not modify the econometric results in any significant way (see results in row 14 in Table 3).
2. A net trust measure seemed adequate as the 'Don't Know' answers varied over a wide range from 0 per cent in Greece in EB 71 to 44.6 per cent in Portugal in EB 51 with an overall mean value of 20.5 per cent. However, it should be pointed out that net trust and trust measures correlate as high as 0.92. For an equation showing how to calculate net trust, see Roth, Nowak-Lehmann D., and Otter (2013, 4).
3. Although the monthly matching methodology by Wälti (2012, 597) correlates as high as 0.99 for the variables unemployment and inflation and 0.95 for the variable growth of GDP per capita, when comparing it to a semester matching methodology, the monthly methodological approach seems to be more adequate to prevent any potential overlap between the explanatory macro-economic variables and the EB data. The exact months of polling for the EBs surveys are displayed in the legend of the x-axis in Figure 1.
4. GDP data were chain-linked, the reference year being 2005, and seasonally adjusted. Data on GDP were missing for Greece from the 2nd quarter of 2011 onwards.
5. Due to inconsistent data on population size and breaks in some country time series within the official Eurostat data, values had to be exchanged by means of interpolation whenever required.
6. Possible measurement errors from the performed interpolation seem improbable as the monthly constructed variables correlate with the semester data as high as 0.95 for growth of GDP per capita.
7. For Greece, time trend data from 2001 onwards were taken. The five countries Slovakia, Slovenia, Malta, Cyprus and Estonia were not analysed as their accession occurred only recently and thus time trend data would not have been available from 1999 onwards.
8. For reasons of adequacy population-weighted trust trends are utilized for the EA-12, EA-4 and EA-8 country sample. However, population-weighted and non-population weighted aggregates are highly correlated.
9. With the exception for Greece's decline in trust in the EC, trust in the ECB has decreased more significantly than trust in the EC and EP in all EA-12 countries from 3-5/2008 to 11/2012. In comparison to the EC and EP, the decrease in trust in the ECB is significantly higher (one standard deviation above the mean) in particular in the three core countries Germany, Netherlands and Finland. In those three countries, the additional trust decline varies from 29 to 38 percentage points of net trust with respect to the EC and 29–32 percentage points of net trust with respect to the EP with Germany showing the largest additional decline of 38 and 32 percentage points, respectively.
10. A pre-requisite for using the DOLS approach is that the variables entering the model are non-stationary and that all the series are in a long-run relationship (cointegrated). In our case, all series are integrated of order 1, i.e. they are I(1) (and thus non-stationary, non-stationarity of inflation and growth of GDP per capita is due to non-stationarity (non-constancy) of the variance of these series) and they are cointegrated. Results for the panel unit root tests and Kao's residual cointegration test can be obtained from the authors upon request.
11. We found first-order autocorrelation to be present.
12. FGLS is not compatible with time-fixed effects but picks up shocks and their influence over short-to-medium term periods. In addition, the potential inclusion of time dummies would not alter our results in any significant manner (see results in row 15 in Table 3), and it could be shown that time-fixed effects do not tackle the problem of autocorrelation of the error term.

13. For a detailed explanation of all steps leading from Equation (1) to Equation (2) within a similar model specification, please see Roth, Nowak-Lehmann D., and Otter (2013, 12–4).
14. The coefficients β_{2p}, χ_{2p}, δ_{2p} and φ_{2p} are linked to the endogenous part of the explanatory variables and do not result in a t-distribution. Since we are not interested in the influence of these 'differenced variables' on trust, they will not be depicted.
15. In addition to the theoretical validity of differentiating a pre-crisis from a crisis period, empirically, a Chow-test showed a structural break between the pre-crisis period (3-4/1999–3-5/2008) and the crisis period (10-11/2008–11/2012). Results can be obtained from the authors upon request.
16. The insignificant relationship between unemployment and trust in the EA-8 is largely driven by the German case in which an actual decrease of the unemployment rate of 2.8 percentage points (from 3-5/2008 to 11/2012) is associated with a significant decline in net trust in the ECB of 48 percentage points (see here also Figure A2). Once excluding the German case from the EA-8 country sample, the relationship between unemployment and trust regains significance (90 per cent level) and the coefficient regains strength (–7.1).
17. This is logical as in the case of Spain trust decreased significantly during the second year of the sovereign debt crisis while its sovereign bond yields remained relatively stable.
18. Whereas our econometric analysis actually still finds a weak (90 per cent level) relationship, Wälti's (2012) findings points towards an insignificant relationship.
19. This is in contrast to the German case where an actual reduction of the unemployment rate is associated with a significant decline in trust in the ECB. A plausible hypothesis for the German case might be that the broadening of the ECB's mandate to assure financial stability throughout the crisis has led to a decline in trust in the ECB.
20. As the decline of trust in the ECB might be interpreted as part of a general crisis of trust in European institutions, it becomes debatable whether other trust variables, such as citizens' trust in the EC and the EP should be included in the model specification. We excluded these variables for two reasons. First, as trust in the EC and the EP is equally determined by inflation, growth and unemployment (Roth, Nowak-Lehmann D., and Otter 2013), it is econometrically incorrect to include these trust variables in the regression, because doing so would lead not only to double counting but also to endogeneity. Second, the Durbin–Watson statistic (being around 2) did not give us reason to worry about omitted variables.
21. It should be mentioned, however, that in 1-2/2009 net trust temporarily reached a value of –1 per cent. In this instance, however, net trust recovered to a value of +14 five months later in 6-7/2009.
22. In contrast to the support for the Euro, the support for the European Union actually declined more strongly (Braun and Tausendpfund 2014).

References

Acharya, V., T. Philippon, M. Richardson, and N. Roubini. 2009. The financial crisis of 2007–2009: causes and remedies. In *Restoring financial stability: how to repair a failed system*, eds. V. Acharya and M. Richardson, 1–56. Hoboken, NJ: John Wiley & Sons.
Banducci, S., J. Karp, and P. Loedel. 2009. Economic interests and public support for the Euro. *Journal of European Public Policy* 16, no. 4: 564–81.
Bellucci, P., and M.S. Lewis-Beck. 2011. A stable popularity function? Cross-national analysis. *European Journal of Political Research* 50, no. 2: 190–211.
Braun, D., and M. Tausendpfund. 2014. The impact of the Eurozone crisis on citizens' support for the European Union. *Journal of European Integration*, forthcoming.
Bursian, D., and S. Furth. 2011. *Trust me! I'm a European Central Banker*, http://papers.ssrn.com/sol3/papers.cfm?abstract_id=1932638.
Clements, B., K. Nanou, and S. Verney. 2014. We no longer love you, but we don't want to leave you: the Eurozone crisis and popular euroscepticism in Greece. *Journal of European Integration*, forthcoming.
De Grauwe, P. 2009. *Economics of monetary union*. Oxford: Oxford University Press.
De Grauwe, P. 2010. The Greek crisis and the future of the Eurozone. *Intereconomics* 45, no. 2: 89–93.
De Grauwe, P. 2013. The European Central Bank as lender of last resort in the government bond markets. *CESifo Economic Studies* 59, no. 3: 520–35.

De Grauwe, P., and Y. Ji. 2013a. Panic-driven austerity in the Eurozone and its implications. *VOX*, 21 February.
De Grauwe, P., and Y. Ji. 2013b. The legacy of austerity in the Eurozone. *CEPS Commentary*, 4 October.
Ehrmann, M., M. Soudan, and L. Stracca. 2013. Explaining European Union Citizens' Trust in the European Central Bank in normal and crisis times. *Scandinavian Journal of Economics* 115, no. 3: 781–807.
Eijffinger, S., and J. de Haan. 1996. *The political economy of Central Bank independence*. Special Papers in International Economics 19. Princeton, NJ: Department of Economics, Princeton University.
European Central Bank. 2010. *The strategic intent of the Eurosystem*. Frankfurt: ECB, http://www.ecb.int/ecb/orga/escb/html/intents.en.html.
European Commission. 2009a. *The Europeans in 2009 — special Eurobarometer 308/Wave 71.1*. Brussels: European Commission DG Communication.
European Commission. 2009b. *Standard Eurobarometer 71*. Brussels: European Commission DG Communication.
European Commission. 2009c. *Standard Eurobarometer 72*. Brussels: European Commission DG Communication.
European Commission. 2010a. *Standard Eurobarometer 73*. Brussels: European Commission DG Communication.
European Commission. 2010b. *Standard Eurobarometer 74*. Brussels: European Commission DG Communication.
European Commission. 2011a. *Standard Eurobarometer 75*. Brussels: European Commission DG Communication.
European Commission. 2011b. *Standard Eurobarometer 76*. Brussels: European Commission DG Communication.
European Commission. 2012a. *Standard Eurobarometer 77*. Brussels: European Commission DG Communication.
European Commission. 2012b. *Standard Eurobarometer 78*. Brussels: European Commission DG Communication.
European Economic Advisory Group. 2010. *The EEAG report on the European economy*. Munich: CESifo.
Farfaque, E., M.A. Hayaty, and A. Mihailov. 2012. *Who supports the ECB? Evidence from Eurobarometer survey data*. Working Paper 2011/092. Reading: Henley Business School, University of Reading.
Financial Crisis Inquiry Commission. 2011. *The financial crisis inquiry report*. Washington, DC: US Government Printing Office.
Fischer, J.A., and V. Hahn. 2008. *Determinants of trust in the ECB*. Research Paper Series 26. Thurgau: Institute for Economics, University of Konstanz.
Fratzscher, M. 2013. The costs for Germany if the Eurozone collapses. *Europe's World*, 1 October.
Gärtner, M. 1997. Who wants the Euro — and why? Economic explanations of public attitudes towards a single European currency. Public Choice 93, no. 3–4: 487–510.
Gesis ZA Data Service. 2005a. *Eurobarometer 1970–2004*. CD-Rom 2, EB 42–EB 51. Mannheim: Gesis.
Gesis ZA Data Service. 2005b. *Eurobarometer 1970–2004*. CD-Rom 3, EB 52–EB 62. Mannheim: Gesis.
Gesis ZA Data Service. 2009. http://www.gesis.org/en/services/data/survey-data/eurobarometer-data-service/data-access/.
Giavazzi, F., R. Portes, B. Weder di Mauro, and C. Wyplosz. 2013. The wisdom of Karlsruhe: the OMT case should be dismissed. *VOX*, 12 June.
Giddens, A. 1996. Leben in einer posttraditionalen Gesellschaft [Living in a post-traditional society]. In *Reflexive Modernisierung*, eds. U. Beck, A. Giddens, and S. Lash, 113–94. Frankfurt am Main: Suhrkamp.
Gros, D., and F. Roth. 2009. The crisis and citizens' trust in central banks. *VOX*, 10 September.
Guiso, L. 2010. A trust-driven financial crisis: implications for the future of financial markets. In *The EEAG report on the European economy 2010*, eds. European Economic Advisory Group, 53–70. Munich: CESifo.

Healy, J. 2001. Financial stability and the central bank: international evidence. In *Financial stability and central banks — a global perspective*, eds. R. Breatly, A. Clark, C. Goodhart, J. Healy, G. Hoggarth, D.T. Llewelyn, C. Shu, P. Sinclair, and F. Soussa, 19–78. London: Routledge.

Jones, E. 2009. Output legitimacy and the global financial crisis: perceptions matter. *Journal of Common Market Studies* 47, no. 5: 1085–105.

Kaltenthaler, K., C.J. Anderson, and W.J. Miller. 2010. Accountability and independent central banks: Europeans and distrust of the European Central Bank. *Journal of Common Market Studies* 48, no. 5: 1261–81.

Khodyakov, D. 2007. Trust as a process: a three-dimensional approach. Sociology 41, no. 1: 115–32.

Kosfeld, M., M. Heinrichs, P.J. Zak, U. Fischbacher, and E. Fehr. 2005. Oxytocin increases trust in humans. Nature 435: 673–76.

Luhmann, N. 2000. *Vertrauen* [Trust]. Stuttgart: Lucius and Lucius.

Nannestad, P., and M. Paldam. 1994. The VP-function: a survey of the literature on vote and popularity functions after 25 years. Public Choice 79, no. 3–4: 213–45.

Roth, F. 2009a. The effects of the financial crisis on systemic trust. *Intereconomics* 44, no. 4: 203–08.

Roth, F. 2009b. Does too much trust hamper economic growth? *Kyklos* 62, no. 1: 103–28.

Roth, F., L. Jonung, and F. Nowak-Lehmann. 2012. *Public support for the single European currency, the Euro, 1990 to 2011. Does the financial crisis matter?* Working Paper 2012: 20. Lund: Department of Economics, University of Lund.

Roth, F., F. Nowak-Lehmann D., and T. Otter. 2013. *Crisis and trust in national and European Union institutions — panel evidence for the EU, 1999 to 2012*. EUDO/RSCAS Working Paper Series 2013/31. Florence: European University Institute.

Sapienza, P., and L. Zingales. 2012. A trust crisis. *International Review of Finance* 12, no. 2: 123–31.

Stevenson, B., and J. Wolfers. 2011. Trust in public institutions over the business cycle. *American Economic Review* 101, no. 3: 281–87.

Stiglitz, J. 2009. *Freefall-free markets and the sinking of the global economy*. London: Penguin Books.

Stiglitz, J. 2012. *The price of inequality*. London: Allen Lane.

Stock, J.H., and M.W. Watson. 1993. A simple estimator of cointegrating vectors in higher order integrated systems. *Econometrica* 61, no. 4: 783–820.

TFEU. 2010. *Consolidated version of the treaty on the functioning of the European Union*, http://eur-lex.europa.eu/LexUriServ/LexUriServ.do?uri=OJ:C:2010:083:0047:0200:en:PDF.

Tonkiss, F. 2009. Trust, confidence and economic crisis. *Intereconomics* 44, no. 4: 196–202.

Torres, F. 2013. The EMU's legitimacy and the ECB as a strategic political player in the crisis context. *Journal of European Integration* 35, no. 3: 287–300.

Tosun, J., A. Wetzel, and G. Zapryanova. 2014. The EU in crisis: advancing the debate. *Journal of European Integration*, forthcoming.

Wälti, S. 2012. Trust no more? The impact of the crisis on citizens' trust in central banks. *Journal of International Money and Finance* 31, no. 3: 593–605.

Wenkel, R. 2008. *10 Jahre Europäische Zentralbank — eine Erfolgsgschichte* [10 Years of European central banking – A success story], http://www.dw.de/zehn-jahre-europäische-zentralbank-eine-erfolgsgeschichte/a-3362376.

Wooldridge, J.M. 2009. *Introductory econometrics: a modern approach*. Mason, OH: South-Western Cengage Learning.

Appendix

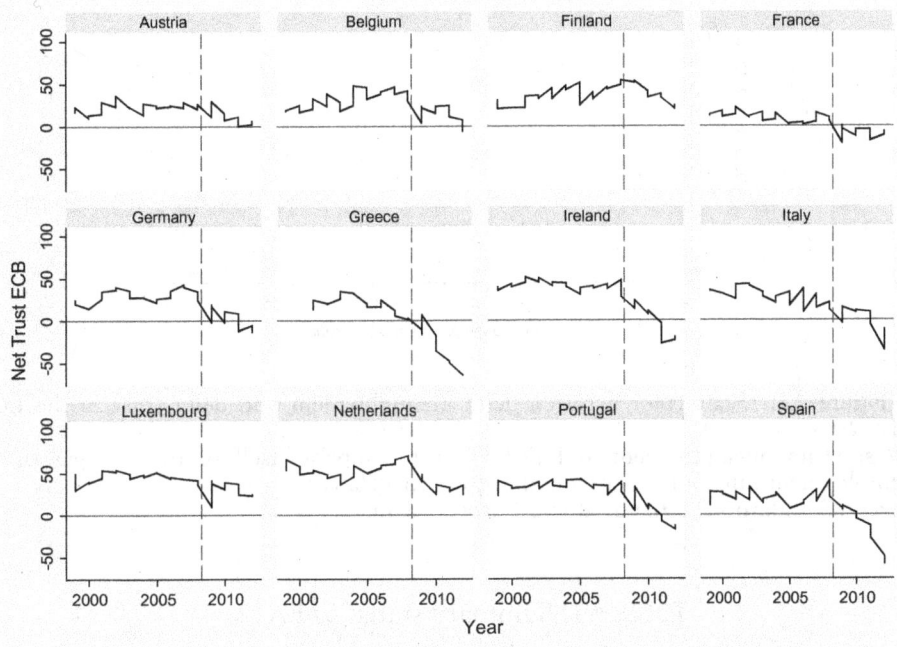

Figure A1. Net trust in the ECB by EA12 countries, 1999–2012.
Notes: For Greece, the time trend is displayed from 2001 onwards. As the figure depicts net values, all values below 0 indicate that a majority of respondents mistrust. The dotted line represents the incidence of the bankruptcy of Lehman Brothers in September 2008.
Sources: Standard EBs 51-78 and Special EB 71.1.

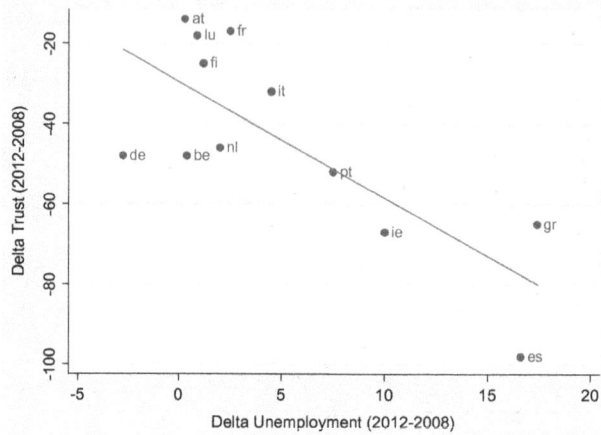

Figure A2. Scatterplot between delta unemployment and delta trust in the ECB, 2012–2008.
Notes: Delta unemployment and Delta Trust comprise itself of the changes of the unemployment rate and Trust from 3-5/2008 to 11/2012.
Sources: Standard EB 69 and 78 and Eurostat data.

Table A1. Summary statistics EA12

Variable	Obs.	Time periods	Mean	Std. dev.	Min	Max
Net trust in ECB	344	29	23.3	21.5	−65	70
Unemployment	344	29	7.9	3.7	1.85	25.4
Inflation	344	29	1.10	0.78	−1.27	3.51
Growth of GDP per capita	341	29	0.6	1.5	−6.6	6.4
Sovereign bond yields	344	29	4.5	2	1.4	23.4

Notes: For Greece the trust trend starts from 2001 onwards and growth of GDP per capita is missing from the 2nd quarter of 2011 onwards.

European Integration in the Euro Crisis: The Limits of Postfunctionalism

FRANK SCHIMMELFENNIG

Center for Comparative and International Studies, ETH Zurich, Zurich, Switzerland

ABSTRACT   The Euro crisis presents a puzzle to the post-functionalist approach to European integration. In spite of unprecedented social hardships, politicization, loss of popular support and political turmoil in the Eurozone, the Euro crisis has produced major new steps of technocratic supranational integration. This article shows that integration during the euro crisis can be sufficiently explained by a neofunctionalist account based on path dependency, endogenous preference change and functional spill over. Finally, it explores three mechanisms that have helped to shield EU-level reform from a constraining dissensus: euro-compatible government formation, avoidance of referendums and delegation to technocratic supranational organizations.

Introduction: The Postfunctionalist Moment in European Integration

In a path-breaking article entitled 'A Postfunctionalist Theory of European Integration: From Permissive Consensus to Constraining Dissensus', Hooghe and Marks (2008) make a powerful argument in favour of moving beyond the dominance of IR-based, elite-focused and functionalist theories to explain European integration. In addition, they provide a coherent framework for the burgeoning research on the domestic and mass-level of EU politics—including public opinion, electoral choice and party politics. Hooghe and Marks (2008) claim that neofunctionalism and intergovernmentalism, the dominant theories of European integration, united by a common focus on the functional, efficiency-based rationale for regional integration, economic preferences and bargaining between interest groups, 'have become less useful guides for research on the European Union' (3). Under the current circumstances characterized by politicization engaging mass publics and extending into the domain of domestic politics, European integration has become salient and contested in public opinion and party competition. As European integration has moved into core areas of state sovereignty and national identity and has produced effects reaching deeply into national economic, financial and welfare policies, public opinion has turned more euro-sceptic. This euro-scepticism has been mobilized by euro-sceptic parties as well as an increasing number of referendums. As a result, EU-friendly elites now regularly face a 'constraining dissensus' when making decisions on European integration. As a consequence of politicization, Hooghe and Marks (2008) 'expect to see downward pressure on the level and scope of integration' (21), a limitation of governments' room to manoeuvre (22) and a mismatch of functionally efficient and politically feasible solutions (23).

In this perspective, the Euro crisis constitutes a 'postfunctionalist moment' in the history of European integration. The triple sequence of financial crisis, debt crisis and Eurozone crisis has triggered an unprecedented politicization of European integration (see also Hutter and Kerscher 2014). First, never before has EU policy had such a directly attributable, visible and negative effect on the welfare of member state citizens as in the austerity measures imposed on the highly indebted Eurozone countries as part of the EU/IMF rescue packages. Wages and pensions were cut, taxes increased, public expenditures and investments reduced as part of the rescue conditionality. In Greece, the hardest hit country, pensions and public sector pay are reported to have decreased by 25% and private sector pay by at least 15%, whereas effective tax rates have increased by more than 20% and unemployment reached 26% at the end of 2012 (Monastiriotis 2013). Second, the Euro crisis has triggered unprecedented mass protest against a European policy. Although the austerity measures are formally decided and implemented by national governments, they are required or constrained by international loan conditionality. Protesters therefore regularly target the 'Troika', the EU or the German government in addition to their national governments.

Third, public opinion surveys show a steep plunge in public support for the EU. According to the Pew Research Centre, 'positive views of the European Union are at or near their low point in most EU nations' after having fallen from 60% in 2012 to 45% in 2013.[1] On the basis of Eurobarometer data, Debomy (2013) concurs that 'the highest level of euro gloom ever observed in the last quarter century has been or is close to being reached' (1). Already in 2012, the Pew Research Centre observed that there were no majorities considering the Euro 'a good thing' in any of the surveyed Eurozone countries.[2] In addition, there are indications of a growing transnational divergence in public opinion of the Eurozone. Attitudes towards the EU have soured most dramatically in the southern European countries hit hardest by the crisis, which brought these traditionally Europhile countries to levels of euro-sceptic public opinion formerly reserved for the UK and the Nordics (Debomy 2013, 7–12; see also Clements *et al.* 2014). According to the Pew Research Centre, the 'prolonged economic crisis has created centrifugal forces that are pulling European public opinion apart, separating the French from the Germans and the Germans from everyone else' (see fn. 1).

Finally, the crisis has been a period of high government instability in the Eurozone (see Table 1). Out of 15 elections in the Eurozone during the acute Euro crisis (between the beginning of 2010 and mid-2013), only five have been regular elections (column 4). In 11 out of these 15 elections, the Euro crisis issue was the issue that triggered early elections and dominated the electoral campaign (column 5). At the height of the crisis, between March of 2011 and March of 2013, every single election was predominantly about the response to the crisis. Only 2 out of 15 elections confirmed the incumbent government: in Estonia in March 2011 and in the Netherlands in December 2012 (column 6). In addition, two governments were changed in Greece and Italy without elections as crisis-driven emergency measures in November 2011.

In sum, the financial crisis has produced all ingredients for a 'postfunctionalist moment' in European integration. EU policy has arguably become more domestically salient, controversial and politicized than ever before. Budget controls and austerity measures demanded by the EU have imposed losses on large groups of people in the debtor countries. They have sparked mass protests, a loss in trust and support for the EU, widespread snap elections and changes in government. According to the post-functionalist scenario, we should have observed a strong constraining dissensus leading to decision-making blockades at the EU level, stagnation and even setbacks in integration or an increase in differentiated integration as a consequence.

And yet, the EU has embarked on a far-reaching reconstruction of EMU resulting not only in the preservation of the Eurozone but also in a major leap of supranational and technocratic integration in fiscal and financial policy. How has this been possible? I propose in this article that governments have been able to shield Eurozone integration from the impact of politicization by forming euro-compatible governments, avoiding and constraining referendums on institutional reform and by delegating competences to supranational organizations. In the next two sections of the article, I briefly outline the integration steps taken during the Euro crisis and claim that they can be explained by a neofunctionalist argument without reference to mass-level domestic politics. I then move on to describe and illustrate the shielding mechanisms employed to limit the impact of politicization on Eurozone policy.

Integration Steps in the Euro crisis

The original design of EMU was characterized by an uneven integration of macroeconomic policies. It combined centralized monetary policy with decentralized fiscal policy and negative financial market integration. Monetary policy was supranationally centralized. The Eurozone countries transferred monetary policy completely to the European System of Central

Table 1. Elections and government formation in the Eurozone (2010–13)

Country	Date	Elections	Regular election	Crisis main issue	Change of Govt.	Eurosceptic party gains	Mainstream government
Slovakia	12/06/2010	Parliamentary	Yes	No		No	Yes
Belgium	13/06/2010	Parliamentary		No		No	Yes
Ireland	25/02/2011	Parliamentary				No	Yes
Estonia	06/03/2011	Parliamentary	Yes	No	No	No	Yes
Finland	17/04/2011	Parliamentary	Yes				Yes
Portugal	05/06/2011	Parliamentary				No	Yes
Spain	20/11/2011	Parliamentary				No	Yes
Greece	11/11/2011	None				No	Yes
Italy	12/11/2011	None				No	Yes
Slovenia	04/12/2011	Parliamentary				No	Yes
Slovakia	10/03/2012	Parliamentary				No	Yes
France	22/04/2012	Presidential	Yes			No	Yes
Greece	06/05/2012	Parliamentary					Yes
Netherlands	12/12/2012	Parliamentary			No	No	Yes
Cyprus	24/02/2013	Presidential	Yes			No	Yes
Italy	25/02/2013	Parliamentary					Yes
Malta	09/03/2013	Parliamentary		No		No	Yes
Germany	22/09/2013	Parliamentary	Yes	No	No		Yes
Austria	29/09/2013	Parliamentary	Yes	No	No		Yes
Luxembourg	20/10/2013	Parliamentary		No		No	Yes

Banks with the European Central Bank (ECB) at its head. The ECB is independent both from the member states and the institutions of the EU and has the exclusive competence to decide and implement the monetary policy of the Eurozone.

In contrast, the member states did not create a fiscal or financial union alongside monetary union. The EU has no right to tax and to get into debt. Because the EU budget runs on contributions by the member states limited to around 1% of GDP, the EU's fiscal room of manoeuvre is extremely limited. The EU does not have a fiscal equalization scheme across member states either. According to the no-bailout-clause of Article 125 TFEU, the Union and the member states 'shall not be liable for or assume the commitments' of other member states. Article 123 TFEU further prohibits the ECB from allocating credit to the EU or the member states.

The original design of EMU did, however, introduce regulation and supervision of national fiscal policy based on the 'excessive deficit procedure' (Article 126 TFEU) and the Stability and Growth Pact. The provisions uphold the deficit limits laid down in the convergence criteria for admission to the Eurozone: the ceilings of 3% of GDP for new debt and 60% of GDP for overall sovereign debt. If a state exceeds these ceilings, the Commission initiates a multistage procedure at the end of which the finance ministers of the Euro group may impose sanctions by qualified majority. These rules however were softened in 2005 and sanctions have never been imposed.

In the area of financial market regulation, the focus has been on negative integration based on mutual recognition and home country control. In 1999, the European Commission issued the Financial Services Action Plan (FSAP), which was approved by the member states in 2000. In 2002, the Lamfalussy Process was introduced to accelerate legislation implementing the FSAP. The goal was to complete the internal market of financial services while leaving banking supervision at the national level. Centralization was minimal, limited to the Committee of European Banking Supervisors established in 2004 as an independent advisory body. Its role was slightly strengthened in 2009 but still limited to issuing 'non-binding guidelines, recommendations, and standards' (Article 3 of Commission Decision 2009/78/EC).

The Eurozone reforms agreed and implemented during the crisis have strengthened both fiscal and financial integration. First, the strict no-bailout policy has been replaced with institutions and practices providing highly indebted Eurozone countries with public credit. A first emergency credit to Greece in April 2010 was followed by the European Financial Stability Facility in May 2010, a private company that issued bonds guaranteed by the highly solvent Euro countries and offered the proceeds to indebted countries under the condition of fiscal and financial consolidation measures. The EFSF was superseded in September 2012 by the European Stability Mechanism—a permanent international financing institution with a capital stock from the Eurozone countries and a lending capacity of 500 million Euros.

In addition to these formal steps, the ECB has intervened on several occasions to provide relief to highly indebted countries and banks. In the context of its Securities Markets Programme, the ECB has bought more than 200 billion Euro worth of bonds of highly indebted Euro countries since May 2010. In December 2010, it doubled its capital stock to hedge the risks of its bond-buying operations. In December 2011 and February 2012, it provided banks with long-term cheap credit of more than one trillion Euros, which they could use to buy government bonds as well. In July 2012, ECB President Mario Draghi pledged to "do whatever it takes to preserve the euro", implying that it would provide unlimited liquidity to keep Eurozone government afloat.[3] Under its Outright Monetary Transactions programme, the ECB is ready to buy bonds without limits from countries receiving EFSF or ESM assistance and complying with financial consolidation conditions. Whereas the mandate of the ECB has not been formally revised and the ECB claims to remain within the confines of its statutes, these commitments and measures effectively supersede the no bailout provisions of the treaties.

Second, fiscal regulation and supervision have been strengthened in a series of legislative acts (most notably the 'Six-Pack' of December 2011 and the 'Two-Pack' of March 2013) and in the Treaty on Stability, Coordination and Governance in the EMU (aka the Fiscal Compact). Fiscal surveillance now starts with ex-ante control of national budgets. Member states are obliged to establish a national balanced budget rule and procedure in addition to EU-level rules and monitoring. The ESM and the ECB only assist countries financially that have introduced such a procedure. In case member states exceed the deficit limits, sanctions enter into force faster: fines are paid at the beginning of the procedure and reimbursed in case of compliance. Sanctions are quasi-automatic: they now require a qualified majority of governments to be stopped rather than imposed.

Finally, the EU has taken steps towards a 'banking union'. As a response to the financial crisis, the EU created a European System of Financial Supervisors including the European Banking Authority in 2010 to establish harmonized standards, create a level playing field and—as a last resort—address decisions to national authorities. This was clearly a move from negative to positive integration in banking regulation and supervision (Regulation (EU) 1093/2010 of the European Parliament and the Council), but it still relied on national authorities. In March 2013, however, the Council and the Parliament agreed on the Single Supervisory Mechanism that assigns supervision of 'significant' banks to the ECB. In December 2013, the Council agreed on a Single Resolution Mechanism based on the progressive mutualisation of national bank resolution funds over a ten-year period.

In sum, the Eurozone has reacted to the crisis by introducing unprecedented collective liabilities, significantly reducing state autonomy in budgetary policy, a core area of sovereignty and by centralizing financial market supervision. Even though the creditor countries have not incurred direct losses so far and the new fiscal sanctioning regime has not been applied yet, these reforms constitute a step change in EMU. These reforms have been predominantly technocratic. They have boosted the role of the ECB as a lender of last resort and supervisor of the European financial system; they have strengthened the Commission in fiscal supervision (Bauer *et al.* 2014), and put in place new, predominantly intergovernmental organizations such as the ESM. In the next section, I argue that we can explain this result without recourse to mass-level politics, on the basis of neofunctionalism instead of postfunctionalism.

A Neofunctionalist Explanation of Reforms in the Euro crisis

Contrary to the claim of Hooghe and Marks (2008) that theories based on elite economic preferences, bargains and on efficiency-driven logic of regional integration 'have become less useful guides for research on the European Union' (3). I argue that national economic preferences, intergovernmental bargains as well as functional dynamics go a long way in explaining the processes and outcomes of integration in the Euro crisis.

Neofunctionalist theorizing on European integration has gone through various stages of development and comes in a number of varieties. After Haas's (1968) initial formulation of the theory, a series of reformulations and qualifications (e.g. Lindberg and Scheingold 1970; Schmitter 1970), and Haas's (1976) sceptical assessment of the 'obsolescence of integration theory', neofunctionalism re-emerged in the 1990s under the heading of 'supranationalism' together with the dynamic growth in European integration following the internal market programme and the Treaty of Maastricht (e.g. Sweet and Sandholtz 1997). What unites the different versions of neofunctionalism is the idea of a dynamic and progressive integration process that transcends its intergovernmental origins as a result of endogenous interdependencies, spillovers and path-dependencies.

I base my analysis on Pierson's (1996) historical-institutionalist model of integration dynamics. Pierson's model starts with an initial institutional and policy outcome based on the constellation of member state preferences, bargaining power and negotiations in an intergovernmental bargaining process. This is in line with Moravcsik's (1998) liberal intergovernmentalist explanation of European integration. Whereas, Moravcsik stops at this point and conceives European integration as a series of intergovernmental bargains each driven by (exogenous) international interdependence and state preferences, Pierson stipulates a two-step process of endogenous change. In the first step, he argues that member states are likely to lose control of the integration processes and institutions they created due to the partial autonomy of supranational organizations, the restricted time horizons of political decision-makers, unanticipated consequences such as overload and spillover resulting from high issue density and unexpected shifts in government preferences. In the second step, member states are unable to reassert control because of supranational actors' resistance, institutional barriers to reform (such as veto powers or high voting thresholds) and prohibitive exit costs.[4] With the possible exemption of shifts in government preferences, this account of a path-dependent integration trajectory relies completely on systemic EU-level conditions and processes.

Preference Constellation

Government preferences in the Euro crisis have been shaped by structural financial and economic positions. The crisis has pitted highly solvent against highly indebted countries. The highly solvent countries have suffered from comparatively moderate sovereign debt, enjoyed the confidence of the financial markets and benefited from low interest rates to service their debts. For these reasons, they were not under strong pressure to engage in painful austerity and financial consolidation measures and did not need external assistance. Conversely, they sought to avoid costly commitments and collective liability schemes to assist the highly indebted countries but pushed for tightly monitored and sanctioned national austerity measures instead. Led by Germany, the coalition of the solvent countries (including Austria, Finland and the Netherlands) has regularly opposed Euro bonds, the expansion of rescue packages and an immediate mutualisation or centralization of bank resolution. They instead demanded automatic sanctions against violators of the excessive deficit rules and strict banking supervision.

By contrast, the highly indebted countries have suffered from high interest rates to service their debts and borrow fresh money, which reflects the weak or lost confidence of the financial market actors in the sustainability of their fiscal position and their ability to repay their debts. Unsurprisingly, these countries have sought external financial assistance and shunned unilateral adaptation. Led by France, the coalition of mainly southern Euro countries was in favour of expanding the rescue funds and of mutualizing government debt in the Eurozone in order to reduce their interest burden. They advocated growth instead of austerity policies as well as direct bank bailouts. Conversely, they opposed automatic sanctions in case of excessive deficits. In sum, government preferences in the Euro crisis have tended to reflect 'national interests' rooted in the structural financial positions of the Eurozone member states. Party positions have only mattered on the margins: changes in the party composition of national governments have not led to changes in substantive preferences or even coalitions.

Incidentally, the preference constellations and coalitions mirror those of the founding period of EMU when traditional hard-currency countries, led by Germany, insisted on EMU to be governed by an independent central bank committed to price stability, whereas traditional soft-currency countries led by France would have preferred intergovernmental macroeconomic governance oriented towards growth. At that time, the constellation of bargaining power favoured Germany because German preferences were closer to the status quo—the existing European Monetary System was dominated by the Bundesbank—and the German government was more constrained domestically because of widespread scepticism toward a single currency. If France wanted supranational monetary integration, they had to accept the German terms.

In the Euro crisis the bargaining situation had changed because of a common and preeminent preference of all actors in favour of the preservation of the Euro and the Eurozone. No Eurozone country has officially questioned the existence of the Euro or its membership in the Eurozone. Chancellor Merkel has repeatedly declared the Euro to be the indispensable core of European integration: 'Europe fails if the euro fails'.[5] She has further vowed to do everything to defend the Euro.[6] Meeting in Paris in July 2012, French President Hollande and Italian Prime Minister Monti also expressed 'their will to do everything ... to defend, preserve, and consolidate the Eurozone'.[7] Finally, all bailout countries have emphasized their preference to keep the Euro.

This common interest of the Eurozone countries is a new and endogenous preference or a preference that has formed as a result of integration and internalized integration into the 'national interest'. In Pierson's terms, the Euro crisis was a 'heavily discounted or unintended effect'. Although there was widespread scepticism among economists and in Germany about the viability of the Eurozone, most member states were eager to adopt the Euro in order to enhance their financial standing and reduce their borrowing costs. Counterfactually speaking however, it is doubtful that the member states would have introduced the single currency in 1999 had they known the situation they would face in 2010. In 2010 returning to the status quo ante was not an efficient option any more. First, the Euro contains considerable 'sunk costs' for states, firms and citizens resulting from introducing a new currency and adapting to a new monetary regime. Second, monetary union strengthened transnational capital movement and interlocking among financial services in the Eurozone. Monetary union thus created additional endogenous interdependence, which increases the incentives to preserve the Eurozone. Third, the institutional hurdles are high: there's no orderly exit procedure for the Eurozone unless a country leaves the EU altogether. Finally and most importantly, all members of the Eurozone were highly uncertain and risk-sensitive about a breakup of the Eurozone. Even the exit of a relatively small economy such as Greece or Cyprus was excluded because of potential contagion effects in the larger southern member states Spain and Italy, which were considered too big to rescue. For an export-oriented economy—such as Germany's—leaving the Eurozone would have entailed the appreciation of the national currency, an export slump and a long and deep recession.[8] And these considerations do not even include the political repercussions for Germany and Europe of the failure of the core integration project of the EU. On balance, then, the common interest of preserving the Euro and the Eurozone was paramount to the different preferences of highly solvent and highly indebted member states. And the costs of preserving and fixing the Eurozone were preferable to the risks of shrinking or even dissolving it. This common interest changed the structure of intergovernmental bargaining and bargaining power.

Bargaining Constellation

The combination of a pre-eminent common interest with secondary opposed interests turns negotiations on Eurozone reform into a 'game of chicken'. In the original game, two drivers race their cars towards each other; whoever swerves first is the 'chicken' and loses. 'Chicken' is a mixed-motives game. Both drivers have a predominant interest to avoid the crash. At the same time, they prefer the other to swerve. Applied to the Euro crisis, no member state wants the Eurozone to break up. But the highly solvent countries prefer the highly indebted countries to pay the price by unilateral financial consolidation, and the highly indebted countries prefer the highly solvent countries to foot the bill and bail them out.

A game of chicken rewards brinkmanship. To win the game, each side must send signals of resolve. Yet, because both sides know that rational players swerve in the end, it pays off to create the impression of irrationality or inability to give in. If the costs of crash are extremely high, then the expectation is for last-minute cooperation or cooperation under pressure. Highly solvent countries and highly indebted countries are not in a completely symmetrical situation. The highly solvent countries are in a better position to survive a crash and can thus afford to demonstrate resolve in principle. The highly indebted countries may, however, not be able to avoid bankruptcy unless assisted, and the fear of contagion provides even small debtor countries with a bargaining chip. At the end of the day, both groups 'swerved': the creditors agreed to bail out the debtors, and the debtors agreed to the strengthening of centralized fiscal and financial market supervision. This linkage is now institutionalized: ESM and ECB assistance is dependent on implementation of the Fiscal Compact.

The rescue measures also demonstrate that even the most powerful country, Germany, was constrained in the modified bargaining situation. First, Germany has been under strong pressure to assist because no other member state could take its place as saviour of the Eurozone. Second, Germany accepted a time-inconsistent deal. Whereas the creditors had to commit to their bailout immediately, it is still unclear whether the stronger monitoring and sanctioning powers will work better than the old Stability and Growth Pact. Third, Germany has been institutionally constrained by the one state one vote rule and majority voting in the ECB Council, which has allowed the other EU countries to outvote the German representatives on several occasions.

The course of the Euro crisis offers rich evidence for a repeated game of chicken. Time and again, the German government has first blocked and then agreed to increasing assistance at the last minute when the situation was critical and recipient governments accepted stronger monitoring and sanctioning. In March 2010, Chancellor Merkel first threatened to exclude Greece as the 'ultima ratio' and postponed financial assistance; then Germany agreed to loans to Greece as the 'ultima ratio' to stabilize the Euro.[9] In 2011 and 2012, the German government has repeatedly put the brake on the expansion of the EFSF or the ESM—only to agree to additional commitments when the crisis intensified. In January 2013, it gave up its resistance against a rescue package for Cyprus. On their part, the debt countries have constantly tried to circumvent supranational monitoring and conditionality. In 2012, for example, the Spanish government delayed a formal request for EFSF funds for several weeks and tried to involve its banks directly rather than via the state budget. Cyprus first tried to obtain Russian credit to avoid the EFSF conditionality; then it tried to spare its financial industry from the rescue conditionality. In the end, Cyprus had to accept harsh bailout conditions in order to avoid insolvency threatened by the ECB.

In line with the neofunctionalist model elaborated by Pierson, the preservation and deepening of the Eurozone has been an outcome of path dependency and functional spillover from a centralized monetary policy to a formerly decentralized fiscal and financial market policy. Renationalizing monetary policy as a reaction to the inefficiencies of EMU was considered too risky and costly, therefore the member states decided to consolidate EMU through an institutionalized bailout regime, a more centralized fiscal policy and more centralized financial market supervision. Path dependencies resulted in an endogenous common preference to preserve and reform the Eurozone. The supranational ECB used its competencies to elaborate and modify the rules of the Eurozone informally. And both preference change and supranational power changed the bargaining situation. The result was a level of integration in fiscal and financial policy that the Eurozone countries had opposed ahead of the crisis.

In sum, the integration outcome of the Euro crisis can be explained on the basis of efficiency problems, state interests modified as a result of international and transnational interdependence, and intergovernmental bargaining in a supranational context. This neofunctionalist account provides a sufficient explanation of integration in the Euro crisis; it is neither dependent on nor confounded by postfunctionalist domestic or mass-level conditions. Whereas there has certainly been a "constraining dissensus" at the level of Eurozone governments about the best policy to save the Euro and about its distributional implications, this dissensus can be explained on the basis of structural national interests.

Shielding Integration: How Governments Contain the 'Constraining Dissensus'

The Euro crisis has featured both major politicization and major steps of technocratic reform. Even though the Euro crisis has made EU policy highly salient, spurred anti-EU protest, significantly reduced public support and trust in the EU, and caused government instability, the Euro countries have agreed on considerable financial commitments and competence transfers to preserve and consolidate the Eurozone. Why has politicization not effectively constrained technocratic integration? I will first discuss two possible counter-arguments that could be raised against the diagnosis of a 'postfunctionalist moment'. My main point will be, however, that governments have learned to contain the constraining dissensus by isolating crisis management from politicization.

The first counter-argument might be that politicization need not be detrimental to European integration but could actually work in its favour (see already Schmitter 1969). It is conceivable that highly valued and salient European policies mobilize citizens and voters to support the EU in a crisis that threatens such policies and benefits. Recent opinion polls show an interesting discrepancy in respondents' views on the EU and on the Euro. Whereas support for and trust in the EU have taken a steep plunge—especially in the hardly hit southern European Euro countries, approval of the single currency has been much less negatively affected. Importantly, whereas support has declined in member states that have not introduced the Euro, the Euro enjoys a stable two-thirds majority of support in the Eurozone countries (Debomy 2013, 20–1). There are no majorities within EU member states wishing to reintroduce national currencies (see fn. 2). Governments determined to preserve the Euro can therefore operate on the basis of widespread support of their citizens. This does not mean that voters have been satisfied with the specific policies implemented to save the Euro and to reduce public debt, or that they have given their support to those politicians that stand most clearly for financial and fiscal consolidation. Wanting to preserve the Euro does not necessarily go together with readily accepting wage and transfer cuts or higher taxation and social security contributions. In the highly indebted countries, voters have regularly ousted incumbent governments—including those governments and parties that had been most strongly committed to the Euro and EU crisis policies: e.g. *Fianna Fáil* in Ireland, President Sarkozy in France, the Monti government in Italy, or PASOK in Greece.

The second counter-argument could be that politicization needs to be exploited by euro-sceptic parties to make a political impact (de Vries 2007; Kriesi 2007). In addition, euro-sceptic parties need to join government or prevent mainstream parties forming a majority government to be able to constrain policy considerably. As Table 1 shows, euro-sceptic parties have not made great inroads in the Eurozone during the crisis. Only in two countries, Finland (True Finns) and Greece (*Syriza*, *Chrysi Avgi*), openly euro-sceptic parties have gained significantly in the elections. The True Finns won 19% of the vote, up from 4% in 2007. On the extreme left in Greece, *Syriza* won more than 16% in May and more than 26% of the vote in the June 2011 elections, up from below 5% in 2009. On the extreme right, *Chrysi Avgi* moved from almost no votes to 7%. Thus, even though there has not been a surge in euro-sceptic parties in the Eurozone, their rise in Finland and Greece had the potential of disrupting the rescue of the Eurozone in a creditor country and in the most affected debtor country. In Italy, both *Cinque Stelle* and Berlusconi's *Popolo della Libertá* have campaigned on a populist, anti-EU platform and won more than 40% of the popular vote together in 2013 but neither can be clearly classified as ideologically euro-sceptic.

To summarize, whereas Euro crisis politicization did not result either in a general mood to abandon the Euro or in a region wide rise of anti-EU parties, voters have been unhappy enough with the rescue and austerity packages to punish mainstream parties, strengthen sceptical parties and potentially disrupt Eurozone reform in a large number of member states. To reduce the impact of politicization, Eurozone governments have therefore used three instruments targeted at different gateways of politicization: euro-compatible coalition formation, avoidance of referendums and supranational delegation. They address the three ways in which intergovernmental policy-making can be constrained domestically: through elections, referendums and parliamentary ratification.

First, Eurozone rescue and reform policies may be disrupted by governments that include parties opposed to such policies. The formation of Euro-compatible government coalitions ensures that such parties are kept out of EU-level negotiations and facilitates parliamentary approval at home. Second, member state referendums on treaty ratifications have proven to be a major potential obstacle to institutional reforms in the EU. Governments therefore seek to arrange institutional reform in a way that reduces the likelihood that referendums will be held or disrupt the reform process. Finally, supranational delegation removes policies and decisions effectively from the purview of domestic politics. In the remainder of this section, I provide examples illustrating how these instruments have been used during the Euro crisis.

Euro-compatible Government Formation

At a time when the Euro crisis was at the top of the policy agenda, or when the liquidity of the state depended on international financial assistance, governments were formed in a way that ensured smooth cooperation with the European partners and compliance with financial assistance conditionality. Indeed, as Table 1 shows, all governments formed during the crisis after elections or changes in government without elections, have been mainstream governments, i.e. governments composed of parties supporting the Euro and further European integration. The Euro crisis period has been characterized by high government instability—elections have mostly been snap elections and incumbents have generally been voted out of office. Yet the new governments formed as a result were supportive of Eurozone cooperation and deepening. This process has mitigated the effect of domestic politicization, even where popular dissatisfaction with the crisis policies has made euro-sceptic parties the big winners of elections.

For instance, the True Finns left coalition talks when it became clear that its partners would remain supportive of the EU's bailout policy. In Greece, the mainstream parties formed a coalition supporting the bailout and consolidation arrangements with the Troika against the big winner of the elections, *Syriza*. In the Netherlands, the election result of December 2012 permitted the coalition of Prime Minister Rutte to form a majority government without the further support of the euro-sceptic PVV, whose opposition to austerity measures had caused the former minority government to call an election.

Avoiding Referendums

Aside from elections and government formation, domestic parliamentary votes and referendums are the other conventional form in which politicization is translated into policy constraints at the European level. Major reforms of EU policies and steps in European integration require treaty revisions, and treaty revisions require ratification in all member states, either by parliamentary vote or by referendum. Since the 1990s, referendums on treaty revisions have been a major venue for euro-sceptic mobilization and mass-level constraints on European integration. They have produced opt-outs (as in Denmark, from EMU), delays in treaty ratification (Irish voters temporarily blocked the entry into force of the Treaties of Nice and Lisbon) and outright treaty failure (as the negative referendums on the constitutional treaty in the Netherlands and France). Avoiding referendums (or limiting their impact) has therefore been the second instrument of shielding the rescue and reform of the Eurozone from constraints of mass-level dissensus.

In a rather dramatic way, this could be seen when Greek socialist Prime Minister Papandreou announced his plan to hold a referendum on the 2011 bailout package for Greece. Intended as a move to circumvent the blockage of the bailout plan by the opposition, the referendum would have prolonged and increased uncertainty about the financial situation of Greece, its membership in the Eurozone, and about the future of the Euro. Papandreou was therefore put under strong pressure by the other EU governments to call off the referendum and pave the way for a grand coalition with the main opposition party New Democracy. His European partners threatened him with Greece's exit from the euro zone and cutting financial assistance: 'French President Nicolas Sarkozy and German Chancellor Angela Merkel warned him that Athens would not receive a cent more in aid until it met its commitments to the euro zone'.[10] As a result, Papandreou stepped down and an interim coalition government of Socialists and Conservatives approved the bailout package.

In general, governments have designed treaty revisions or new treaties in a way that minimizes the need to hold referendums or the negative consequences of failed ratification. Normally, new treaties or treaty revisions require the unanimous ratification of all participating countries. Each country thus has a veto. For the new intergovernmental treaties agreed during the Euro crisis, this practice was fundamentally changed. Neither the ESM Treaty nor the Fiscal Compact required ratification by all 17 Eurozone countries to enter into force. The Fiscal Compact required ratification by 12 member states only, and the ESM Treaty could enter into force with 90% of the ESM's capital stock. This would already have been the case if the eight largest Eurozone countries had ratified the Treaty. As a consequence, one or a few small member states could not block further integration. In addition, ESM assistance was made conditional on prior implementation of the Fiscal Compact.

Furthermore, the Eurozone governments have generally been reluctant to use the occasion of the Euro crisis to embark upon a major revision of the treaties. This can be seen in the procedure to establish the ESM which was in part designed to minimize the likelihood of ratification by referendum by keeping a low profile and avoiding a formal increase in supranational competence. First, the ESM was established by an intergovernmental treaty rather than an upgrade of EMU. Second, when anchoring it to the EU's treaty framework, the member state governments used the 'simplified revision procedure' (Article 48(6) TEU) for the first time. This procedure allows for revisions of the policy-related provisions of the TFEU by the European Council without an intergovernmental conference provided that a treaty change does not increase the competence of the Union.

Although it is difficult to make a causal inference, these moves have worked: Ireland was the only Eurozone country to hold a referendum on the Fiscal Compact. And for the first time since the Treaty of Amsterdam, the Irish voters approved a European treaty in the first round. Ireland did not hold a referendum on the ESM Treaty.

Supranational Delegation

Delegation to non-majoritarian technocratic supranational organizations is the third major instrument to shield European policies from the fallout of domestic politicization. According to theories of integration in a functionalist tradition, credible commitments to international cooperation shielded from political pressures and incentives for defection are the major reason for governments to agree to supranational integration (Moravcsik 1998). By transferring competences to supranational organizations, governments effectively tie their own hands and remove decisions from the domestic arena. Intergovernmentalism and neofunctionalism only differ on the question whether supranational delegation increases the net power of governments and remains in the confines they determine, or they create supranational autonomy that supranational organizations then use actively to expand their competences and scope.

During the Euro crisis, governments have either delegated new tasks to the ECB (in banking supervision) or accepted the informal expansion of the ECB's mandates. Financial assistance via the rescue funds required intergovernmental agreement between countries with different preferences and approval by sceptical parliaments on the part of the creditors as well as the debtors. The alternative, i.e. bond-buying operations and the provision of cheap liquidity by the ECB, only required a majority in the ECB Council without any involvement of domestic political actors. The highly indebted countries have therefore demanded that the ECB play a pro-active role. Even the German government did not object to the ECB's crisis intervention programs. Although it contradicted its macroeconomic principles, the monetary goals Germany had anchored in the Treaty and the position of Germany's highest officials in the ECB (who were outvoted on the occasion). This is because the German government had been obliged by the Federal Constitutional Court to ask the Bundestag for permission for each financial commitment to the rescue funds. In addition, there has been a vociferous minority in the party groups of the coalition in the Bundestag that rejected the rescue programs. The government was therefore uncertain about being able to mobilize its own majority without the help of the Social Democrat and Green opposition parties.

To conclude, governments have been able to shield their crisis policy and deepening of Eurozone integration, first by excluding euro-sceptic parties from government, second by designing new treaties and the treaty-making procedure so that the threat of referendums and ratification failure was minimized, and third by further empowering supranational organizations or agreeing to the informal expansion of their mandate. In the Euro crisis, when the survival of the Eurozone was at stake, governments have been able to circumvent the constraining dissensus produced by the 'postfunctionalist moment' in the history of European integration.

Conclusions

In this article, I have analysed the Euro crisis to probe into the limits of postfunctionalism. My argument does not contradict the basic assumption of postfunctionalism: European integration is becoming more politicized. Indeed, politicization has been peaking during the Euro crisis and put the EU under severe stress. But politicization has not decisively affected the integration outcomes on this most likely occasion. The process of technocratic integration during the crisis has largely followed neofunctionalist instead of postfunctionalist expectations, and governments have proven capable of limiting the impact of politicization by isolating policy-making at the European level from the constraining dissensus through Euro-compatible government formation, avoiding or taming referendums, and supranational delegation.

To be sure, Hooghe and Marks (2008) anticipated that political leaders would respond to the challenge and that politicization would stimulate institutional reform, including the suppression of controversial referendums and 'shifting decisions to non-majoritarian regulatory agencies' (22). However, if governments are able to respond as effectively as under the conditions of extreme politicization at the height of the Euro crisis and if integration dynamics still follow the neofunctionalist model when the constraining dissensus should be paramount, then there is reason to question the explanatory relevance of postfunctionalism as a theory of integration. Put differently, whereas explanations of European integration need to take into account mass-level domestic politics in the member states, the constraining dissensus appears to shape integration *outcomes* to a lesser extent than it shapes the integration *strategies* of elites and the integration *process* that leads to the outcomes. In this way, member state governments were able to turn a potential obstacle to integration into an opportunity (Tosun *et al*. 2014).

The big caveat is that the Euro crisis may either reappear or that it may have set in motion processes that will continue to have an impact once the crisis over. Even though the financial crisis of the Eurozone has calmed, debt, recession and mass unemployment in the highly indebted countries remain. This may lead to a further decline in support for the EU—and the Euro as well. People may turn in greater numbers to euro-sceptic parties so that government formation without such parties will become more difficult. Moreover, governments may have been willing to protect EU-level policy and institutional reform under the immediate impact of the crisis—often accepting severe losses in electoral support. They may be less willing to do so once the biggest threat has passed.

Notes

1. http://www.pewglobal.org/2013/05/13/the-new-sick-man-of-europe-the-european-union/.
2. http://www.pewglobal.org/2012/05/29/european-unity-on-the-rocks/.
3. http://www.ecb.int/press/key/date/2012/html/sp120726.en.html.
4. See also Author; Yiangou, O'Keefe, and Glöckler (2013). For a different historical-institutionalist account focusing on how initial responses to the crisis shaped subsequent institutional choices, see Gocaj and Meunier (2013).
5. Government declaration, 27 February 2012 (http://www.tagesschau.de/wirtschaft/bundestaggriechenland108.html).
6. http://www.angela-merkel.de/page/103_686.htm.
7. http://www.lemonde.fr/economie/article/2012/07/31/hollande-et-monti-determines-a-tout-faire-pour-consolider-la-zone-euro_1740722_3234.html.
8. Compare e.g. the scenarios in Straubhaar (2011, 30–1) and *The Economist*, 26 May 2012, 26–7.
9. See http://www.euractiv.com/priorities/merkel-wants-scope-expel-eurozon-news-354178; http://www.euractiv.com/euro-finance/german-consent-helping-greece-st-news-375148.
10. http://www.reuters.com/article/2011/11/03/us-g-idUSTRE7A20E920111103.

References

Debomy, D. 2013. *EU no, Euro yes? European public opinions facing the crisis (2007–2012)*. Paris: Notre Europe.

de Vries, C. 2007. Sleeping giant: fact or fairytale? How European integration affects national elections. *European Union Politics* 8, no. 3: 363–385.

Gocaj, L., and S. Meunier. 2013. Time will tell: the EFSF, the ESM, and the Euro crisis. *Journal of European Integration* 35, no. 3: 239–53.

Haas, E.B. 1968. *The uniting of Europe: political, social and economic forces, 1950–57*. Stanford: Stanford University Press.

Haas, E.B. 1976. Turbulent fields and the theory of regional integration. *International Organization* 30, no. 2: 173–212.

Hooghe, L., and G. Marks. 2008. A postfunctionalist theory of European integration: from permissive consensus to constraining dissensus. *British Journal of Political Science* 39, no. 1: 1–23.

Kriesi, H. 2007. The role of European integration in national election campaigns. *European Union Politics* 8, no. 1: 83–108.

Lindberg, L.N., and S.A. Scheingold. 1970. *Europe's would-be polity. Patterns of change in the European community*. Englewood Cliffs, NJ: Prentice-Hall.

Monastiriotis, V. 2013. Austerity measures in crisis countries — results and impact on mid-term development. *Intereconomics* 48, no. 1: 4–32.

Moravcsik, A. 1998. *The choice for Europe. Social purpose and state power from Messina to Maastricht*. Ithaca, NY: Cornell University Press.

Pierson, P. 1996. The path to European integration: a historical institutionalist analysis. *Comparative Political Studies* 29, no. 2: 123–63.

Schmitter, P.C. 1969. Three neo-functional hypotheses about international integration. *International Organization* 23, no. 1: 161–6.

Schmitter, P.C. 1970. A revised theory of regional integration. *International Organization* 24, no. 4: 836–68.

Straubhaar, T. 2011. Drei Euro-Zukunftsszenarien [Three future scenarios for the euro]. *Die Volkswirtschaft* 11: 30–33.

Sweet, A., and W. Sandholtz. 1997. European Integration and Supranational Governance. *Journal of European Public Policy* 4, no. 3: 297–317.

Yiangou, J., M. O'keefe, and G. Glöckler. 2013. 'Tough Love': How the ECB's monetary financing prohibition pushes deeper euro area integration. *Journal of European Integration* 35, no. 3: 223–37.

Index

accountability 11
Acharya, V. 110
advocacy coalition framework 6
Africa 95
age: public opinion in Greece 55, 64, 67
Anderson, C.J. 38, 39, 40, 41, 63, 64, 68
Anderson, J.E. 21
Apostolides, A. 4
apparel sector 96, 99
Aquascutum 96
Armingeon, K. 2, 11, 39, 41, 43, 44, 48
arms embargo 104
Asia 95
Australia 95
Austria 81, 102, 113, 115, 133; citizens' support for EU: impact of Euro crisis 43

Balance of Payments (BoP) assistance 22–3
Baldwin, R. 3
Banducci, S. 111
banks 3, 4, 8, 98, 134, 136; central *see separate entry*; Chinese 96, 102; financial sector supervision 29–31, 131, 132, 133, 135–6, 141
Bauer, M.W. 32, 38, 132
Baumgartner, F.R. 6
Bechtel, M. 2, 4, 11
Belgium 93, 102, 113
Bellamy, R. 11
Bellucci, P. 112
Berlusconi, Silvio 138
bilateral investment treaties (BITs) 92, 105
Birkland, T.A. 6
Boomgaarden, H.G. 41, 49
Bornschier, S. 77
Borsodchem 99
Börzel, T.A. 22
Bosch, A. 40
brands 96
Braun, D. 69
Brautigam, D. 95
Bright Foods 97, 99–100

budgets: deficits 2, 3, 21, 54, 134; of EU 21, 23, 130; monitoring of national 9–10, 21, 27, 129, 131–2
Bulgaria 43
Burgoon, B. 90, 95
Bursian, D. 118
Buti, M. 9, 10, 40

Cameron, David 101
Canada 95
capital markets: Commission 23
Capoccia, G. 6
Carey, S. 38
Castles, F.G. 38
central banks 110, 129–30; European Central Bank (ECB) *see separate entry*
Central and Eastern European countries 102
China: foreign direct investment into Europe *see separate entry*; sovereign wealth fund 101
China Three Gorges Corporation 97, 100
Chinese Investment Corporation 101
citizens' support for EU: impact of Euro crisis 37–8; conclusions and implications 47–9; data and methods 41–2; empirical analysis 43–7; theory and hypotheses 39–41; *see also* public opinion in Greece
citizens' trust in European Central Bank 1999–2012 11, 13, 14, 109–10, 120, 125–6; descriptive statistics 113–15; discussion of results 118–19; econometric analysis 115–18; independence, importance of 111, 119, 120; measurement of data 112; model specification 112–13; research design 113; theoretical links 110–12
citizenship and residency rules 104
Clements, B. 38, 43, 119, 129
Clift, B. 75, 80, 86
Commission *see* European Commission
Committee of European Banking Supervisors 131
competition, regulatory 105, 106–7

INDEX

constraining dissensus 6, 32, 69, 74, 127, 128, 129, 141–2; shielding integration: how governments contain 137–41
Copeland, P. 20
cost-benefit calculus 7
Costa Lobo, M. 54
Council of the EU 9, 12, 23, 29, 30, 132
Court of Justice of EU 27, 28
Crum, B. 4
cue model of public opinion 7, 48, 63, 64, 67, 68
cultural identity 106
Cyprus 4, 104, 135, 136; citizens' support for EU: impact of Euro crisis 43, 44
Czech Republic 27, 102; citizens' support for EU: impact of Euro crisis 43

De Grauwe, P. 110, 111, 114, 119
de la Porte, C. 29
De Ville, F. 7–8
de Vreese, C.H. 63–4
de Vries, C. 138
De Wilde, P. 10, 73, 75, 76
Debomy, D. 128, 129, 137
democracy 2, 10–12, 14
Denmark 102, 139
Dinan, D. 8
dissensus, constraining 6, 32, 69, 74, 127, 128, 129, 141–2; shielding integration: how governments contain 137–41
Down, I. 38
Draghi, Mario 4, 131
Drake, H. 75, 80, 86
Duisenberg, Wim 111

Easton, D. 41
economic factors and public opinion 7, 13, 63–4, 68; citizens' support for EU: impact of Euro crisis see separate entry
economic and financial crisis: main characteristics and conceptual clarifications 2–5
economic governance and the Commission 9, 12, 14, 19–21, 31–3; analysing the multifunctional Commission 21–2; coordination of national policies 28–9, 31, 32; economic policy surveillance 25–8, 31, 32; financial stability support 22–5, 31, 32; supervision of financial sector 29–31, 132
economic growth 3, 12, 91, 111, 115–16, 119, 120
economically-based opposition from far left 75, 79
Ehrmann, M. 110, 118, 119
Eichenberg, R.C. 38, 40
Eichler, S. 4
Eijfinger, S. 111, 119

elderly 55
elections 2, 127, 129, 137, 138, 139, 142; politicization of Europe in France 1974–2012 see separate entry
Enderlein, H. 4
Energias de Portugal 97, 100
enlargement and foreign policy 8
Estonia 102, 129
Euro bonds 133
Euro Plus Pact 28–9
Europe 2020 28–9
European Central Bank (ECB) 2, 3, 4, 9, 14, 24, 26, 27, 68, 98; bond buying 131, 141; citizens' trust in European Central Bank 1999–2012 see separate entry; Cyprus 136; Fiscal Compact 131–2, 136; Greece 3, 24, 55, 68; independence 111, 119, 120, 130; lender of last resort 111, 132; majority voting on Council of 136, 141; monetary policy 130; national balanced budget rule and procedure 132; Outright Monetary Transactions programme 131; Securities Markets Programme 131; Single Supervisory Mechanism (SSM) 30, 132; supranational delegation and 'constraining dissensus' 141
European Commission 8, 9, 12, 14, 19–21, 31–3, 96; 1999 Financial Services Action Plan (FSAP) 131; agenda-setting role 9, 20, 21, 31, 33; analysing the multifunctional 21–2; bilateral investment treaty with China 105; coordination of national policies 28–9, 31, 32; economic policy surveillance 25–8, 31, 32; financial stability support 22–5, 31, 32; Greece 3, 24, 55; monitoring compliance with EU law 23, 24, 25; policy cycle approach 21–2; supervision of financial sector 29–31, 132
European Council 3, 8, 20, 25, 29, 98, 140; President of 2
European Financial Stability Facility (EFSF) 24, 25, 44, 131, 136
European Financial Stabilization Mechanism (EFSM) 23, 24
European Neighborhood Policy 8
European Parliament 9, 20, 24, 30, 132
European Stability Mechanism (ESM) 24–5, 32, 85, 131, 132, 136, 140
European System of Financial Supervision (ESFS) 29–30, 132
European Systemic Risk Board 9, 30
Eurostat 29
Excessive Deficit Procedure 26, 27–8, 130–1, 133
exit costs 133
exogenous shocks and integration: theoretical expectations 5; integration

INDEX

theories 5–6; theories of policy and institutional change 6, 105; theories of public opinion change 6–7

Fabbrini, S. 20
Farfaque, E. 118
Featherstone, K. 9
Fehlker, C. 9
Ferretti 99
Fianna Fáil 137
financial and economic crisis: main characteristics and conceptual clarifications 2–5
financial sector supervision 29–31, 131, 132, 133, 135–6, 141
financial services 131
Finland 102, 113, 115, 133, 138; citizens' support for EU: impact of Euro crisis 43; euro-sceptic parties 138, 139
Fiscal Compact 27–8, 32, 131–2, 136, 140
Fischer, J.A. 112, 118
Fligstein, N. 11
focusing events and integration: theoretical expectations 5; integration theories 5–6; theories of policy and institutional change 6, 105; theories of public opinion change 6–7
foreign direct investment into Europe, Chinese 12, 14, 89–91, 105–7; economic mechanisms: European crisis and 'bargain basement' prices 97–100; EU-level political bargains 105; incentives 102–4; internal Chinese motives for investing in Europe 94–7; investment promotion 101; minority investments 106; national political bargains 104; political mechanisms: European crisis and lessened political resistance 100–5; recent patterns of FDI in Europe 91–4; regulatory competition 105, 106–7
France 26, 29, 69, 113, 129, 137, 139; foreign direct investment 93, 95, 100, 101, 102–4, 106; investment promotion 101; politicization of Europe in France 1974–2012 see separate entry; preference constellation 134; referendum 139; Sino-French investment fund 102
Fratzscher, M. 111, 119

Gabel, M. 39, 40, 49, 54, 63, 68
Gärtner, M. 112
Geely 96
gender: public opinion in Greece 64
General Mills 100
Genschel, P. 10
Germany 10, 11, 13, 26, 75, 81, 87, 113, 128, 129; bargaining constellation 136; Euroscepticism 4; Federal Constitutional Court 141; foreign direct investment 90, 93, 95, 101, 102, 104; investment promotion 101; preference constellation 133, 134, 135
Giavazzi, F. 111, 119
Giddens, A. 110
global economic crisis 1, 3, 38, 39, 44, 47–8, 57; foreign direct investment 92
Gocaj, L. 6
Gómez-Reino, M. 77
Gourevitch, P.A. 74
government bonds 3, 99, 104, 111, 131
Greece 3, 9, 22, 24, 129, 131, 137, 138; bargaining constellation 136; citizens' trust in European Central Bank 1999–2012 113, 115, 117, 118–19; euro-sceptic parties 138, 139; foreign direct investment 99, 101, 102, 104; pensions 128; preference constellation 135; privatization 98, 99, 102; public opinion in see separate entry; referendums, avoiding 139–40; wages 128
Green-Pedersen, C. 74, 75, 76, 80
greenfield investment 92
Gros, D. 11, 110
gross domestic product (GDP) 42, 46–7; citizens' trust in European Central Bank 1999–2012 and growth of 111–13
Grunberg, G. 77
Guinaudeau, I. 76, 77, 78
Guiso, L. 109

Haas, E.B. 132
Haier 96
Hall, P.A. 6
Hallerberg, M. 25, 29
Hanemann, T. 90, 93, 95, 96, 99
Healy, J. 110
hedge funds 8
Helbling, M. 82, 84
Hennessy, A. 30
Hewlett, N. 75, 80, 85, 86
historical institutionalism 6, 10, 133
Hix, S. 38
Hobolt, S.B. 10
Hodson, D. 3, 4, 20, 25
Hollande, François 75, 101, 134
Hong Kong 95
Hooghe, L. 6, 7, 10, 32, 38, 41, 54, 63, 64, 69, 73–4, 75, 76, 77, 127, 128, 132, 142
Howlett, M. 6
Huawei 93, 97
human rights 104
Hungary 3, 22, 23, 97, 102, 104
Hutter, S. 10, 49, 69, 75, 76, 81, 82, 128

Iceland 3
identity-based opposition from far right 75

INDEX

Illing, F. 39
Industrial and Commercial Bank of China 96
inflation 111; citizens' trust in European Central Bank 1999–2012 111–13, 115–16, 119
intellectual property 104
interest rates 133–4
intergovernmentalism 5, 8, 20, 25, 27, 28, 32, 132, 135, 137; European Stability Mechanism (ESM) 140; foreign direct investment 12, 14; macroeconomic governance 134; neofunctionalism and 127–8, 133; supranational delegation 140–1; unanimity 140
International Monetary Fund (IMF) 2, 22, 24, 98, 128; Greece 3, 24, 55
Ireland 3, 4, 23, 24, 55, 68, 137, 140; citizens' support for EU: impact of Euro crisis 43; citizens' trust in European Central Bank 1999–2012 113, 117, 118–19; foreign direct investment 98, 99, 101, 102, 104; investment promotion 101; referendums 139, 140
Italy 93, 99, 102, 113, 129, 137, 138; political parties 138; preference constellation 134, 135

Japan 90
Jones, C.O. 21
Jones, E. 110

Kaltenthaler, K. 110–11, 118, 119
Kassim, H. 20
Khodyakov, D. 110
Kingdon, J.W. 6
Knapp, J. 95
Knill, C. 21
know-how 95
Koenig, T. 75
Kosfeld, M. 111
Krastev, I. 55
Kriesi, H. 74, 76, 78, 79, 80, 138
Kudrna, Z. 8

Laffan, B. 32
Lamfalussy Process 131
Latin America 95
Latvia 22, 102
Laulom, S. 10
Le Pen, Jean-Marie 80–1
legitimacy 10, 111, 119, 120; input 55; output 11, 55
Lehman Brothers 3, 109, 113
Lenovo 96
Lequesne 75, 80, 86
Li Keqiang 104
Lindberg, L.N. 132

Lipsey, R. 91
Lisbon Treaty 9, 84, 105, 111, 139
Llamazares, I. 54
Longo, M. 11
Loveless, M. 39
Luhmann, N. 110
Lütz, S. 24
Luxembourg 24, 113, 115; citizens' support for EU: impact of Euro crisis 43

Maastricht Treaty 3, 77, 133
McLaren, L.M. 38, 39, 41, 54, 63, 64
Macroeconomic Imbalance Procedure 26
Mair, P. 55
Mavris, Y.E. 54
Menz, G. 20
mergers and acquisitions (M&A) 91–2
Merkel, Angela 134, 136, 140
Merler, S. 24
Meunier, S. 4, 105
Monastiriotis, V. 128
Monti, Mario 134, 137
Moravcsik, A. 5, 10, 11, 133, 140
multiple streams framework 6
mutual recognition 131

Nannestad, P. 112
national security 91, 106
neofunctionalism 5, 9, 12, 14, 33, 127–8, 129, 132–3, 136–7, 140–2
neoinstitutionalism 6
Netherlands 102, 113, 115, 129, 133; citizens' support for EU: impact of Euro crisis 43; euro-sceptic PVV 139; referendum 139
New Century Financial Corporation 3
Nice Treaty 139
Nicolaïdis, K. 11

Ondarza, N. v. 20, 29
opt-outs 139
overview of state of research 7; implications for democracy 10–12; implications for institutions and governance 8–10; implications for policies 7–8

Pandya, S. 91
Papandreou, Giorgos 3, 139–40
Parliament, European 9, 20, 24, 30, 132
parliaments, national 138, 141
PASOK 137
Passino, C. 99
path dependency 6, 10, 133, 136
pay 128
pensions 128
Peterson, J. 20
Pierson, P. 133, 134, 136
Poland 102

INDEX

policy subsystem adjustment model 6
politicization of Europe in France 1974–2012 13, 73–5, 85–7; actor expansion 76, 80, 81–2; empirical results 80–5; European Constitution 77, 78, 81, 82; index of politicization 76, 80–1; issue salience 75–6, 80, 81–2, 83, 85, 86, 101; media data and core sentence approach 79–80; multi-dimensional concept of politicization 75–6; paradigmatic case 76–9; polarization 76, 80, 81–2, 83, 85, 86
politicization and how governments contain 'constraining dissensus' 137–8, 141–2; avoiding referendums 139–40; Euro-compatible government formation 138–9; supranational delegation 140–1
portfolio investment 91, 98
Portugal 3, 4, 23, 24, 68; citizens' support for EU: impact of Euro crisis 43, 44; citizens' trust in European Central Bank 1999–2012 113, 117, 118–19; Energias de Portugal 97, 100; foreign direct investment 97, 98, 100, 101, 104; investment promotion 101; privatization 98
postfunctionalism 6, 12, 14, 49, 73, 86, 105, 107, 127–9, 141–2; avoiding referendums 139–40; bargaining constellation 135–7; Euro-compatible government formation 138–9; integration steps in Euro crisis 129–32; limits of 127–42; neofunctionalist explanation of reforms in Euro crisis 132–3; preference constellation 133–5; shielding integration 13, 137–41; supranational delegation 140–1
private equity 8
private sector pay 128
privatization 98, 99
process-tracing approach 5
protectionism 8, 85
public expenditure 2, 128
public opinion 4, 6, 14–15, 74, 127, 128–9, 137; citizens' support for EU: impact of Euro crisis *see separate entry*; investment promotion 101; public opinion in Greece *see separate entry*; theories on change 6–7; *see also* citizens' trust in European Central Bank 1999–2012
public opinion in Greece 13, 43, 44, 53–4, 68–9; EU and Greece: changes in group attitudes, 2003–2007 and 2007–2011 59–62; EU and Greece: changing face of public opinion over time 56–9; EU and Greece: multivariate analysis 62–4; Eurozone crisis and Greece: re-emergence of European integration as a contested issue 54–5; investment promotion 101; results and discussion 64–8

public sector pay 128
Puetter, U. 20

Quaglia, L. 8, 54
qualified majority voting, reverse 25–6, 27–8, 132

Rabinovitch, S. 98
Rattinger, H. 39
Ray, L. 41
referendums 128, 129, 138, 139–40, 141, 142
regional funds 8
regulatory competition 105, 106–7
relational content analysis of newspaper articles *see* politicization of Europe in France 1974–2012
residency and citizenship rules 104
Robert Clergerie 96
Romania 22; citizens' support for EU: impact of Euro crisis 43
Roth, F. 11, 38, 68, 110, 114, 119
Ruiz Jiménez, A.M. 54
Russia 95, 136
Rutte, Mark 139

Sabatier, P.A. 6
Sakoui, A. 101
Salines, M. 9, 10, 20, 32
Samaras, Antonis 101, 102
Sánchez-Cuenca, I. 64, 68
Sapienza, P. 109
Sarkozy, Nicolas 75, 84, 86, 137, 140
Schäfer, A. 38
Scharpf, F.W. 3, 11, 38
Schimmelfennig, F. 5, 20, 28, 32
Schmitter, P.C. 5, 132, 137
Schwarzer, D. 8–9, 10, 14, 20, 25
semester, European 9, 25, 29, 32–3
Serricchio, F. 11, 38, 39, 48, 49, 54, 78
Shambaugh, D. 95
Shambaugh, J.C. 4
Shandong 99
simplified revision procedure 140
Single Resolution Mechanism (SRM) 30, 132
Single Supervisory Mechanism (SSM) 29–30, 132
Slovakia 43
Slovenia 26, 102; citizens' support for EU: impact of Euro crisis 43
social security 137
socio-economic status: public opinion in Greece 64–7
soft law 28–9
solar sector 96
sovereign wealth fund 101
sovereignty, national 4, 27, 28, 55, 128, 132; politicization of Europe in France 75, 77, 79, 84, 85, 86

INDEX

Spain 3, 4, 24, 26, 68; bargaining constellation 136; citizens' support for EU: impact of Euro crisis 43, 44; citizens' trust in European Central Bank 1999–2012 113, 115, 117, 118–19; foreign direct investment 98, 99, 102, 104; preference constellation 135
spillovers 9, 91, 133, 136
Stability and Growth Pact (SGP) 3, 28, 29, 32, 130–1; Six-Pack 9, 25–6, 28, 131–2; Two-Pack 26–7, 131–2
state aid 21, 24
Statham, P. 74, 76, 78, 79
Steed, A. 104
Stevenson, B. 112
Stiglitz, J. 110, 118
Stock, J.H. 115
Strecleck, W. 85
Sweden 57, 102
Sweet, A. 133
Switzerland 81, 90, 93
Szczerbiak, A. 54, 58

Taggart, P. 10
Tausendpfund, M. 41
taxation 128, 130, 137; incentives to attract foreign investors 102–4
technology 95
theoretical expectations: exogenous shocks and integration 5; integration theories 5–6; theories of policy and institutional change 6, 105; theories of public opinion change 6–7
Tibet 104
Tonkiss, F. 109
Tonnelier, A. 102
Torres, F. 119
Tosun, J. 8, 32, 38, 69, 119, 142
trade barriers 96
trade liberalization 8
Treaty on Stability, Coordination and Governance (TSCG)/Fiscal Compact 27–8, 32, 131–2, 136, 140
Trondal, J. 20

True, J.L. 6
trust 4, 11, 14, 137; citizens' trust in European Central Bank 1999–2012 *see separate entry*
Tsingtao Beer 96
Tsoukalis, L. 3
Tuo, Y. 93
Turkey 75, 82, 86

unemployment 40, 42, 46, 55, 68, 106, 128, 142; citizens' trust in European Central Bank 1999–2012 111–13, 115–19, 120, 126
United Kingdom 3, 27, 58, 81; citizens' support for EU: impact of Euro crisis 43; foreign direct investment 93, 100, 101, 102, 104; investment promotion 101
United States 3, 4, 110; foreign direct investment 90, 92, 93, 95, 96, 97, 98, 99, 106; government bonds 99

Van Der Eijk, C. 74
Van Rompuy, Herman 2
Verney, S. 54
veto powers 133, 140
Visser, P.S. 7
Volvo 96

wages 128, 137
Walter, S. 2, 4, 5, 13
Wälti, S. 4, 11, 13, 110, 112, 118
Wanhua 99
Weetabix 97
Weible, C.M. 6
Wenkel, R. 111
Whitman, R.G. 8
Wooldridge, J.M. 115
World Trade Organization (WTO) 96

Yiqi, Y. 99
Yoplait 99–100

Zhejiang Xuebao Fashion Co 99
Zhu Weixiang 99